Conversations with Ellen Gilchrist

Literary Conversations Series
Monika Gehlawat
General Editor

Conversations with Ellen Gilchrist

Edited by Tracy Carr

University Press of Mississippi / Jackson

The University Press of Mississippi is the scholarly publishing agency of
the Mississippi Institutions of Higher Learning: Alcorn State University,
Delta State University, Jackson State University, Mississippi State University,
Mississippi University for Women, Mississippi Valley State University,
University of Mississippi, and University of Southern Mississippi.

www.upress.state.ms.us

The University Press of Mississippi is a member
of the Association of University Presses.

Publisher: University Press of Mississippi, Jackson, USA
Authorised GPSR Safety Representative: Easy Access System Europe -
Mustamäe tee 50, 10621 Tallinn, Estonia, *gpsr.requests@easproject.com*

Library of Congress Cataloging-in-Publication Data

Names: Carr, Tracy editor
Title: Conversations with Ellen Gilchrist / Tracy Carr.
Other titles: Literary conversations series
Description: Jackson : University Press of Mississippi, 2025. |
    Series: Literary conversations series | Includes bibliographical references and index.
Identifiers: LCCN 2025030746 (print) | LCCN 2025030747 (ebook) |
    ISBN 9781496859686 hardback | ISBN 9781496859693 trade paperback |
    ISBN 9781496859709 epub | ISBN 9781496859716 epub |
    ISBN 9781496859723 pdf | ISBN 9781496859730 pdf
Subjects: LCSH: Gilchrist, Ellen, 1935—Interviews | Women authors, American—Interviews |
    Women novelists, American—Interviews | Women poets, American—Interviews |
    Authors, American—Southern States—Interviews | Women and literature—
    Southern States | American literature—Southern States—Women authors
Classification: LCC PS3557.I34258 Z46 2025 (print) | LCC PS3557.I34258 (ebook)
LC record available at https://lccn.loc.gov/2025030746
LC ebook record available at https://lccn.loc.gov/2025030747

British Library Cataloging-in-Publication Data available

Books by Ellen Gilchrist

Poetry

The Land Surveyor's Daughter. Fayetteville: Lost Roads Press, 1979.
Riding Out the Tropical Depression. New Orleans: Faust Publishing, 1986.

Fiction

In the Land of Dreamy Dreams. Fayetteville: University of Arkansas Press, 1981.
The Annunciation. New York: Little, Brown and Company, 1983.
Victory over Japan. New York: Little, Brown and Company, 1984.
Drunk with Love. New York: Little, Brown and Company, 1986.
The Anna Papers. New York: Little, Brown and Company, 1988.
Light Can Be Both Wave and Particle. New York: Little, Brown and Company, 1989.
I Cannot Get You Close Enough. New York: Little, Brown and Company, 1990.
Net of Jewels. New York: Little, Brown and Company, 1992.
Starcarbon. New York: Little, Brown and Company, 1994.
Anabasis. Jackson: University Press of Mississippi, 1994.
The Age of Miracles. New York: Little, Brown and Company, 1995.
Rhoda: A Life in Stories. New York: Little, Brown and Company, 1995.
The Courts of Love. New York: Little, Brown and Company, 1996.
Sarah Conley. New York: Little, Brown and Company, 1997.
Flights of Angels. New York: Little, Brown and Company, 1998.
The Cabal and Other Stories. New York: Little, Brown and Company, 2000.
Collected Stories. New York: Little, Brown and Company, 2000.
I, Rhoda Manning, Go Hunting with My Daddy. New York: Little, Brown and Company, 2002.
A Dangerous Age. Chapel Hill: Algonquin Books, 2008.
Nora Jane: A Life in Stories. New York: Little, Brown and Company, 2009.
Acts of God. Chapel Hill: Algonquin Books, 2014.

Nonfiction

Falling Through Space: The Journals of Ellen Gilchrist. New York: Little, Brown and Company, 1987.
The Writing Life. Jackson: University Press of Mississippi, 2005.
Things Like the Truth: Out of My Later Years. Jackson: University Press of Mississippi, 2016.

Contents

Introduction

Ellen Gilchrist (1935–2024) was an American poet, short story writer, novelist, and essayist who published twenty-six books during her long career, which spanned from the 1970s through the 2010s. Known for her witty, sometimes irreverent recurring cast of characters, including Rhoda Manning, a character closest to Gilchrist in broad biographical bullet points, Gilchrist won the 1984 National Book Award[1] in fiction for her collection *Victory over Japan*. She later was a commentator on National Public Radio's then-new *Morning Edition*, making her a nationally known personality. While she published six novels, the short story was her preferred domain, and the realm in which she received the most critical acclaim. In a review of her first collection, *In the Land of Dreamy Dreams, The Washington Post* said that "it's difficult to review a first book as good as this without resorting to every known superlative cliché—there are, after all, just so many ways to say 'auspicious debut.'"[2] Later, in reviewing *The Courts of Love*, the same paper said that "the characters live and breathe. One cannot seem to shake the feeling that they are alive, that their lives flow parallel to ours." The reviewer buries the lede: "Ellen Gilchrist should be declared a national cultural treasure."[3]

Born in Vicksburg in 1935—the nearest hospital to her family's plantation in Issaquena County—Gilchrist spent her childhood in various Midwestern and Southern towns as her father worked for the Army Corps of Engineers during World War II. After starting college at Vanderbilt in 1953, she enrolled at the University of Alabama in the fall of 1954 and then went to Auburn University in the spring of 1955. That summer, she eloped with Marshall Walker, with whom she had three sons, but not before divorcing him, marrying and divorcing someone else, remarrying Walker, and then divorcing him again in 1963. She was married to Frederick Kullman, a New Orleans attorney, from 1968 to 1981.

The marital status report isn't just interesting; it's a vital part of when and how Gilchrist started writing. While she had written all her life, she began writing seriously when her children were teenagers. Because she had her first child at age twenty, in 1955, however, she wasn't exactly middle aged. Her experience of multiple marriages and divorces informs her characters' pasts as well, especially Rhoda Manning, whose story closely follows Gilchrist's.

Several of the earlier interviews in this collection remark on the wonder of Gilchrist's "advanced age"—she was around forty before she began writing seriously and was forty-six when her first book of short stories was published. She was even included in a book called *Late Achievers: Famous People Who Succeeded Late in Life* (Libraries Unlimited, 1992), which also included information on Grandma Moses and Dr. Ruth Westheimer. There is little acknowledgment from the interviewers that women who have children, and especially those who had children in the 1950s before daycare or other childcare solutions were normalized and necessary, perhaps do not have the time or bandwidth to focus on their creative lives. Expressing wonder at the fact that she was in her forties before she had the opportunity to devote time to writing reinforces the patriarchal idea that writers are men, and young ones at that. The collection is a capsule of time in which a writer over forty was a novelty and something worth asking about.

Gilchrist seems to generally take this in stride and responds to this in the 1986 American Audio Prose Library interview with Kay Bonetti, explaining that she began writing during a period of time in which her children were running amok: "I think I did it because my two oldest sons were real wild teenagers and I had lost control of them, and this was during the seventies when no one had any control over their children and I was horrified all the time that my children were going to die . . . and I went into the cave where you write books in order to pass the time while I waited to see if my children would grow up." Despite their tumultuous teenage years, her views on her children and motherhood are consistently glowing. It was the best decision she ever made, and her family never stopped being her very favorite thing. In the interview with Melissa Biggs, Gilchrist says, "The major creative act of my life was the birth of my children."

Gilchrist occasionally talks about how not only was her decision to become a mother a wonderful one, but motherhood should be every woman's default setting; it's good for the reader to remember that however forward thinking Gilchrist was, she was also a person born in 1935 and was very much a product of her generation. In the Bonetti interview, Gilchrist says, "I can't imagine a healthy young woman turning down being in love, having babies, all the richness, the madness of those years, to go sit in a room and do what it takes to write books. Long, long periods of solitude and introspection. . . . It's incomprehensible to me that anyone would do that."

For however incomprehensible Gilchrist thought the idea of not wanting children, questions regarding her status as a woman writer were not her
favorite. In 1988, Gilchrist was part of a panel discussion at Furman University with fellow authors Josephine Humphreys, Louise Shivers, and Gloria
Naylor called "The Woman as Writer and Reader." The first question was
"Do you think of yourself as a woman writer?" The answers from the panelists are all polite, but also let it be known that asking women writers if
they consider themselves women writers is not only kind of a silly question,
but also one that assumes, as Gloria Naylor says in her response, there is a
norm, and "anything that's not in that norm has to explain their existence
and explain what they are doing." Gilchrist responds that she thinks of herself not as a woman as she's writing but as "part of the physical universe
which includes the reaches of the stars and the sub-atomic particles."

Gilchrist veers into similar science talk in several interviews—she did,
after all, name a story collection *Light Can Be Both Wave and Particle*—and
refers to her interest in genetics, namely the idea that it's possible, as she
told Kyle Kellams in 1998, that people "could have the memory in our genes
of everything up to the moment of conception of all of our ancestors."

There is a short feature from *People* magazine that I wish I'd been able to
reproduce in its entirety, but I was unable to obtain permission for it. However, there is one paragraph that is notable. In "Southerner Ellen Gilchrist
Is the Book World's Belle"[4] the author describes the moment Gilchrist won
the 1984 National Book Award for *Victory over Japan*: "The dark horse, Ellen
Gilchrist, a saucy 49-year-old southerner, was poised for action in a ruby-
red velvet suit. As the crowd burst into applause when her name was called
out, Gilchrist trotted to the microphone to claim the award and $10,000 in
prize money. After graciously acknowledging her competition, she stopped
and the audience stirred expectantly. Apparently at a loss what to do next,
Gilchrist then blurted out, 'Uh, I brought my Lionel Richie tape with me, if
anyone wants to listen to it.'"

I read and reread the line about the Lionel Richie tape. It's such a weird
thing to say any day of the week, much less at the moment that you win a
National Book Award. What happened next, though, was surely attributable
to the Lionel Richie moment: she was approached by Jay Kernis and Bob
Edwards and asked to become a regular contributor to *Morning Edition*.
At the time, Fayetteville, Arkansas, did not have a public radio station, and
Gilchrist hoped her work would change that. (Whether it was her work
or not, Arkansas got a public radio station in 1985.) Gilchrist wrote and

recorded weekly essays in 1985 and 1986 until, she said, it stopped being fun. (The lesson is, of course, stay weird.)

Gilchrist mentions in various interviews the column that she wrote for the Franklin, Kentucky, newspaper while in high school: "Chit 'n' Chat 'Bout This 'n' That." (For the record, that apostrophe explosion is in fact the correct punctuation.) These weekly columns were a glimpse into early 1950s' teenage life. In the April 12, 1951, *Franklin Favorite*, the editor writes, "Last week we introduced a new column at the lower corner of this page. . . . Her column appears again this week and will continue each week at the same spot. If you are interested in the mysterious workings of the teenage mind or in teenage news and views, the column is a weekly must." The column would continue through 1952 and usually ended with a poem written by Gilchrist, Dorothy Parker's influence apparent, like in "That's Love" from the May 31, 1951 column, which ends with "That's love and it's better / Than a room full of gold / And I'd try it again / If I wasn't so old."

In the Arkansas Memory Project interview, she tells a story about having written a paper on Dorothy Parker for her future husband, Marshall Walker, on which he got an A:

> I know the father of my children, the man at Georgia Tech that I—the young man at Georgia Tech that I fell in love with—one of the first things I did for him before we ran away and got married was I wrote him a book report on Dorothy Parker. I loved Dorothy Parker. I knew all her work by heart. And his probably gay professor kept him in after class—this big, strapping, athletic KA—and said, "Oh, Mr. Walker, I would never, never have thought you were a fan of Dorothy Parker. This is just wonderful. Made my semester." And he gave him an A on it. [*Laughter*] God knows I'd give anything to have a copy of it.

(Coincidentally, I also wrote a paper for my boyfriend in college—on Ellen Gilchrist.)

In 1968, Gilchrist won the Mississippi Arts Festival's poetry prize for "Legerdemain." She talks about this in the Educational Television interview: "I was sitting under the hair dryer at Joseph's Beauty Parlor and someone came up to me and said, 'You're the poet laureate of Mississippi. You just won this contest!'" What she doesn't mention is a factoid that is random and divine: "Winners were announced in the statewide competition by film star Joan Crawford during the fifth annual festival."[5] (I am sorry to say that I cannot explain how Joan Crawford came to be involved, though it is one of those details that makes research a gift.)

I was unable to acquire permission to reprint a short interview from Mary A. McCay's *Ellen Gilchrist*, a volume from the Twayne author series, but I thought it worthy of inclusion because the tone was so sharply different than any of the other interviews. There is little trace of the effusive and forthcoming person who shows up to all the other interviews. A sample:

> **MARY McCAY:** What influence did the following people have on your work: Jim Whitehead, Bill Harrison, and Frank Stanford?
>
> **ELLEN GILCHRIST:** Bill Harrison showed me the form of the short story. Jim Whitehead is one of my two best friends. Frank showed me how to put a book together and how to believe in my instinctive sense of what a book should be.[6]

The terse responses could have been for any reason, including the fact that an interview published in a book of literary criticism lasts forever or because McCay was the only interviewer to ask about the poet Frank Stanford, Gilchrist's friend and founder of Lost Roads Press, which published Gilchrist's first book of poetry, *The Land Surveyor's Daughter*, the year after Stanford's death by suicide in 1978. For more on their relationship, see James McWilliams's *The Life and Poetry of Frank Stanford* (University of Arkansas Press, 2025).

In 1992 or so, I wrote a fan letter to Ellen Gilchrist. I have no idea what it said, but I memorized her response: "What a long, strange time it's been making up all these people." I remember being slightly outraged that she dared to say she made them up, since one didn't have to look far (even in the pre-Internet days) to discover the similarities between Rhoda and her creator.

Many, if not all the interviewers, in their way, ask about the autobiographical nature of her work, especially in regard to Rhoda Manning. Gilchrist settled upon the perfect response along the way: that she gave Rhoda all her childhood memories. While this is almost exactly the same thing as basing a character on yourself, somehow it sounds different enough that the interviewer accepts it and moves on.

While Gilchrist is open about sharing her memories and experiences with Rhoda and other characters, she does make it clear that other things influenced her work: a spate of suicides in New Orleans inspired "Rich," the first short story she ever wrote; and a friend's experience giving up a child for adoption inspired *The Annunciation*. In the *Clarion-Ledger* in 1983, Lela J. Davis writes, "Although *The Annunciation* is not a biography, many aspects of Amanda's strong will and unconventional lifestyle are mirrored in Ms. Gilchrist's life. 'Thank God, I have never had the tragedy of losing a child and I certainly couldn't have kept it a secret . . . but Amanda does have the good parts of my personality,' Ms. Gilchrist said." The best and most convincing argument I can think of to prove that a thing didn't happen to you is that you are too much of a blabbermouth to have ever kept it a secret.

There were other interviews over the years—writing twenty-six books over forty-plus years means a lot of opportunity for interviews—but the ones chosen for this collection represent those in which Gilchrist has something to say: a tidbit that's not shared in other interviews, an interesting way of telling a story she has shared before, a contradiction to an earlier statement, or being in conversation with a group of people that's unique in some way.

The collection opens with a brief profile in the *Clarion-Ledger* upon the 1983 publication of Gilchrist's first novel, *The Annunciation*. It's a quick sketch, catching up the public on Gilchrist's career (and personal life—the multiple marriages are hard not to mention). She is cautious, perhaps aware that the capital city's newspaper will be read by her parents, and so is careful to stay within the lines. There is still a little Gilchrist sparkle when she talks about living in New Orleans and not quite fitting in with the culture: "I can't imagine anything more boring in this world than having to be with people who are exactly like you. You can't teach each other anything."

In 1984, Mississippi's Educational Television featured Gilchrist on an episode of *PostScripts*, hosted by Edward Cohen and filmed at her parents' house in Jackson. This is the first in-depth interview Gilchrist would give and the first time the public at large would have heard not only her voice but her way of speaking. She is excitable and enthusiastic and appears to be having the time of her life. Most of the interview is about her as a person, not her writing life, and she talks a lot about her childhood. Here, she's talking about how she slept very little as a teenager: "I guess if I were a teenager now they would have me in therapy and they would give me some tryptophan, or they'd do something to make me sleep, or they'd regulate my diet. I lived on sugar. They'd make me eat bread and vegetables and I'd sleep eight hours like everybody else and I never would've read all those books and I'd be a nice, normal housewife somewhere. Well, that's fine. That's not what happened with me!"

This was the first interview that I transcribed; I feel like it was fitting that it was both of our firsts in a way. At first the way she stops, starts, and changes direction made me a little crazy. But once I listened and listened again, I learned her patterns, which seem random and chaotic but are rhythmic and lyrical. It might be a funny thing to put in the introduction to a book, but reading her words is no match for listening to her speak. A portion of this interview is on YouTube and is worth seeking out.

Gilchrist is comfortable and unreserved with Kay Bonetti in the 1986 American Audio Prose Library interview, which is one that I transcribed from unedited audio. Bonetti has a gentle, yet focused interview style that Gilchrist responds to. Gilchrist touches on some interesting topics, most of them focused on her writing, including her decision to include the character of Traceleen, a Black servant, in her fiction: "[Writers] wouldn't do it because we thought it was wrong. And finally I made up my mind that we'd turned our back on one of the great and beautiful things that Black people had been able to do. Had been able to take the condition of servitude and turn it into a beautiful thing. . . . I was taking a big chance when I wrote a Black character as a servant."

Gilchrist also gives Bonetti a wonderful explanation of the autobiographical nature of all her writing: "Oh, in the heat and passion of the creative moment, I just grab anything that's handy. I just give them anything that's in the room. You know, I always give my characters my clothes, my car, my living room furniture, my baby grand piano. I give them the nearest thing because it's the story, I want to serve the story. . . . What you want is the music."

Gilchrist also talks a little about the kind of trance she's in while writing: "When you're really on, you're not there. You're just the servant, serving the vision, giving a gift to the world, although Bill Harrison told me he was going to throw up if I ever said that in public."

Like many author interviews, Gilchrist is asked about her influences in almost every one and generally mentions Eudora Welty and William Faulkner. Of special interest is the 1987 interview with Melissa Biggs, "Ellen Gilchrist: A Voice of Southern Conflict." Gilchrist breaks from the usual and states, "I think the primary influence on my writing and on the way I write and the forms I choose to write in is J. D. Salinger. After I've come back around to him from everywhere. I don't even think of Salinger as modern because he's been gone for so long." While this is the only time that she cites Salinger as an influence, readers can easily draw a line from Salinger to Gilchrist style-wise once the seed is planted.

In this interview Gilchrist also, in response to a question about if she ever took any formal writing classes, says that she "took a class with Eudora Welty once. But she didn't teach us anything. She was just a kind and lovely old woman. But like all great writers she couldn't teach writing because she doesn't know how she does it." In later interviews, she tells a different story (and repeats it almost verbatim) about her time in Welty's Millsaps seminar.

Her commentaries on NPR's *Morning Edition* made her a nationally recognized personality, and on December 29, 1989, Gilchrist was invited to be a part of the *MacNeil/Lehrer NewsHour*'s panel on "Evaluating the Eighties." Among the other artist panelists asked to weigh in on the close of the decade were playwright August Wilson, violinist Isaac Stern, and novelist Robert Stone. At one point, Stone is asked if there's a symbol of the eighties, and he opines that style-wise, bohemia has disappeared among artists: "When I was younger, I mean, we had to externalize our sacred mission and we lived in holy poverty and the girls wore black and now it seems as though writers and politicians and gangsters and stock brokers are all in the same restaurants and they're all pursuing the same style of life." Asked for a response, Gilchrist says, "I have on black. Mr. Stone should come to Fayetteville, Arkansas. We still have Bohemians there." Gilchrist's role among the panel of serious culture makers seems to be to provide a bit of fun or comic relief.

In a radio interview with James McKinley in 1991, Gilchrist talks about the writing process, the problem of too many characters to juggle, and the folly of thinking up a plot and sticking to it during the actual writing: "The river does not run straight." She also mentions Salinger, but only in reference to talking about reading books while driving. She mentions that she cruised around reading *The Catcher in the Rye* as a teenager. She was sixteen when it was published in the summer of 1951, which means she read this brand-new book with its fresh, modern narrator whose voice is both hilarious and tragic at the moment it was becoming a cultural touchstone.

Gilchrist was featured in a 1992 story in *Publisher's Weekly* and speaks more about returning to writing after the years raising children: "I began to have this recurrent dream of being in my house in New Orleans and opening a door to find all these rooms that I didn't know were there, full of chests with the drawers full of treasures. Nothing had been touched in a long, long time, and I had this feeling that I wanted to get other people in the house and show them these rooms. So I began to write." She also talks about how she is embracing writing novels.

In an interview with Martha Wilson and Gwen Sell of Macon College in 1995, Gilchrist covers a variety of topics but really focuses on how much she dislikes writing novels:

[The novel is] not a demon, it's a dinosaur—it's this huge thing that should have died years ago, and it's always gnawing at your back. A publisher will give you three times as much money for a novel as a book of short stories, and besides that—it just—all of a sudden something starts turning into a novel and you think, "No—down—down!" God, what I hate is putting them together—when they get almost to the end and you've got all these chapters and things, and it takes up a whole room just to have the whole sets of papers sitting all over the place. You can't leave town because if the house burns down, there are no copies.

By 1998, in a radio interview with KUAF's Kyle Kellams, Gilchrist seems to have made her peace with the novel—due to something a friend said: "I said, '*Why* aren't you satisfied with the collections of stories? Why do you want a novel?' And she said, 'Because I want to be able to take a book with me to bed and have it there night after night. I don't want it to be finished in one night.' And I kept thinking about that, and I thought, 'You know, that's the best argument I've ever heard for why I should want to write a novel.' But a novel is a huge investment in time and energy and hope—it's an investment in hope and self-confidence."

In 2004, Paul Mandelbaum interviewed Gilchrist for his book *12 Short Stories and Their Making*, in which they discuss "Rich." This is a deep dive into one of Gilchrist's most famous stories—and one of her first, which contains scenes that Gilchrist says she doesn't regret, exactly, but she doesn't want her grandchildren to read. This interview puts in one place all the things Gilchrist has said about this story over the years (and more). One of the best parts is when Mandelbaum says she balances some of the shocking images in the story by comparing them to something beautiful, and Gilchrist's response is "I know it. Because I'm not a horror writer."

The hours-long Arkansas Memories Project interview, a remarkable piece of historical information, was conducted by Scott Lunsford for the David and Barbara Pryor Center for Arkansas Oral and Visual History at the University of Arkansas. Conducted in 2010 when Gilchrist was seventy-five, it's an incredibly detailed account of her life. The interview focuses more on her biography than her writing, which makes it a great source of information and fills in the gaps for the curious. The Pryor Center's transcript methodology is to transcribe exactly what the interviewee says, including every "um," "er," and false start. While the portion of the interview used in this volume is still rather long, the entire thing is not reproduced here, but it is available on the Pryor Center's website for the interested.

In 2013, Luke Lampton and Scott Anderson met with Gilchrist for an interview that appeared in their literary magazine's premiere issue. The

China Grove interview is a treat to read: Lampton and Anderson clearly adore Gilchrist, and she basks in their attention. They recite poetry together, read aloud from a play, and seem to truly enjoy each other's company. It's a delight to read, though you may experience a bit of envy at not having been invited to the party.

The final interview in this volume is from the 2022 Mississippi Book Festival when Gilchrist was in conversation with former festival executive director Holly Lange. Gilchrist was eighty-seven at the time and holds court like a queen. Gilchrist relates several behind-the-scenes stories, like about how Gilchrist almost didn't show up to her first poetry reading at Jackson's Lemuria Books, what her parents thought of her much-younger boyfriend when she was in her fifties (hint: they were not impressed), and the story of her exit from the University of Arkansas English Department after some controversy about teaching *Go Down, Moses* by William Faulkner. In a meeting with the dean of Arts and Sciences, after she had an attorney friend write a somewhat scary letter, Gilchrist said she walked in and said, "I want you to know that I'm here for one reason only, because I was called a racist and a misogynist by the head of the creative writing program. And I'm going to defend myself about that and tell you what I did during the civil rights movement." She then sums up with this: "And so actually, in street talk, I got fired for teaching Faulkner."

My intent in choosing this selection of interviews was not only to provide a compendium of information about Gilchrist in her own words for scholarship purposes but also to delight and entertain her readers. As I listened to and transcribed hours of interviews with Ellen Gilchrist, I came to feel that I knew her in a way that I know is impossible—but when I read these interviews now, I hear her voice in my head and know that however smooth and edited a written sentence may be, there's a good chance she started and stopped a few times, too excited by all of the potential answers available for a particular question to immediately settle on one.

I could not have completed this project without the help of librarians and archivists, who perform magic every day, notably Ally Mellon at the Mississippi Department of Archives and History, Elizabeth Engel at the State Historical Society of Missouri, James Kennedy at Millsaps College, and Betty Moore and Elisabeth Scott at the Mississippi Library Commission. Librarians and archivists are virtuosos of information and access; I am beyond grateful for their help, determination, and professionalism.

A special thanks is given to all of the interviewers and publishers who granted permission for their work to be collected in this volume. Thanks also to my household support group, who were patient and kind during the various stages of putting this book together, including when I had to replay audio clips over and over at full volume to make sure what I heard was what Gilchrist was saying. (No thanks is given to my cats, who walked on my keyboard and knocked papers off my desk.)

From the moment I discovered *Victory over Japan* on the shelf at the Nicholson Memorial Library in Garland, Texas, in the summer of 1990, I've been a fan of Ellen Gilchrist. I hope she would have appreciated this volume, which was an honor to put together. While we did have occasion to be in the same room together a handful of times during Mississippi Book Festival events, I did not meet her or know her. (Did I surreptitiously take a couple of photos of her at the Eudora Welty House? Perhaps.) But after reading this collection, I hope you feel, as I do, that you know and understand Ellen Gilchrist's work and life a little better. As she said about her own writing in 1994, "And then there's another kind of epiphany. You begin to understand your work in its relation to your life and you begin to see what it was you were doing and how the two forces played, or helped each other, played against each other, played off of each other, and used each other, and fed upon each other."

TC

Notes

1. From 1980–1987, the National Book Awards were renamed the American Book Awards, so interviews may reflect both names.

2. Susan Wood, "Louisiana Stories: The Debut of Ellen Gilchrist," review of *In the Land of Dreamy Dreams*, by Ellen Gilchrist, *Book World–The Washington Post*, March 21, 1982: 4, 13.

3. Hart Williams, review of *The Courts of Love*, by Ellen Gilchrist, *The Washington Post*, February 15, 1997.

4. Harriet Shapiro, "Southerner Ellen Gilchrist Is the Book World's Belle," *People* 23, no. 6 (February 11, 1985): 75.

5. "Winners in Fest Literary Competition in Five Areas," *Clarion-Ledger*, April 28, 1968, 54.

6. Mary A. McCay, *Ellen Gilchrist* (Twayne Publishers, 1997), 109.

Chronology

1935   Born February 20 in Vicksburg, Mississippi, to Aurora Alford
          Gilchrist and William Garth Gilchrist Jr.
1951–1952 Writes a weekly column in *The Franklin Favorite* newspaper
          (Franklin, Kentucky) called "Chit 'n' Chat 'Bout This 'n' That."
1953   Graduates high school from Southern Seminary and Junior Col-
          lege in Buena Vista, Virginia. Enrolls at Vanderbilt University for
          freshman year of college.
1954–1955 Enrolls in the University of Alabama for the fall semester. Enrolls
          in Auburn University in the spring semester.
1955–1963 Marries Marshall Peteet Walker. Has two sons, Marshall
          Peteet Walker Jr. and Garth Gilchrist Walker. Divorces Mar-
          shall Walker. Marries and divorces James Nelson Bloodworth.
          Remarries Marshall Walker. Has third son, Pierre Gautier
          Walker III. Divorces Marshall Walker.
1965   Enrolls in Millsaps College. Publishes a poem and a short story
          in Millsaps's *Stylus* literary magazine.
1967   Graduates from Millsaps College with a bachelor of arts in phi-
          losophy. Receives honorable mention at the Southern Literary
          Festival for "Six Poems."
1968   A poem, "Legerdemain," wins the Mississippi Arts Festival's
          poetry division. With Jane Petty, adapts Eudora Welty's short
          stories into a play, "A Season of Dreams," for New Stage Theatre.
          Marries Frederick Sidney Kullman and moves to New Orleans.
1976   Writes for the *Vieux Carre Courier* as a contributing edi-
          tor. Enrolls in the Creative Writing Program at the University
          of Arkansas in Fayetteville and splits her time between New
          Orleans and Fayetteville.
1979   *The Land Surveyor's Daughter* published by Lost Roads Press
          (Fayetteville, Arkansas). Wins a National Endowment for the
          Arts Fellowship grant in fiction.

1981   *In the Land of Dreamy Dreams*, a collection of short stories, published by University of Arkansas Press. Divorces Frederick Kullman.

1982   Wins the Mississippi Institute for Arts and Letters award for literature.

1983   *The Annunciation*, a novel, published by Little, Brown and Company.

1984   *Victory over Japan*, a collection of short stories, published by Little, Brown and Company, which is nominated for and the winner of the 1984 National Book Award for Fiction. Begins weekly broadcasting during *Morning Edition* on National Public Radio.

1985   Wins the Mississippi Institute for Arts and Letters award for literature.

1986   *Drunk with Love* (short stories) published by Little, Brown and Company. *Riding Out the Tropical Depression* (poetry) published by Faust Publishing.

1987   *Falling Through Space: The Journals of Ellen Gilchrist* published by Little, Brown and Company. Receives an honorary doctor of letters degree from Millsaps College.

1988   *The Anna Papers* (novel) published by Little, Brown and Company.

1989   *Light Can Be Both Wave and Particle* (short stories) published by Little, Brown and Company.

1990   *I Cannot Get You Close Enough* (three novellas) published by Little, Brown and Company.

1991   Wins the Mississippi Institute for Arts and Letters award for literature. Receives an honorary doctor of humane letters degree from Southern Illinois University at Carbondale.

1992   *Net of Jewels* (novel) published by Little, Brown and Company.

1994   *Starcarbon* (novel) published by Little, Brown and Company. *Anabasis* (novel) published by the University Press of Mississippi.

1995   *The Age of Miracles* (short stories) and *Rhoda: A Life in Stories* (short stories) published by Little, Brown and Company.

1996   *The Courts of Love* (short stories) published by Little, Brown and Company.

1997   *Sarah Conley* (novel) published by Little, Brown and Company.

1998   *Flights of Angels* (short stories) published by Little, Brown and Company.

2000   *The Cabal and Other Stories* published by Little, Brown and Company. *Collected Stories* published by Little, Brown and

	Company. Receives an honorary doctor of arts and humane letters degree from the University of Arkansas. Serves as visiting professor at the University of Arkansas during the fall semester.
2001	Begins work as associate professor of creative writing at the University of Arkansas.
2002	*I, Rhoda Manning, Go Hunting with My Daddy* (short stories) published by Little, Brown and Company.
2004	Wins the Thomas Wolfe Award from the University of North Carolina at Chapel Hill and the Thomas Wolfe Society.
2005	*The Writing Life* (essays) published by University Press of Mississippi. At Tulane University, is chosen as the Andrew W. Mellon Fellow, serves as the Mellon Chair, and is the Zale Writer in Residence at Sophie Newcomb College in the spring of 2005.
2008	*A Dangerous Age* (novel) published by Algonquin Books of Chapel Hill.
2009	*Nora Jane: A Life in Stories* published by Little, Brown and Company.
2014	*Acts of God* (short stories) published by Algonquin Books of Chapel Hill.
2016	*Things Like the Truth: Out of My Later Years* published by University Press of Mississippi.
2017	Wins Mercer University's Spencer B. King's Center for Southern Studies' Sidney Lanier Prize for Southern Literature.
2022	Wins the Richard Wright Literary Excellence Award at the Natchez Literary and Cinema Celebration.
2024	Dies at her home in Ocean Springs, Mississippi, on January 30.

Conversations with Ellen Gilchrist

State Native's First Novel Parallels Pains of Her Life

Lela J. Davis / 1983

From the *Clarion-Ledger*, June 2, 1983. Copyright Lela J. Davis—USA TODAY NETWORK. Reprinted by permission.

"When a writer writes a book she is answering all the books she's ever read," said Ellen Gilchrist, as she lounged in blue jeans and shirt on the floor of her best friend's spacious living room in Jackson.

Ms. Gilchrist, whose latest reply is *The Annunciation*, her first novel, was in the city recently to promote the book at area bookstores.

She said the novel, which has been in bookstores across the nation for about three weeks, is "receiving favorable reviews."

The Annunciation "simply tells the story of a woman who had to give her child away," Ms. Gilchrist, forty-eight, said.

But far from being simple, the book unfolds the complex tale of an Issaquena County girl, Amanda McCamey, who at age fourteen has an illegitimate child fathered by her cousin, Guy.

Amanda is quietly whisked from the family plantation and taken to a New Orleans convent where the baby is born and immediately taken from her.

However, the memory of the child provokes constant sorrow in Amanda's life as she grows to become the rich and bored wife of a Louisiana lawyer.

The decadent life of the New Orleans aristocracy holds little fascination for her and she returns to school to become "the best middle-aged Middle French translator ever."

Given the opportunity to engage in a competition to translate the sonnets of an obscure eighteenth-century poetess whose life parallels her own, Amanda quits the city and her husband to "hightail it" to the Arkansas Ozark town of Fayetteville.

While in Fayetteville working on the poetry translation, she falls in love with and becomes pregnant by a local man some twenty years younger than herself. The crux of the story comes when Amanda, now age forty-four, must decide whether to have the child.

Although *The Annunciation* is not a biography, many aspects of Amanda's strong will and unconventional lifestyle are mirrored in Ms. Gilchrist's life.

"Thank God, I have never had the tragedy of losing a child and I certainly couldn't have kept it a secret . . . but Amanda does have the good parts of my personality," Ms. Gilchrist said. "I gave her things from my own life."

Ms. Gilchrist, who was born in Vicksburg, spent part of her childhood in Issaquena County, as did Amanda.

She now lives in Fayetteville, where she has lived "off and on since 1976."

"My perception of Fayetteville is much the same as Amanda's; it is an artists' colony," Ms. Gilchrist said.

She said she moved to Fayetteville because she had a lot of friends there, and it was inexpensive.

"Making a living as a writer is a chancy business. . . . Nobody expects you to be able to have a lot of money, or drive a big car or to get dressed up," she said.

Like the strong-willed Amanda, Ms. Gilchrist said her life "for a long time was caught up in marriages."

At twenty, she ran away from home, married, had three boys and followed her first husband, an engineer, from city to city.

She later divorced and returned to Jackson to study at Millsaps College where she received a degree in philosophy. While at Millsaps Ms. Gilchrist took writing classes under Eudora Welty, whom she says "was my inspiration and encouraged me." During this time she also married, and was divorced from, her second and third husbands.

She then spent fourteen years in New Orleans with her fourth husband, who like Amanda's husband, is a lawyer. They have since divorced.

Unlike Amanda, Ms. Gilchrist says, she was not part of the "New Orleans aristocracy."

"I was probably expected to be a part of it, to accept those limitations . . . but I can't set limits of the type of people I love or am interested in. I can't imagine anything more boring in this world than having to be with people who are exactly like you. You can't teach each other anything."

After New Orleans came Arkansas and "serious writing," she said.

Ms. Gilchrist said her marriages and "life constantly calling me back to it" kept her from "writing seriously" until she was forty years old.

"I would write for a while, win an award, and be satisfied," she said. "I'd get married again and go back to being a normal person."

But Ms. Gilchrist, who says she has been writing for as long as she can remember, thinks of herself as a "professional writer."

"When I was doing research for the book in the library, I went through the stacks and got to the Gs and realized in a short time my novel is going to be here," she said.

The Gilchrist name is no stranger to library shelves. *The Annunciation* will join her book of poetry, *The Land Surveyor's Daughter*, published in 1979, and *In the Land of Dreamy Dreams*, which won the Mississippi Institute of Arts and Letters fiction award, on the shelves. *In the Land of Dreamy Dreams* was published in 1982.

Ms. Gilchrist enthusiastically speaks about the new novel she has started and of several short stories she is "in the middle of." One of them, she said, is about "a girl who leads a slave rebellion."

She is slower, however, to talk about the many literary awards she has won, including two "Pushcart Awards" from the Pushcart Press in New York and a "Prairie Schooner Award" from the University of Nebraska for her short stories. She also was awarded a grant from the National Endowment for the Arts that "helped to support her" while she wrote *The Annunciation*.

"I think the awards are just a way of people saying, 'We love you and keep on writing,'" she said. "And as long as they like it, I will."

PostScripts No. 7: Ellen Gilchrist

Edward Cohen / 1984

From interview on television program *PostScripts*. Used by permission of Mississippi Public Broadcasting. Copyright 1984, Mississippi Authority for Educational Television. Transcript by Tracy Carr.

Ellen Gilchrist: I'm what I'm writing about, I'm a part of it. I think that's why it's an interesting and a happy profession for me because it's not hard for me to go in the closet and put on my Superman suit.

Narrator: Ellen Gilchrist is the author of a volume of short stories, *In the Land of Dreamy Dreams* and *The Annunciation*, a novel set in the Mississippi Delta, New Orleans, and Fayetteville, Arkansas.

Gilchrist: I was born in the Street Clinic in Vicksburg, Mississippi, a small hospital where many people whose mothers were from the Delta, people would come up there to have their babies, and my mother had given birth to my older brother at home, at Hopewell Plantation with my uncle as the physician. I mean, you know, he was the only physician in three counties. By the time she was pregnant with me she decided that maybe she would go to a hospital, which was something that ladies didn't like to do in nineteen hundred and thirty-five because it meant that they would have to, for example, take off their clothes in front of strangers. But then when I was four days old, my mother and grandmother and father took me—I guess, no, I think that my father was a professional baseball player and I think that he was playing—I could go in the other room and ask my mother—I think that he was playing baseball in Nashville when I was born. Anyway, they took me to a plantation down in Issaquena County, deep in the Delta, and I was there until I was four or five.

Edward Cohen: What were you like when you were a teenager?

Gilchrist: Genetically I'm a very energetic person who doesn't have to sleep a lot. I had a lot more hours to live as a teenager than almost anyone I know. My friends when I was young remember me as someone who always got up at dawn and woke them up. They remember that they spent the night with me or let me spend the night with them anyway. I really didn't sleep very much. I had a lot more time on my hands than people that—I guess if I were a teenager now they would have me in therapy and they would give me some tryptophan, or they'd do something to make me sleep, or they'd regulate my diet. I lived on sugar. They'd make me eat bread and vegetables and I'd sleep eight hours like everybody else and I never would've read all those books and I'd be a nice, normal housewife somewhere. Well, that's fine. That's not what happened with me! What happened with me is that I ate all the sugar I wanted, I slept very little, I had an enormous amount of energy, I was a cheerleader, I was yearbook editor, and I wrote the school newspaper—I literally wrote the features sections. Read books all the time, dreamed all the time. I had boyfriends, but I never took any one of them seriously. I was always in love with someone who was in college or something and that would be the major romantic interest of my life. And all the nice boys my own age that I went out with I would teach to dance, lecture on physics . . . I used to worry about myself. I always had all these boys that were my good friends, and my quieter, less restless friends would have steady boyfriends and they'd walk arm in arm and hand in hand up and down, and they always knew who they were going to have a date with, and life was not uncertain.

Cohen: Well, were you something of a nonconformist?

Gilchrist: Oh yeah, I was the ringleader of the rebellion. But within bounds, in the fifties you just didn't—I did things like—my idea of, you know, really being rebellious was to lead a bunch of people and we'd play hooky and go swimming. I had to be the first person swimming every spring. Or we would borrow a pickup truck, tell everybody that we were forming a literary society, and then we would go to the library and three of us would keep the librarian busy while the fourth got the books that she wasn't supposed to let us take out and off we would go to a cave. But we would never read the books, we would just climb through the cave.

Cohen: Were the books illicit literature?

Gilchrist: I was pregnant with my second child when somehow or other I got into my hands through a series of people giving to others a copy of *Lady Chatterley's Lover*. I was about eight months pregnant laying on the sleeping porch of a summer house reading the first book I'd ever read like that. I could see why they hadn't let us have it sooner.

When I was in the second or third grade, I went to the library every Saturday of my life. All—everything—most of the things that I did with other people . . . I mean, I like to have two or three other people around.

My mother let me have people spend the night with me all the time, and I always had one or two close friends, and somebody spent the night with me every night. My brother would be upstairs having four people spend the night with him. But there was this lonely thing that I did all my life and that was read. But my mother's a big reader and one of my grandmothers. You know, I had people I could discuss books with, and I always had secret relationships with English teachers in that I would stay after class and talk to them. I even read poetry and I read philosophy. I read everything that was in the Carnegie libraries.

Cohen: How did your school experience affect your writing?

Gilchrist: I read poetry a lot. Oh, I remember, I'd been reading a sad poem with a Greek name about how a poet, probably a seventeenth-century poet, had lost his best friend. And instead of going to the funeral, he'd gone off to the woods to have a private *whatever this big Greek word was* that meant, you know, that he would stay there.

I was in love with a boy that was a lot older than I was, and I thought he was going to die of cancer. And I must've been thinking about that. I'd been out there, you know, with my same-age boyfriends. So I went hiking off into the woods and the sun was going down and it was a cold, dark, late fall day. And finally, you know, I went up over the rise of the hill and I was sitting up on top of that hill—I probably had the book of poetry with me too—reading the book of poetry to myself and imagining the death of this person, you know, who's a very healthy, fifty-four-year-old at the moment and did not, thank God, die of cancer or anything. And then I probably, I mean, I remember that I did write poems all afternoon. I wrote on one. I know it was a lot of writing and in that writing I was a person grieving over the death of a person. There'd been no deaths in my family except you know very old people that I was not greatly saddened by. And then when I was satisfied with that and the sun was almost down or completely down, I'd be walking back home in a strange sort of state. And by the time I got to my yard, I'd be myself again. And I'd go in the house and go in the kitchen. Everybody'd say, "Why are you late to dinner?" and "Why weren't you here?" and "Where have you been?" And then I'd eat about fifteen pieces of cinnamon toast and drink a whole lot of milk, and I'd be a child again.

But I think that that's true of my writing then, and it's true of it now. When I write, I mean, you know, I get up out of bed and I make some coffee and all this, and I'm my nice, normal self. And if my grandchild's been spending the night, I take him home and then I go into the room where I work and I'm someone else. I'm what I'm writing about. I'm part of it. I think that's why it's an interesting and a happy profession for me because it's not hard for me to go in the closet and put on my Superman suit.

Cohen: Was there ever one special person that really helped you to become a writer?

Gilchrist: So many people all my life, but in the sixties when I lived in Jackson, when I began to publish some poetry when I would write it, Patti Black[1]—who is the director of the museum here, who's a close friend of mine—used to come grab my poems and say, "These are wonderful, write some more poems." Patti took a bunch of my poems one time and sent them off to the first Mississippi literary competition and one day about two months later, I was sitting under the hair dryer at Joseph's Beauty Parlor and someone came up to me and said, "You're the poet laureate of Mississippi. You just won this contest!"[2] Patti's kind of wonderful about that anyway. I wrote a play about her once called "Come Back, Little Fatty Whitey" about how everybody in Jackson was so relieved she'd gone to live in New York because now we didn't have to paint and write and sculpt and do good. [*Laughs*]

Cohen: What other Mississippi writers do you enjoy the work of?

Gilchrist: Well, of course Eudora, I mean I worship Eudora and William Faulkner, and I love Ellen Douglas's books, and I love the writer Joan Williams, who has another book of short stories that will be out soon, and Barry Hannah—oh, I think he's the funniest man in the world. I think *North Towards Home* by Willie Morris is one of the most important books in my life. During the sixties when my ideas were not shared by my family, that was one of the books that told me that "hey, it's all right, it's all right to know that segregation is wrong." You know, "Here, I'm a smart man, I'm the editor of *Harper's* magazine, and I, Willie Morris, am telling you it's okay." That was important; it propped us up, gave us strength.

Cohen: Do you feel that Mississippi's past of racial injustice has helped Mississippi's writers to have a lot to write about?

Gilchrist: Oh, yes, oh yes. An endless subject and it isn't over now. And I don't think much has changed. I thought everything would change, but I don't think it's changed. No, that's not true, that's not true. We integrated the school system. Thank God we did that. I forgot until I saw a program on Medgar Evers recently that there was a time in my lifetime when the public library of Jackson, Mississippi was integrated. That is devastating information. [*Pause*] I mean, was segregated—excuse me, excuse me. I can't even bear to use the word.

Cohen: Do you have a love/hate attitude towards Mississippi?

Gilchrist: Toward this state? I don't have any hate toward this state or anything else, I hope. I consider evil to be ignorance. From my point of view, all right, evil is stupidity, it's an inability, or perhaps a refusal, and then it's fear, when it's refusal, it's fear. It's an inability to be able to think of your vested interest as anything larger than your circle of friends. And that's just stupidity. And so I haven't got time to hate anything because it's my job in the world to pass on good ideas and information that other people gave me.

Cohen: So, do you then feel an obligation to, not to be didactic, but to have a moral message in your writing?

Gilchrist: I wish I didn't; no, that's not true. I'm me. I'm whatever I am. A series of events created me. I can't conceive of anybody bothering to write anything if they didn't think it was going to . . .

No, that's not true, because I'm perfectly happy to write some Rhoda stories that I think of as a way that I'll amuse other people. Some Sunday afternoon when somebody doesn't have anything to do, they'll be sitting on the couch laughing their head off at something Rhoda does. But if I get into a serious piece of work, I'm opinionated. So, um . . . I'm selling my opinions when I write fiction; I know that.

Cohen: Is there a—

Gilchrist: It's subtle and I'm not thinking about it while I'm writing. I'm thinking about characters and plot and event, but it's always there. It's like a thumbprint. It's all over a writer's work. And I think the public in general, or even the very small audience for poetry, knows when they read a writer's work whether that writer wishes them well, and I think they accept or reject your work on the basis of that as they do, as we do one another in real life. Do you think that's true?[3]

Cohen: Do you follow a daily schedule of writing, or just sort of wait for the inspiration to strike?

Gilchrist: I started writing seriously in 1976 or '75, I can't remember. And from that time 'til this, five or six or seven days a week, more likely seven, unless I start worrying about being obsessive, and then I make myself stop doing it, I get up in the morning, and go to my typewriter. I go from the moment I wake up, I go to my work and I don't do anything else till about 2:00 in the afternoon. I have to interrupt that for periods of time because my mind will get—I have to leave the work alone, force myself to go off and just see my friends and do things like that. But I think that's what . . . that looks and sounds like self-discipline, but it's not self-discipline. It's exactly what I want to do. I'm doing exactly what I want to do because once a piece of writing gets started, I can't wait to finish it because I don't really know what's going to happen. I may have written down a plot outline, but I don't really know what's going to happen until I write it because the characters are always full of surprises. God knows, at any moment they may tell you anything that you didn't know you knew.

Cohen: So in some ways they almost write it themselves?

Gilchrist: Oh yeah. Kierkegaard said that they get up off the page and take the pencil out of your hand, and Salinger quoted him as saying that. And in both of their cases it's true and I hope that occasionally it's true in mine. Because that's when the conscious mind and the ego has really gotten out of the way of the story.

Cohen: Do you keep a notebook or journal?

Gilchrist: I've just got a million yellow legal pads laying all over the place.

Cohen: But do you write things down as they occur to you, or they happen, and then you go back to them and thieve from that?

Gilchrist: Not in any systematic way. That's an especially good thing for a poet to do. When I get through writing for the day, I just live in the real world from then on. I forget my profession for the rest of the day, I mean, if I can. I mean, I'm thinking all the time and if anything happens to me that's in any way threatening or in any way sad there's a little piece of my mind that always says, "Nothing's ever lost on a writer." So, you know, I'm keeping the information. I have a good memory. I don't have to write it all down.

Cohen: How do you react to criticism?

Gilchrist: Harsh criticism?

Cohen: Well, there's a couple of kinds, there would be the criticism of critics in a newspaper or whatever, and then criticism from an editor.

Gilchrist: Editorial criticism I consider help and I understand it to be help and I am very good at taking it. I pride myself on being able to listen to whoever my first reader is or my editors. I pride myself on being able to get completely objective about that. Criticism of my work, written criticism of my work . . . I've never—this is honest—I've never really had to deal with it until about two weeks ago, no one has ever written anything about my work but pretty much unqualified praise, and a reviewer for *Harper's* magazine took a whole page to review *The Annunciation* and he loved it and at the beginning he said that he couldn't help loving it, and at the end he said he couldn't help loving it, and in the middle he said he couldn't help loving Amanda. But all around that, he was parodying the extreme romanticism of my mind. And I was so proud of myself because I opened the mailbox and there was *Harper's* and I knew Taliaferro[4] was going to do the book, and I know what a mean blankety-blank-blank-blank he's been to many writers, I mean, I know his clear, crisp, analytical, critical mind. And I couldn't wait, I ran in the house and I opened it up and I started laughing my head off. If I had set out to parody, to attempt to parody Amanda I couldn't have done a better job. At one point he says, "Holden Caulfield would've loved her." [*Laughs*] I thought, my God, I handled it, I did it! I read it and I thought it was funny! And it was okay.

Now on the other hand, if someone really attacked a piece of writing of mine, in fact, whenever anyone writes anything about my writing the first thing I want to know is, who wrote it? Someone taught me that and it was a good lesson. Who is my critic? The best thing you can learn as a writer is not to criticize your critics, but to critique them, at least. Who is this person, where are they coming from? What have they done that gives them the right to criticize my work?

Cohen: How do you feel when someone asks you to read something they've written and you read it and you really feel it's not any good—what do you tell them?

Gilchrist: I would never encourage anybody to do this unless they were truly talented and unless they had the kind of health and energy and enthusiasm that would get them through those long arduous processes. I mean, it's not just a lonely life, but there's a long time after you finish writing something before you see it in print. There's a lot of real hard clerical work that has to be done on the way, and all that time you've got to also be able to believe in yourself and that takes a lot of physical health. Just being real strong and real optimistic. But I sort of, I try to arrange it so that I'm never in that position unless I already know enough about the person, and a lot of times I could pick out in the room the writer by the way they walk and talk and move around. Or it seems to me, and I'm usually right. I wouldn't get myself in a position where I was supposed to be the judge of whether some other person was going to get to do this wonderful dreamy thing.

Cohen: When you start writing something, is the entire plot already in your mind, or does it form gradually?

Gilchrist: I have a vision, or a *conception*, that's a good enough word. I'll conceive of a piece of work and I'll do that very quickly, and my mind will have the structure of it, like a model of DNA, but that doesn't mean that my mind yet has the interior workings of all the neutrons and protons and all this, that, and the other. Once I see that picture, once I see that novel or I see that story, it never occurs to me that I won't be able to find the other parts to it or know the rest. It doesn't appear just in the form of a character . . . it depends. It'll appear in the form of a character or characters involved in either some seminal event or a series of events. The mind is wonderful. You can literally see a short story in about five minutes. And then you've got many long days of remembering the pieces and finding the rest of it, but that's . . . now I'm getting mystical, excuse me. [*Laughs*]

Cohen: That first flash, is it a picture in your mind or is it a series of words? What is that first flash?

Gilchrist: Eudora calls it the lyrical urge, the urge to call up to praise. It's just like I say, "Oh my God, I'm going to write about that," or "I'm going to tell that story!"

Cohen: How important is rewriting to you?

Gilchrist: That's another part of my mind. That's the part of my mind that's—I'm a good editor and I'm real cold and analytical about it. And I don't care what Miss Rhoda K. Faust⁵ thinks about her beautiful line in paragraph three; if it takes away from the story or if it slows down, *ckkkkk* [*sound effect to indicate it's cut*]. And I don't save it to use someplace else. Tough luck, Rhoda, you know, it's just gone.

Cohen: Can a person make a living at this sort of thing?

Gilchrist: I was talking to Melanie this morning about that. Success for an artist, and I really believe this, if you can feed yourself, keep a roof over your head, and take care of your family, if you have one, you're a successful artist. And if you can also buy health insurance you're real successful, OK? So it depends on what you consider a living. I think it's a good thing for a young writer to have another profession. Teaching's, you know, the ordinary one, but it would be nice to be able to be a carpenter or something along the way.

[*Reads from* The Annunciation]

Notes

1. Patti Carr Black, author of numerous books about aspects of Mississippi history and culture. Black was also director of the Old Capitol Museum in her thirty-year career with the Mississippi Department of Archives and History and one of the founders of New Stage Theatre in Jackson.

2. This is most likely referring to Gilchrist winning the 1968 Mississippi Arts Festival's poetry division for her poem "Legerdemain."

3. There is an awkward edit to the interview here that makes it seem like Cohen is ignoring her question.

4. Frances Taliaferro, review of *The Annunciation*, by Ellen Gilchrist, *Harper's* (June 1983).

5. Rhoda K. Faust, owner of Maple Street Bookshop and Faust Publishing of New Orleans. Faust Publishing published *Riding Out the Tropical Depression* in 1986.

Ellen Gilchrist Interview

Kay Bonetti / 1986

From Ellen Gilchrist interview; a.c. 369. *American Audio Prose Library* (C3851), the State Historical Society of Missouri Research Center—Columbia. Used by permission of the American Audio Library. All rights reserved. Transcript by Tracy Carr.

Kay Bonetti: The following is an interview with Ellen Gilchrist conducted by Kay Bonetti for the American Audio Prose Library in February of 1986 at the author's home in Jackson, Mississippi. Ellen Gilchrist was born in Mississippi in 1935, the child of an engineer who, at the beginning of World War II, because of his work, took his family on a somewhat nomadic life into the small towns of Indiana, Illinois, and Missouri, much like her character Rhoda, who Gilchrist says she gives her childhood memories to in those stories, which are some of her best. Her early life, again like that of some of her characters, was spent in the bosom of a loving extended family on a plantation near Greenville, Mississippi. Ellen Gilchrist came to writing late, in 1975, and after a divorce from her third husband, a New Orleans lawyer, she moved to Fayetteville, Arkansas, encouraged by her novelist friend Jim Whitehead and has since that time published one novel, *The Annunciation*, and two collections of short stories, *In the Land of Dreamy Dreams* and *Victory over Japan*, which won the 1984 American Book Award. Gilchrist's special gift is for voices, frequently including those of mostly spoiled and awesomely willful Southern white women who find themselves out on some kind of a limb and commenting on the view, as one critic aptly put it. And one of Gilchrist's most interesting narrators, a Black maid named Traceleen, describes these women and what Gilchrist is doing in her stories best of all: "Some people just meant to be more trouble than other people, demand more, cause more trouble, and cause more goodness. Got to study them so we see how things are made to happen."[1]

Ellen Gilchrist: I've been all my life a poet and a philosopher—those are the things that I read. I don't read fiction; I haven't read fiction in years. I read poetry and I read philosophy and I read books by scientists. And I view life very philosophically and I view life as a wild, burgeoning process which I find good. I think of life as good. My parents are in their late seventies and they're very healthy, strong people; they're going to live another ten, twenty years. People in my family live long, happy lives and there're many, many people in my family. I have many cousins. And I think of life as being wild and beautiful and burgeoning and exciting.

KB: Well, let's talk about your life as a writer. You're very interesting to me and a lot of other readers because you, officially anyway, started writing late. I wonder if you could tell us—

EG: I wrote when I was a young girl—I had a newspaper column when I was a sophomore in high school in a real newspaper, and I wrote all my life. After I reached puberty and started falling in love and then during my childbearing years, I never gave it a thought. I can't imagine a healthy young woman turning down being in love, having babies, all the richness, the madness of those years, to go sit in a room and do what it takes to write books. Long, long periods of solitude and introspection. I mean, unless you were sick or something or couldn't get a boyfriend [*laughs*], I can't imagine anybody doing that, and there are young women all over the United States that are, you know, turning in their lives to be—

KB: Mh-hmm.

EG: —writers, painters, all sorts of things. It's incomprehensible to me that anyone would do that. I mean, it didn't even ever occur to me. I knew that I could write. Anything that I wrote was always successful. All my life, whenever I would write something, it would be published. Actually, I think now in retrospect, if I really think about it very seriously and very deeply, I think I, when I did begin writing, I think I did it because my two oldest sons were real wild teenagers and I had lost control of them, and this was during the seventies when no one had any control over their children and I was horrified all the time that my children were going to die. I didn't know where they were, I couldn't control them, their father couldn't control them, their stepfather couldn't control them, and I went into the cave where you write books in order to pass the time while I waited to see if my children would grow up. I'm sure, I'm absolutely sure, that the most important thing to me in the world is the life of my children, and I had the first one when I was twenty, and since that moment, you know, I'd burn up everything I've ever written to save one joint on one finger of one of my children or one of my grandchildren. It's utterly paramount to me. I'm extremely interested in genetics. All the members of my family resemble each other. I mean we marry people who resemble us. And a child will turn up two generations later that looks exactly or acts exactly like someone two generations ago. And a long time ago, I began to hate the idea of death. And in this wonderful burgeoning process that is a family or a tribe there seems to be the only hope for immortality that makes any sense to me.

KB: Is your children—

EG: It's nice to leave books on the shelf. It's wonderful to leave books on the shelf for people to read 100 years from now. And that's interesting to me, but those books aren't really my creation. Those books are creations that I made out of a common language that was created by millions of minds over thousands of years. Those books contain a million stories in lives and words that are the common creation of all mankind. But my children and grandchildren and nieces and nephews and cousins are my thumbprint. And I'm not at all sure but that we don't inherit our parents' memories up to the moment of conception.

KB: Hmm.

EG: Everything I know about the little miniature programs that go into computers tells me that the human brain shouldn't contain everything that's ever happened to the species. This is a lot more interesting to me than literature. Literature's a little side trip I've been on for about the last ten years. And it's interesting to me, but I really think that very soon I won't write any more fiction.

KB: Is that right?

EG: I'll write, I've finished a book of short stories and I have a historical novel almost finished, and then I think I'll write one more big novel. And after that I'll go back to writing poetry or I'll write nonfiction or I'll write essays.

KB: What, to you, *is* the value of literature?

EG: Oh, I agree with Tom McGuane when he says that the high mission of art is the way we teach our best ideas. You can't preach to people and teach them anything. You can teach people things in the form of a poem or a short story and it will make an important and lasting impression. And I probably learned many things, that, uh—I don't think it's as important as the people who practice it want to pretend that it is. As much as I love poetry, and I love high poetry, I love great poetry, I love the Greeks, I love the great English poets, I love the great American poets, but I also like the lyrics of country and western songs and I like the lyrics of rock and roll and I'm not at all sure that one's more important than the other.

KB: Why is that?

EG: I just think that most of the people who are walking the face of the earth that have enough to eat and have a roof over their head are well meaning. Love the universe, love each other. Wish to be good. Wish to leave behind good things.

KB: One of your characters, Traceleen, she's one of my favorite voices in your stories—

EG: God, isn't she wonderful?

KB: Yeah, says that some people just are meant to be more trouble than other people. Is she speaking for you there?

EG: No, she's speaking for herself. Traceleen is a character that I created in order to give form and shape to something that Nietzsche said that I believe. He said that the greatest creativity is the least resentment. Traceleen has no resentment. She resents nothing. Traceleen loves and serves. There's been all down, all through the history of literature there've been great servants. The idea of being able to serve with no resentment. It's one of the great forms that the human spirit can take. And Black people in the South have done that many, many times. And for many years after the civil rights movement no one could cast a Black person as a servant in a piece of literature. We wouldn't do it because we thought it was wrong. And finally I made up my mind that we'd turned our back on one of the great and beautiful things that Black people had been able to do. Had been able to take the condition of servitude and turn it into a beautiful thing. And people who've lived in the South know, have all seen it happen over and over again. I was taking a big chance when I wrote a Black character as a servant.

KB: You've done it several times, though, in *The Annunciation*, too.

EG: Yeah.

KB: The friendship between—

EG: That was where I got the idea, was from the character in *The Annunciation*. I thought, I'm gonna really turn that idea loose.

KB: The reason I brought that up is because you've said that you think people are basically good, they like to love each other and that sort of thing, and yet, you do write—and people have commented on this—about characters that are like Crystal Manning who demand more and they cause more trouble, but as Traceleen says, they cause more goodness. So I guess what I'd like to know is, where do these people come from?

EG: Within any group of people, everybody has picked out a role to play. Perhaps we do about 90 percent of what we do for excitement. Psychoanalysts say that the great motivating forces are fear and excitement. People do anything for excitement. People in my family'll do anything for excitement. And by my family I mean my large extended family. Oh yeah, that's why I run around with my grandchildren, especially my little four-year-old grandchild, because he's one of the most exciting people I've ever been with in my life. It's like, I was thinking the other day, I woke up with him in the bed with me and I thought, being with this child is like living in a microwave oven. [KB laughs] He just keeps it all stirred up all the time. Even when he's asleep I can feel the force of it, and he's just full of good ideas. He says, "Oh yeah, well, let's go do this, let's go do that." He's got an idea every minute. That's probably what it means to be old. Old people are people who don't have any more good ideas, [who] don't get excited. We need to get 'em some four-year-olds to stir 'em up.

KB: But that would be a good description of a lot of your characters, wouldn't it? People who like to stir things up, get a lot of good ideas.

EG: Right.

KB: Such as Crystal Manning. Is she supposed to be kin to Rhoda Manning?

EG: Yeah, she's Rhoda's cousin. And they've got another cousin out on the West Coast, Leelee Arnold, that I'm writing about right now. Leelee's a hardboiled reporter.

KB: Well, now, Leelee, is that the same Leelee that's in—

EG: —yeah, Leelee's out on the West Coast now living in Sausalito.

KB: I see, is she out there hanging out with Nora Jane? [Laughs]

EG: No, she's out there having an affair with a rugby player, but he never calls her up. [Laughs] She's about to give up on him.

KB: So you do have a sense of the interrelatedness of all your characters.

EG: My characters are so jealous of each other, the only way they'll let a new person in the acting troupe is by having them be kin to them. That's what I finally decided. [Laughs] They've either got to be kin to 'em or an old friend or they won't let 'em come over.

KB: Well, does a story start for you, like, with a voice you hear?

EG: I don't know, I think each one starts differently, since my stories are like little novels. The story "Rich" that begins In the Land of Dreamy Dreams, which is the darkest thing I've ever written and which was caused in my mind by a rash of suicides in New Orleans which is still going on. Since I've been back in Jackson I've heard about three or four suicides in that world down there, one just worse than the other. I think it's caused by the climate. I think the climate makes this happen—either that or too much whiskey. Or the things put together. I was just horrified by these suicides and I'm sure that was the underlying, unconscious motivation that made me write this story, but I was having dinner one night with Jim Whitehead² and we were talking about something. We were in Fayetteville, Arkansas, and after he left, he and his wife went home, I sat down at the table to write this story for Jim—for some reason I thought it was going to be funny to begin with. And I wrote, "Tom and Letty Wilson were rich in everything." And the story grew from that and all the darkness of all these suicides rose up out of my unconscious mind and became one suicide, one terrible, desperate suicide.

KB: You've also written in that story and in *The Annunciation* the question of the loss of one's child, the loss of one's natural, biological child and that that theme is also—

EG: —I knew a beautiful woman for many years and one day over lunch she told me that she'd given a child away when she was fourteen or fifteen years old. I was absolutely stunned and horrified by this story. I love my mother so much. I am so crazy about my mother and I am so crazy about my children and my grandmothers and all of this mothering that I've had. The very idea of being taken from your natural mother.

KB: Was that the source of *The Annunciation*, that story?

EG: I think so, because for a long time, I'd tried for a long time to write a short story called "Cargo" about a mother who gave a child away for adoption and learns by a newspaper story that it died in an accident. Because that's what I kept thinking: what would happen if you had to give a child away, what would happen? And I thought that I would get up every day and wonder if it was alive? I would need to know—I need to know every day of my life that my children are alive. It's paramount to me. I think I've finally gotten old enough to realize that there's a will to life that a loving mother instills in a child. If you love your child, the child loves himself so much he's not going to get killed, he's keeping himself from getting killed with the same ferocity that you would if you were there.

KB: So how did you get up to Fayetteville, Arkansas, finally, after you started writing, you went up to Fayetteville to live.

EG: I wrote poetry all summer when I started writing, and I sent a big box of it to my friend Jim Whitehead, and he read it and it was wild, wild poetry. And he said, "Ellen, you can't do this in a vacuum, come up here and be with us for a while." So I went up there for a semester and studied poetry, but I had to go back—I could only stay a semester and then I went back home. Then later, about a year and a half later when my youngest son—I had to go back home because my youngest son was still in high school and I wanted him to go up there with me, but he didn't want to do it. Naturally, he didn't want to leave his high school. So after a semester, I went back home, but I always wanted to go back up there. And then when I decided to write seriously for a while, I needed to live in a place [where] it was inexpensive to live. Also I wanted to be with Jim and I wanted to be up there with Bill Harrison,[3] a good friend of mine who runs the writing program. I was never in the writing program or anything, but I liked to be around there. It was just a good place to be.

KB: Have you found that being around other writers that are your friends has been a helpful force in terms of your productivity?

EG: More than anything else, it was a way to understand the business of writing, the business part. Contracts and agents and what goes on in New York City and how it's done and why not to talk to movie people on the telephone.

KB: I take it from what you've said that you feel that writing is essentially something you kind of have to teach yourself.

EG: You have to learn to do it by doing it.

KB: I am curious about that. You are a kind of writer that has been quoted, anyway, as saying that you have a character, you have a voice, they start talking. But then how do you get it into shape? How does it end up shaping itself into a self-contained story that can stand by itself?

EG: The best ones write themselves. But I think I'm able to do that because of the ones I labored over that I probably threw away. You just learn how to do it. It's not that complicated a craft. Actually, it's not that complicated to learn to write anything. If you can read a sonnet, you can pretty much figure out how to write it. You know, someone points out to you the technical parts and you understand it or you don't. It's just not that hard to do. A good piece of writing will bring its own form with it.

KB: But do you take notes? Do you use overheard conversations, lines, things like that?

EG: No, I trust my memory to do it. You'll remember the good parts. I think if you take notes, you'll end up with a lot of stuff. The things that the mind remembers are the best parts.

KB: To what extent do you give things from yourself and your own life to your characters in your work?

EG: Oh, in the heat and passion of the creative moment, I just grab anything that's handy. I just give them anything that's in the room. You know, I always give my characters my clothes, my car, my living room furniture, my baby grand piano. I give them the nearest thing because it's the story. I want to serve the story. Faulkner never researched anything. I would never research anything while I was writing. I would never stop writing to look something up in the dictionary or the encyclopedia. I mean, I would just put anything there and I can do the research later. What you want is the music. The more I write the less I understand the process, so I just real deliberately never think about it. I think I've internalized whatever amount of craft I know or want I've internalized.

KB: One's tempted if she looks up a few of the basic facts of your biography to guess or think that maybe the character Rhoda Manning is perhaps the one that's closest to you in terms of—is that just coincidental—

EG: Oh, yes, she really is, because I gave Rhoda all my childhood memories.

KB: Right, that's what I wondered.

EG: I can feel Rhoda. Of all my women characters or female characters, Rhoda's the one that I can feel and smell and touch. I can see things through her eyes.

KB: To what do you attribute your gifts for getting inside the heads of children of all ages. Is it just your memory?

EG: I just like children; I'm interested in them. I think they're wonderful. I think they're hilarious. They never lie, children never lie. Children are way up, probably in the first grade, before they start lying.

KB: The thing that happens in the story that you read today, "Revenge," is that little girls—certainly parallels my upbringing—little girls are told what they can't do. In order to participate in the fullness of life, which was male life, they had to, like Crystal, give up, you know, trade in to fail and anything that meant anything in order to fly that silly . . .

EG: Yeah, I've been thinking about it a lot, I think that—my parents, our parents, parents of people my age, were still Victorians and this was a very well-meant way to protect children, to protect girls from their own sexuality. My mother's generation watched women die in childbirth, and they loved us—they didn't want us to die in childbirth, and they didn't want anyone to impregnate us. They didn't want anyone to have intercourse with us before we were married or after we were married. They'd put up with it after we were married because they couldn't stop it. They wanted us safe and they didn't want us dying. And they didn't want us impregnated because it was a real fear. It wasn't some fantasy fear, or some—I mean, that's why the Victorians put those long skirts on their daughters. That's why supersensitive men in those cultures went into monasteries in order not to be the one. Those men, men of that generation had watched women die of childbirth. Childbirth was a terrible and frightening thing that often killed people. Go out to any cemetery in this part of the country, which is all I know well, and there'll be one man and three women who died in childbirth. That man wasn't doing some mean thing to these women. That was a terrible way for him to live. This was sad for everybody. I think what they were trying to do, I think everything that they were trying to do was to protect us. It made us mad and it confused us. And so from our point of view, you know, it was one thing but their point of view, it was just loving us and trying to protect us.

KB: Well, when you write about these things, are you writing just to describe what is, or are you writing with a point of view or opinion about it?

EG: I don't know, I just serve whatever vision comes to me. Whatever story comes to me, I'm just the typist. I trust myself to be delivering good messages.

KB: How've you been received down here?

EG: You know, people down here love my work. They think it's funny. There's a wonderful woman who lives in Jackson named Beth Jones who says that as long as all the cards are on the table, you can deal with them. I think that's true in a marriage, or it's true in a friendship, or it's true in a culture. Which is why more and more I think that I'll probably be working in some kind of news media and why I enjoy working with National Public Radio because we have to keep the cards on the table. When the cards are on the table, you can deal with them. When they're under the table, trouble begins.

KB: Do you think you write to understand people that aren't like you or understand behavior that's not like yours?

EG: Well, I think the subconscious or unconscious mind does the writing. It's either trying to understand something or it's praising something.

KB: Is there any one thing or some things that you can tell us that you think you are definitely praising in your work? Would life, the force of life itself be one thing?

EG: Yeah, just life itself. Anytime people have a good idea and carry it through.

KB: Seems like there's just—

EG: —Or acts of heroism. I don't have much luck writing about acts of heroism, but I try. I heard a story on the radio about three years ago. I was in a little restaurant on Dickson Street in Fayetteville, and there was a radio on in the back where they were cooking the food. A young man about twenty-one years old had woken from a dead sleep in the middle of the night in some place like Alma, Arkansas, and the house next door was on fire and there was an infant inside. And the mother and father—it was impossible for them to get back inside and the fire department couldn't get back inside, and without even putting on his clothes, he got out of bed wearing a pair of boxer shorts, walked next door, walked into the burning house, picked up the baby, and walked back out. He did it all just in a state, just one of those incredible states that you read about. Just a state of pure zen. He walked in there past the firemen and the people, got the child, carried it back out, and handed it to them. And then all the newspapers and radio stations and television stations in the state started converging on him trying to make him into a hero and he said, "Get out of my house. Don't you dare make me into a hero. I don't even know what I did. I don't know how I did it, and I definitely don't want to talk about it, and don't you dare put my name on the radio." [*Both laugh*] Isn't that wonderful? I tried to give that act of heroism to Freddy Harwood and I think I succeeded, but I didn't really succeed because nothing can touch the wonder, the exotic quality of real acts of heroism in the world.

KB: For our listeners: who's Freddy Harwood?

EG: Freddy Harwood is a bookstore owner out on the West Coast. He owns the largest and least successful bookstore in Berkeley, California. Well, that's how he . . .

KB: And he falls very much in love with Nora Jane Whittington.

EG: Right, he is fated to be in love with Nora Jane Whittington.

KB: Who wants nothing to do with him.

EG: She likes him just fine; it's just that her heart has been captured by a young man named Sandy. She knows enough to want to be in love with Freddy Harwood, but it's too late.

KB: Are we going to hear more about her and her baby?

EG: Yeah, except they are identical twin girls named Tammili and Lydia.

KB: Aha. So that's who Tammili is at the end of that story, then because she's been saying it's going to be Lydia if she has it and it's Tammili who speaks at the end of that story.

EG: Right, it's Tammili and Lydia.

KB: I wanted to ask you about that, as to who that is there. She's going to have twin girls.

EG: They're identical twin baby girls.

KB: Is she going to start doing more with her voice, Nora Jane? Is she going to sing?

EG: I don't know. I don't know. I can't get Nora Jane to do that. Nora Jane doesn't want to have her name in the papers. Nora Jane doesn't like for people to look at her. Nora Jane just likes to go around the world just being herself and not having a lot of people know who she is. And that's why she won't use her voice.

KB: And that's why she has six Dynel wigs and can change herself.

EG: Nora Jane is very shy.

KB: What's going to happen to Sandy? Is he out of it now?

EG: I don't know. I don't want to tell 'cause it's all in my new book.

KB: Ahh.

EG: I want to sell at least ten copies of my new book.

KB: Is this the novel, or is this another set of stories?

EG: It's a book of short stories called *Drunk with Love*. It's all being put to bed in Boston right now and will be published in October by Little, Brown. May be my last book of short stories.

KB: And Sandy and Nora Jane are back in it?

EG: Sandy and Nora Jane, and Traceleen is in the book telling the true story of how Miss Crystal quit drinking.

KB: Is Freddy going to be back in it, too?

EG: Yeah, in fact there's one extra story that we may still put into the manuscript. The title story is about Freddy Harwood. "Drunk with Love" is a Freddy Harwood story. And there's another story that may also be there called "The Starlight Express," but we haven't decided. Because the book's already been sold in Europe and England as it is with the fourteen stories. This is a fifteenth story that we may add to the American edition.

KB: You're one of those writers that really came out well with an academic press book. *In the Land of Dreamy Dreams* came out by the University of Arkansas Press, and it was a success, and that's kind of unusual. What happened? Did they really push that book?

EG: No, I finished it one afternoon and Bill Harrison wanted to take it to New York and give it to his agent. And I told him that I didn't want him to do that 'cause I didn't want—at that time I didn't know what a nice place the publishing world in New York was. It was a nice place and a lot of nice people are in it. They're wonderful, they're fun to talk to, they're fun to work with, they're just like all of us. But at the time I didn't know that and I said, "No, I don't want you to take that book to New York," and he said, "Well, if I can't take it to New York, let me take it over and give it to Miller[4] because he's just started a press for the university and he needs a work of fiction." And I said, "Oh, ok, well, you can take it over there because I know those people." So he took it over and gave it to Miller and they called me in a few weeks and told me that they definitely wanted to publish it. And then I just forgot all about it because I didn't think anyone would pay any attention to a book of short stories from a little university press. And the next thing I knew, it was published and *The Washington Post* gave it a rave review,[5] and it started selling like crazy and they just kept making more and more printings of it, and it was passed around by word of mouth essentially through the academic community. Which partly they loved the book, but I'm sure they also liked the idea that a university press had done that well with a book.

KB: What do you think it is about Mississippi? Some people say that Mississippi seems to be a breeding ground for writers. Do you think there's any truth to that? Do you have any thoughts on that one way or another?

EG: I think it's the language, the beauty of the language, the musical quality of the English language is achieved down here.

KB: It has seemed to me that Mississippians tend to revere their writers. Do you think that's just a coincidence with two of them having been world figures like Faulkner and Welty? Or do you think there's any kind of appreciation for writing as a vocation down here?

EG: Mississippi's good to its artists, not just its writers, its artists. Mississippians worship beauty, or the people in Mississippi that I come from, and that I've known all my life worship beauty. In the human face, in literature, in their homes, they want things to be beautiful and they make things beautiful.

KB: Are there some things that you really can't write about? I think you said something about yoga being something—

EG: Oh. Yeah. There are some real wonderful things that have happened in the world you can't write about. You can't write about sexual intercourse; you can't write about yoga. You can't really write about wonder; you can circle it.

KB: Would you call, say, for instance, the scene where Amanda has her baby in *The Annunciation* that's a case kind of circling wonder, isn't it there?

EG: Yeah, and it's Christmas Eve. So I guess I circled wonder.

KB: And it's funny. I mean, she's on stage.

EG: Right.

KB: [*Laughing*] It's a great performance. She's performing this birth.

EG: I wrote that scene on Christmas Day, early in the morning. I wrote the last chapter of that book.

KB: So would you agree, I mean, would you be comfortable if I as a reader said to you that that was a way you circled wonder there, that humor is one way to circle?

EG: Right. But I sort of write in a dream, not in a real state when I'm writing. I can't talk about it afterwards. It makes perfect sense to me; I know what I'm trying to create. And then I just do the best job that I can. When you're really on, you're not there. You're just the servant, serving the vision, giving a gift to the world, although Bill Harrison told me he was going to throw up if I ever said that in public. He said, "Do not say that art is a gift to the world." But it is a gift to the world and he knows it and he gives it, too. Ginny Stanford[6] says that art is a gift to the world. She just finished the painting that's going to be the cover of my new book. I never had Ginny paint a painting to be a cover. My imagination or my mind would choose a painting that I knew of hers, and as soon as I'd make the title for a book, I always know which of her paintings that I want to go with it. But this time she had to repaint the painting because the painting was sold, the painting that I want for *Drunk with Love* was sold to a psychiatrist in Texas, and we don't know where it is. And we only had a bad slide of it with the light falling across the subject's face in a bad way so Little, Brown couldn't use it. So Ginny repainted the painting from the slide. And she called me up yesterday from the banks of the swollen Russian River in Sebastopol, California, to tell me that she finished the painting the day before the rain started to fall. I can't wait to see it; it's this wonderful, hilarious painting.

KB: What does a real editor do for a writer, at least for you?

EG: Mostly, editors want me to write more about something. They want me to expand something. I have a poet's sensibility about writing—I'm always trying to say it in as few words as possible, and an editor wants you to tell more about something. I usually go on and do it. Why not?

KB: I take it you write to entertain yourself, too, don't you?

EG: Oh, I really do. I do it because I like to do it. I mean, there are twenty-four hours in a day and I'm awake about most of them. I gotta have something to do with all that time. One of the things that I've found to do that amused me is to write stories.

KB: Well, how good a judge do you consider yourself of your own work?

EG: Probably better than I used to be. I can tell what it feels like when I'm writing it whether it's going to be good or not. If it's making me really happy and making me laugh when I'm writing it like the Traceleen stories did, then I'll probably elicit the same response from my readers. And I don't write things anymore that make me sad. At whatever cost to my work, or to my reputation as a writer, I'm not going to write junk that makes me sad. I mean, if it's making me cry—who wants to make people cry? Life is short and sweet.

KB: Ellen Gilchrist's books are *In the Land of Dreamy Dreams*, *The Annunciation*, and *Victory over Japan*. They're all available from Little, Brown. The American Audio Prose Library is a comprehensive collection of distinguished writers reading and discussing their work. It's produced by Kay Bonetti and Ed Herman. The music is from Tommy Dorsey. For information about other writers in this series, write us, the American

Audio Prose Library, at the address printed on the label of this tape. This project is made possible by the National Endowment for the Arts and the Missouri Arts Council.

Notes

1. From "Traceleen's Telling a Story Called 'A Bad Year,'" published in *Victory over Japan*, Little, Brown, 1983.

2. Codirector of the creative writing program at the University of Arkansas.

3. Codirector of the creative writing program at the University of Arkansas.

4. Miller Williams, the author of over thirty books of poetry, scholarship, and translation, founded the University of Arkansas Press.

5. Susan Wood, "Louisiana Stories: The Debut of Ellen Gilchrist," review of *In the Land of Dreamy Dreams*, by Ellen Gilchrist, *Book World–The Washington Post*, March 21, 1982: 4, 13.

6. Ginny Crouch Stanford, an artist whose paintings served as the covers of *In the Land of Dreamy Dreams*, *Victory over Japan*, and *Drunk with Love*. She was married to the poet Frank Stanford, a close friend of Gilchrist whose press, Lost Roads Press, published her first book of poetry.

Ellen Gilchrist: A Voice of Southern Conflict

Melissa Biggs / 1987

From *In the Vernacular: Interviews at Yale with Sculptors of Culture* (McFarland, 1991), 85–91. Reprinted by permission.

When Ellen Gilchrist's grandchildren come to visit her in Arkansas, they all sleep together in a big bed and tell each other stories. The tales that fill that crowded bed probably approach the beauty of the ones that fill the pages of her books. Gilchrist begins her stories to her grandchildren with "Once upon a time." The stories of her books also reflect the Southern literary tradition's reliance on the evolving narrative voice. The author of two novels and three books of short stories, Gilchrist has recently published an autobiography, *Falling Through Space*.

Gilchrist was born on the banks of the Mississippi—what she affectionately calls the Delta. At fourteen she wrote a column called "Chit 'n' Chat 'Bout This 'n' That," for a local Franklin, Kentucky, paper. Though she continued to write occasionally, it was not until she was forty that her writing career took off. She became the editor of a New Orleans paper and later enrolled in creative writing classes at the University of Arkansas.

Her first published book was a collection of poems entitled *The Land Surveyor's Daughter*. In 1981 a collection of her short stories, *In the Land of Dreamy Dreams*, was published to immense critical acclaim. And her next collection of stories, *Victory over Japan*, won the 1984 American Book Award for Fiction.

Gilchrist writes predominantly about the South. Her protagonists are usually upper-class women struggling with society's constricting mores. Trapped between their own desires and the demands of Southern society, these women grow desperate and destructive. On a scorching Arkansas day in the summer of 1987, Gilchrist spoke over a crackling phone line to Melissa Biggs about her works and life as a writer.

Melissa Biggs: When did you first start writing?

Ellen Gilchrist: Oh, I've done it all my life. I could read and write before I went to school. I was raised in the Mississippi Delta and there wasn't anything else to do. When I was little, I pretended to read and write before I could read. I don't even remember how I learned how, I wanted to do it so much. People in my family are all literate people. My grandfather was always sitting at his desk writing, and my father walked around with pencils and paper in his pockets. There was this solitary thing that all the members of my family did; they would be sitting somewhere at a desk writing and I always did that. I don't think what I do now is qualitatively very different from what I did when I was four years old. It's a perfectly natural thing for me to do, to re-create reality and express joy or horror or whatever by sitting down at a desk and doing it.

Biggs: What writers do you think have influenced you the most?

Gilchrist: I think the primary influence on my writing and on the way I write and the forms I choose to write in is J. D. Salinger. After I've come back around to him from everywhere. I don't even think of Salinger as modern because he's been gone for so long. See, I approve of everything he's ever done. I love the way he quit. He said, "Fuck you," to everybody. They published a book of critical essays about his work, in which a whole bunch of assholes, who later went on to become sort of half-shot writers, all sorts of people who couldn't even touch his wings, were taking off against him.

Biggs: Is that when he stopped writing?

Gilchrist: Yes, they published all of this criticism against *Franny and Zooey*. He obviously thought, "I don't need this," and just stopped. And all he's been doing since is living a sort of wonderful normal life. So I am influenced by how he's led his life as a writer, because it's true to what he wrote. It's true to what he told me he knew about human existence. He told me he wasn't going to fuck with assholes and I believed him.

Biggs: Can you define what you want to get out of writing?

Gilchrist: I want to have a good time and make other people have a good time. And if there are bad guys I want to hate them and if there are good guys I want to love them and that's it. That's what I want to do in life; that's what I want to do as a writer. I already know who I want for my audience. I want people with a sense of humor. People who don't have a sense of humor can't read my work. Because even the darkest thing I ever wrote is funny.

Biggs: What do you consider the darkest thing you've ever written?

Gilchrist: The story "Rich." That story's not really funny. It's about New Orleans and the decadence and sadness and disease of that culture that I lived in and that many of my cousins still live in. It's why those people jump off the bridge every day. Wealthy, wealthy people who have everything in the whole world kill themselves every year in New Orleans. Always the most beautiful ones kill themselves.

Biggs: That is an incredibly powerful story.

Gilchrist: It's about the disease of that city. Writing the story cured me of that. It was a hard story to write.

Biggs: Have you taken any formal classes in writing?

Gilchrist: I took a class with Eudora Welty once. But she didn't teach us anything. She was just a kind and lovely old woman. But like all great writers she couldn't teach writing because she doesn't know how she does it. I can't teach it either. I tried once. I can help someone occasionally. I can tell them what I like.

Later I went up to the University of Arkansas to study poetry with Miller Williams, and there Bill Harrison showed me how to write a short story. He literally showed me how to write a short story in about two months. And then I didn't study it anymore, because he showed me what I needed to know. He told me that it had to have a beginning, a middle, and an end and a couple of other things. And that was all I needed to know. I wrote "Rich" for him. I think I was curing myself of the years I put in in that swamp.

Biggs: Do you adhere to any sort of writing routine?

Gilchrist: During the years that I created that body of fiction that is my work, I was working from dawn until past noon and not doing anything else, except maybe going out to run. But I'm not working that way now. I mean I've gotten to the point now where if I'm in the middle of something I still work like that, but I don't work like that when I'm developing ideas. Now I can be developing ideas down at the Station restaurant talking to my friends. But when you're beginning you don't trust yourself. When you're beginning anything you have to pay your dues, and it's real hard. I lived by myself a lot of that time which is really unusual for me, living all my life in a house full of people, and I'll never do that again. But it was important at the time.

Biggs: You started writing poetry?

Gilchrist: My ambitions were always to be a poet. Although, that was the thing Bill Harrison taught me. He taught me that you can contain poetry within fiction. That fiction contains poems, that it can contain poems. And what he told me, and this is interesting and can be useful. He told me that you have to write the *libretto* before you can write the *aria*. Wasn't that wonderful?

Biggs: How have criticism and acclaim affected your approach to writing or haven't they?

Gilchrist: Well, I was very fortunate, because I was in my forties when that began to happen, and I was old enough and I had good enough friends who were established writers to be wary of it and to take the good parts, but I mean I am sure that it exacted a price on my writing and my life but not a big one and not anything I can't get back. I just shudder to think of what would have happened to me if I'd been young when that happened or what would happen to anyone, because I would have believed what they had said instead of what I knew in reality. Someone's subjective judgment of you and your work is their subjective judgment, whether it's praise or not. Writers have to become good judges of their own work. You have to keep trusting your own mind about it.

You know, I have more fans and greater reviews in London than I do from any place in the world, and my stories have been translated into many languages. The British really understand what I'm doing, and they will over and over and over again pick out the stories to praise that are the ones that I know are the best pieces of work. The ones that the American reviewers a lot of the time don't like at all.

Biggs: That's fascinating. Why do you think that is?

Gilchrist: I don't know. I think it's because I've read more British literature than I have American literature. I really think that's why, because I'm more on their wavelength. My ancestors considered themselves Englishmen and Scots. They came here in the seventeenth century but they considered themselves Scots. I don't know why that is, but it's the language, the language of Shakespeare and the language of the King James version of the Bible. I've been reading Shakespeare all summer, and my God, it is so wonderful. My son tells me that there are a lot of studies now that say a *lot* of people think that Shakespeare wrote part of the King James version of the Bible. He was a contemporary and he was the reigning language expert. All of those guys were in it together back then and they were doing it right.

Biggs: Having written a novel and short stories, do you find one genre more interesting or more difficult than another?

Gilchrist: Well, the novel is not fun. The novel demands from a poet's mind or short story writer's mind that we write things that we would never leave in. You have to write passages that I would never leave in a short story or a poem, because they're boring prose. And your editors and people say, "You have to tell us this and you have to tell us that." And I don't think that I have to, but sooner or later you make those compromises in the novel form. I never read novels. I mean I read a novel like *One Hundred Years of Solitude*; that's one of the great novels.

Biggs: You've said that you feel your writing is on a British wavelength, in any way do you feel a part of a Southern literary tradition?

Gilchrist: Well, I love William Faulkner and I love Ms. Welty's work. I don't like her novels but I like her short stories. I like William Faulkner's novels and Ms. Welty's short stories, and surely I learned from both of them that it was alright to use my own voice. But there wasn't any Southern literary tradition for a long time. It's just making a comeback, because we weren't allowed to talk about anything. We were just supposed to lie there on the floor and say we were sorry that our great-great-great-grandfathers had slaves if they did.

Biggs: You write about so many stages and ages of women's lives, is there one in specific that you are particularly drawn to in your writing?

Gilchrist: I think for a long time I was really fascinated with early adolescence, around thirteen, fourteen. Because I know during that time when I was writing, I think the Rhoda stories pretty much coalesce around that age, and I would see little girls waiting for the streetcar in New Orleans with their little Roman Catholic plaid skirts and their socks rolled down and a bit of pouty lip, and I think, "Oh God the power, the power that is in a thirteen- or fourteen-year-old girl." I mean they are just so wonderful. There's a wonderful little girl who is the daughter of a friend of mine here, who is just going to be about twelve. She's just got her braces. There's almost a radiation about her. It's almost like an aroma hovering around her. She's got a twelve-year-old buddy who looks like she's seventeen. I see the two of them together and it's just a wonderful sight.

Biggs: When you write about someone like Rhoda who appears at different ages and in different collections of stories, is it hard to pick her up again?

Gilchrist: No, it's like a friendship, like someone you haven't seen in a year and they show up and you pick up the conversation where you left off.

Biggs: Do you ever think of gathering all of the Rhoda stories into one collection or writing a novel about Rhoda or Nora?

Gilchrist: My agent's always thinking that up, but I think it would be boring. I put the stories together the way they are because that's how they entered me. I think it would be really boring to have all the stories together in one volume.[1]

Biggs: The dynamics of relationships play a large part in your stories, and it seems that often parents are forming intimate relationships with children, specifically fathers and daughters. Do you see that in any way as a reflection of adults' inadequacies in their own relationships?

Gilchrist: I would never use that word, because I don't think we're inadequate. I think we're wonderful and I think it's an amazing thing that goes on between parents and children, an amazing thing. You are the children. The children aren't you. They've got an open end and you've got an open end where your parents are concerned. In the sense that children don't think about their parents, except, "Oh God, I should call my mother." But parents from the moment their children are born direct their energies towards you all. The major creative act of my life was the birth of my children. And the most exciting thing in my late life has been the birth of my grandchildren. Literature doesn't hold a candle to it. Literature and the arts and bridge building is what men do because they can't do that, except now we're letting them. It's an amazing, amazing thing to be a father. I mean amazing.

You know, I keep thinking I have this father who was a great professional athlete and I have brothers whom he is so close to. He's eighty now and my brothers if they are not nearby in any two weeks, my older brother will come from anywhere in the world and just pass through Jackson, he lives in Mississippi, and just to be with Daddy. He's going to be with my father in the last years of his life. But I don't have that relationship with him, because I was a beautiful, attractive young girl and my father is such a good father that he wasn't even very nice to me after I got to be thirteen years old. That's the way they're supposed to treat us. That's an act of love and of caring for us.

There's a scene in a Rhoda story that is the most insightful thing I've ever written about it, and after that I haven't thought about it, because I got what I wanted. I mean that's as much as I think I can know. It's when Rhoda and her father are together in the woods, and they look at each other, and they love each other so much that there's nothing to do but start an argument. That's how he protects her. That's all I know, and that's as much as I'm going to know about it, because that's all I need to know. When I wrote that I knew something about my father.

Biggs: In *Drunk with Love*, many of the characters fall in love but then they're separated or subject to a tragedy. Does that reveal a dark view that you have of love?

Gilchrist: Well, after I began to conceive of the stories as a book, I just thought, well, I am just going to write all of the love stories that I can think of.

Biggs: But they're all so sad.

Gilchrist: Well, a lot of the time a happy ending to a story just doesn't work. And at the very best the love just disappears and turns into friendship or the people run a family together. But the kind of madness that we call romantic love doesn't last. Isn't that a shame? It's the crazy stuff at the start, and then the next spring everybody's right back at work, trying to do it again. Just for that week or that month. The thing I hate about it is waiting for that phone to ring. I could never wait for people. I always called them up. Even when it was never, never done to call a boy, I always just called them up.

Biggs: Do you feel that women have different experiences and roles as writers than men do?

Gilchrist: Oh, I think it's more individual than gender. I mean writers are separated by galaxies. Anyone who is really talented or has a shot at really doing it is going to create their own reality. They're going to create the whole show. That's one of the reasons to do it.

Biggs: How much of your writing is autobiographical?

Gilchrist: Well, everything everybody does is autobiographical writing in one way or another. I mean all you have is your own experiences. It just depends on how much you're going to try to disguise it.

Note

1. *Rhoda: A Life in Stories* was published by Little, Brown in 1995.

The Woman as Writer and Reader: A Group of Award-Winning Women Writers Discuss Issues of Special Interest to Women

Furman Studies / 1988

From *Furman Studies* 33, no. 1 (Winter 1989), 12–21. Reprinted by permission of Jake Grove.

College students and professors, high school students and teachers, avid readers young and old—approximately 500 of them gathered in Daniel Recital Hall last March 24–26 from as near as the Furman dormitories and from as far away as Virginia and middle Georgia. The occasion was a symposium, "The Woman as Writer and Reader." Furman had often hosted individual writers, but had never assembled a group of significant literary figures to interact with each other. For a number of years several people had been eager to have Furman sponsor such a gathering. When funds finally became available, it seemed appropriate to focus on women writers since much of the serious work being published today is written by women, some from this region. In addition, the Emrys Foundation of Greenville was sponsoring a month-long celebration of women in the arts, and Furman wanted to make a contribution. Josephine Humphreys, whose first novel, *Dreams of Sleep*, won the Ernest Hemingway Award and second novel, *Rich in Love*, has been widely acclaimed, opened the symposium to a packed auditorium on Thursday night, March 24. Friday morning's activities included a reading by Louise Shivers, author of *Here to Get My Baby Out of Jail*, which was named best first novel of 1983 by *USA Today*. Shivers was followed by Furman English Professor Willard Pate, one of the organizers of the conference, who read Sally Fitzgerald's paper, "The Level Gaze of the Artist." Fitzgerald, editor of [Flannery] O'Connor's collected works and letters and biographer of the late author, was to have attended the symposium, but was detained in Italy for personal reasons.

Friday afternoon began with a talk by Barbara Hardy, professor of English at Birkbeck College of the University of London. Hardy, author of numerous scholarly works about Dickens, George Eliot, and Virginia Woolf, spoke about her own reactions to the works of fiction written by the other participants. American Book Award–winning Ellen Gilchrist, author of *Victory over Japan*, *In the Land of Dreamy Dreams*, and *Drunk with Love*, closed Friday's activities with a reading that evening. Then Gloria Naylor, also an American Book Award winner for *The Women of Brewster Place*, read from her recently published *Mama Day* on Saturday morning. Two panel discussions gave the participating writers an opportunity to exchange ideas with each other and their readers in public. The first panel, moderated by Pate on Friday afternoon, focused on the question, "Do You Think of Yourself as a Woman Writer?" The second, moderated by Dr. Ann Sharp, another organizer of the symposium and a member of Furman's English faculty, addressed the issue of "The Place of Women Writers in the Literary Tradition." By all accounts, the symposium was a major success. One member of the audience commented, "I could hardly believe the good fortune of having this in Greenville. The person sitting next to me had driven from Charlotte for the day. This exposure is so valuable for 'would be' writers . . . and pure heaven for readers." Another wrote, "Thanks for a stimulating symposium! Encore!" Edited versions of the two panel discussions appear in the following pages.

Willard Pate: We would like first to have all four of you entertain the question, "Do you think of yourself as a woman writer?" Then we will ask for supplemental questions from the audience.

Louise Shivers: Well, I don't know how to answer that question but maybe as we talk, more will come to me. I really do try to write stories. I am a woman and I'm, at this point in my life, very happy about being a woman. So that's the way it's going to come out, but I really don't think about it that much.

Ellen Gilchrist: I wrote an answer down but I wouldn't have had to because Louise just said what I'm thinking. That doesn't mean that it isn't a good title for a panel discussion, but I decided that if I do this I have to tell you exactly what I think whether I am popular with you or not. Because like all well-raised children, I was raised to try to get people to like me. But I don't think of myself as a woman when I write because I think of myself—I wrote this down—"As part of the physical universe which includes the reaches of the stars and the sub-atomic particles." I think it's a terrible mistake for a writer to start limiting their conception of themselves. But Louise just said exactly the same thing much more simply and probably more beautifully.

Gloria Naylor: This is a question that has only been asked of writers in the last twenty years or maybe even fifteen years. I cannot imagine anyone having said to Richard Wright, "What is it like to be a Black, male writer?" or to John Irving, "Tell me, how is it to be male and a writer?" Because we assume naturally that anything that is indeed male writes. So, therefore, in texts you will have the writer, he uses the pen and uses metaphor. That's a problem that does not exist with the people on this panel. It exists with the way we perceive things in this society. If we make the assumption that there is a norm, and if that norm is indeed male or if that norm is indeed white, upper middle-class male, then anything that's not in that norm has to explain their existence and explain what they are doing. The whole process of writing, folks, before the word processor, took a piece of paper and a pencil, and it took a desire to have something to say. From Homer on, every writer has articulated through their own particular experience. Shakespeare's Egyptians, his Venetians, his Caribbeans all spoke like Elizabethan English people. Because that was what Shakespeare was. But now, lo and behold, Alice Walker will come along and she will articulate through her experience and will be asked to explain, "Why did you write from that perspective?" You know it is like saying, "Why do you breathe, Gloria?" "Why do you breathe, Josephine?" And I don't take exception to it; I am not insulted by it. But I am a bit put out by the closed-mindedness of our society that has not accepted the reality that women have been here writing about their experiences at the same time men have been writing. And that is what we have to change.

Josephine Humphreys: I never considered this question at all while I was writing my first book. But suddenly after publishing and talking to people and having people react to my work, I realized it is a question. At first it annoyed me every time it came up. I didn't want to talk about being a woman writer, and I didn't like the distinction made between a woman's book and a man's book. However, in an insidious kind of way all of that thinking has made me think the opposite. There are some things in my own personal life right now—a lot of emotional turmoil that I think is related to being a woman, and in particular with children—that affects my writing a lot. So I hesitate to say that I'm not affected by the female experience and that it doesn't affect my writing.

In a way, though, writing affects my femininity more than femininity affects my writing. It's sort of an opposite thing for me. Writing has changed my life in so many ways, and that's one of them. It seems to be constantly modifying my perceptions of myself and of what I am doing.

Questioner: I'm curious to know how you are able to write, as well as cope with the many demands in women's lives—children, family, husbands, dogs.

Humphreys: This is part of my whole problem now. When I began writing I handled the problem by becoming schizophrenic and dividing my life completely down the middle. Doing children half my time and writing the other half. Well, children and family, but everything else disappeared out of my life, including friends. And that is the worst loss. Everything else too—all my contact with community. At the time I was clearly glad to be rid of it. But this is ten years down that road now, and I find that the lack of friends and the lack of contact with the human community is killing. It really is very, very difficult to maintain over that long period of time. And though I give some thought and effort to restoring myself in that respect, I have a feeling that I will cut back even further, so that I'm eventually going to cut back on the things that are crucial and important to me and that I love. So it's frightening to me that there seems to be, to me anyway, almost a danger in writing.

Naylor: I understand what Josephine is saying. That's one of the reasons I teach. Because it forces me to leave my home and to reach out to people and listen to what they are saying and communicate. Because as a writer you are rewarded for staying inside, for becoming a recluse. That's one of the ironies of the whole process. The more you hold yourself off from the world, the better you're able to re-create the world that you've sort of shut off. Unlike the women on my left and right, I don't have to worry about the nuclear family. There was a husband once, but I got rid of him, and so there are no small children who are dependent upon me. So there's even a greater danger that there'll be no one demanding my time outside of me. And you don't want that. You want to be a whole human being if you possibly can, but it becomes a fight.

Gilchrist: I'll tell you what I was thinking about when Gloria was saying that. My first book of fiction was supposed to be published the same month that my first grandchild was being born in New Orleans. I've always thought what a lucky and fortunate and star-created situation that was for me because it saved me. I remember I called Eudora Welty sometime in August, and she said something about I know you're excited about your book, and I said I am. And then I said, "Eudora, the baby's going to be born exactly the same time, and I don't know which one to be more excited about." And she said, "Oh, Ellen, they're not in competition." Oh, wasn't that wonderful? And they aren't; and I thought about it a million times. But they are. Since I am an obsessive person, I have to do what Josephine used to do—I have to go from obsession to obsession, but I've been doing it for fifty-three years, and I'm real comfortable with that.

Shivers: Even though my children were late teenagers by the time I started writing, I still have almost the same problem I think Jo was talking about. We have a very close family and even though they're now grown people with husbands and wives and I have a grandchild, they're constant, everyday problems. I mean, they still are your children. I was so intense about finally getting the chance to be a writer and not wanting to miss the chance to tell these stories that I finally found out I could tell, and at the same time wanting to keep the family. That's all—I don't do anything else. I'm either writing or with the family, and there are some relationships and friendships that hurt to give up, but you do have to give up some things if you are a writer. That's for sure, and I've been there. It's worth it.

Gilchrist: I've learned a wonderful thing from having that happen to me, though. I've learned what it is when a man becomes obsessive about his work. I know now he doesn't dislike me, he's not tired of me; he's excited about something he's doing, he's moving toward a goal that he has created for himself, real or imaginary. And not only a man. I say men because I have sons, and my sons are at the age where they're beginning to really fulfill their mature lives, and I see them get an idea in their head and start going toward it, and nobody else is going to exist for them for weeks or months. And it's wonderful to know that that's okay. They're going to come out the other end and say, "Where are my friends? Where are my children? Where's my mother?"

Questioner: Mrs. Shivers, it seems to me that both Roxy and Georgeanna, whom you shared with us in your reading this morning, seem to be very aware of their roles in society as far as being mothers and taking care of their houses. You mentioned that you married very early and that you didn't start writing until you were about forty, and I wondered if their experiences and your experience are parallel, if you're trying to send a message about a woman's place in society through Roxy and Georgeanna, and the difference now from then.

Shivers: I probably am. Neither one of them really had much choice. Georgianna certainly, in the late eighteen hundreds, didn't have any choice. There were no libraries and bookmobiles. There she was in this little town and she was raised to—you know, you're a wife and a mother and you cook meals and take care of the men and there you are. That's your life. And then Roxy came on in 1930 and did the same thing. Well, I was raised the same way. I'm sure most of y'all were raised that way. The woman steps back. You give the man the biggest piece of meat and you wait until he eats. Yes, I am still working out something in myself about that. And I see it in my daughters, though they've already gone far from it. I think I started giving them a message pretty strong, "Get out there and go." But I still have some problems with myself, and, of course, I'm writing through those problems.

Gilchrist: Nobody ever told me that women were supposed to take a back seat to anybody. I just didn't even perceive it as being between men and women. You went out there and fought with your brothers for whatever you wanted—this is the kind of stuff I say that makes me unpopular. I saw being the only girl in the family as a position where I was the only one who could run to my mother and grab hold and hide behind her and say, "He hit me! He hit me!" I always started it!

Questioner: This question is directed to Mrs. Shivers. I heard you say at another workshop that the tender trap for most Southern girls was being daddy's little girl or something to that effect. That it was a trap that was very difficult to get out of.

Shivers: It was for me. I did have this wonderful father, and he was just very tender and sweet. And then I had all these brothers. It helped me stay a victim a lot longer. Because they were protective, I was safe. I was really safe. I had Daddy and the boys. And that's not all bad. My daddy was a sweet thing, and I do think of him as sweet. I didn't start writing until after my father died. And that's part of the thing that made me go on to do it, I'm sure. One of the things that feels so good about all this is I know how proud he would be that I finally did it. But I also know now that he would have been proud if I had gone ahead and done it a long time before I did. You know, I like men and I never had any big awe about men. I was surrounded by them all the time, not only the ones at home but all the boys who worked at the funeral home, so it wasn't any great mysterious thing. But somewhere in there I had just gotten that message from the time I was born: "Keep quiet and be sweet and they'll love you better." I have a part in the new novel I just finished where I say, "Maybe that kind of compassion and all this Southern, loving way is just another way to say fear." Maybe it was just another word for fear. So I'm still trying to figure all this out.

Gilchrist: It's another word for Oedipus complex, if you say all that. Now that is amazing. All that a female child can do from the time she sits up and walks and talks is repeat that relationship that she had with her daddy. And all that a male child can do is repeat the one he had with his mama. And it's not bad. It's just how the human mind works, but you can never finish sounding the mysteries of the Oedipus complex.

Humphreys: I had no brothers at all and no boys my own age to talk to and went to a girls' school. So my father was the only male in my life. And though I couldn't wait until he died to publish, he wishes that I had. The messages to me when I was growing up were you need not compete with men, and women can do anything that men can do. And you must get all A's in school and you must be the best that you possibly can, but never let anyone know how smart you are. Especially don't let men know. And never . . . let's see, the things that you could do that might ruin your life included number one, getting pregnant, number two, going on the stage, number three, publishing something. And those were explicit rules.

Pate: This is very Southern.

Naylor: Yeah, very Southern. Although my folks are from Mississippi and I was conceived in Mississippi and they moved to New York a month before I was born, I grew up in somewhat of a Southern home. But not quite as Southern as what I am hearing. I'm the oldest of three girls. My dad wanted sons and my mother told us that he told her when I first came, "Okay, okay, I'll give you that one, but I want sons." And then the middle sister came and the baby sister. My mother said, "Then I closed up shop." So he reconciled himself to the fact that he was going to be raising females. And that was good for us because we were taught by a father that you can do anything you want to do. He was so afraid that we would have to become dependent upon men that we learned how to change tires. I learned how to unchoke my car, that sort of thing. And also just to go out and do what I had to do in the world. But, somehow you knew that after you did all that, you did get married. Become very independent so in case he leaves you, you can take care of yourself. There was supposed to be a he who would be there. That's the kind of home it was. But as far as my writing is concerned, I never had any worry about my parents' having to be senile or dead before I could say the things I've said. They've been quite proud of the fact that I do write. I think a lot of that comes from their background. They didn't have the privilege of going on to college or even being allowed to use the public libraries where they were.

Questioner: If you had advice to give to a person who wants to write, what would you tell them?

Humphreys: If you are twenty, I would tell you to read as much as you possibly can. That would be the first thing to do. If you are thirty, I would tell you to work as hard at writing as you possibly can. And I think those are two things that all writers should do, all beginning writers and all practicing writers also. Hard work is the secret to me and it is the way that you get to page 300, which is always the crucial thing. You just have to keep at it.

Shivers: I would say learn to respect yourself, and respect that desire to do it. Read and write, and just write about things that you are passionate about. And do it. It really comes down to being that simple. The day came when I said to myself, if I am going to do it I've got to do it and not keep talking about it.

Naylor: I have found that if you have to tell a person to read, they're normally not a writer by inclination, because all writers begin as voracious readers and then somehow just spring off from that. You also want to articulate your own story. So the reading is just natural, more than even desire—an almost unquenchable passion for you. You just absorb language. To reiterate, it's hard work. And you have to understand the loneliness of it. We have this Hollywood conception about what it means to write, but it takes tremendous hours and not just hours where you are sitting around, but hours of intense concentration and self-examination. That's work. But if you have a story you feel is worth telling, you don't mind that sacrifice of friends, of community, of time and even having it be all wrong sometimes. And then you have to have the courage to start over and to keep believing that somehow that story is in you.

Pate: This would be something that would be true for a man or a woman.

Naylor: Exactly. That's the whole thing about this panel. Ninety-nine and forty-four one-hundredths of the process is indeed not only genderless and raceless, it's even humanless at times. It's about dredging up things that are down there in the human spirit, in the gut. Yes it's words, it's language, which is the province of everyone. It just becomes problematic when you begin to filter it through thousands of other perceptions or assumptions.

Questioner: When you want to write about something that involves people you know, is it a problem? Do you say, "I am going to do it; I don't care who's offended?" How much of that kind of editing do you do as you write?

Naylor: It's really censorship you are talking about.

Questioner: Yes, censorship. Self-censorship.

Naylor: What will happen is that I will often see the character start to evolve and take on a life of his or her own. I might catch glimpses of people in my family, perhaps, or of friends in that character, and I just simply let it go. Because if you step in and say, "Oh, God, this is my mother. This is a story she told me when she was twenty. She'll kill me. She'll cut me out of her will. She'll cancel her insurance policy." If you do, if you pull yourself in and you say let me chop this off, then the writing becomes flat.

And I think psychologically something happens because you know that you cheated. After that it's like playing dominoes, everything will fall flat. It takes a lot of courage and I think understanding from the people around us. You can only write from what you know. And things you've imagined and things you wish to meet. And they'll have to understand that it's not them. Perhaps it may be just little bits of them. And if it is them, I think it's a compliment. You know what we have told you about how hard it is to write, and you spend that much time talking about your mother? She should be glad.

Humphreys: Also, the thing you are writing about tends to change as you write and to become less a true event or a true person and more your own creation or own mixture of the two. In the end it's something new.

Questioner: I have heard different writers refer to a character they had created taking on a life of its own, speaking to them. If you've had such experiences, could you share them with us?

Humphreys: I used to hear people say that, and I thought it was baloney. That's before I was writing. And now I get that same feeling. I think what happens is that when I am writing, part of my rational brain shuts down. That's almost necessary in writing and is what we call inspiration. It is not really that at all, but it is something coming from part of the brain that we are not always in control of or in good touch with. And so it seems as if the book is writing itself or your character is taking over. Obviously that doesn't happen; it's obviously the creation of your imagination, but you may not know exactly how it's working.

Gilchrist: It's like, "Who is driving this car? Who's skiing down this hill?" You are not really thinking about it. It may not be as difficult to write a book as we would like to think. Once you get past all the inhibitions and fears and problems and questions—you just write. It feels like memory, which means you thought it up very fast and you are just remembering the parts.

Questioner: As an aspiring writer, I wonder when do you make the differentiation between talent or lack of talent? Is there a certain number of rejection slips that tell you that?

Naylor: That should be the least of your concerns. That, or even reviews. If you are literate, you have a talent for putting words on paper. Though it becomes a bit more than that—things we have been telling you about— dedication, willingness to hang in there, the passion for language itself. If anything, that is what separates the girls from the women.

Ann Sharp: Today, we'd like to talk about the place of the woman writer in the literary tradition. In recent years, there has been a growing concern about past failures to include women writers in standard collections like the Norton Anthology. And there has been an effort to have more women included. Would you tell us what women writers you read when you were growing up?

Gilchrist: I'll start with Pearl Buck who I think won the Nobel. And Edna St. Vincent Millay, wonderful, wonderful sonnets which I think will some-day be revived. She's represented in anthologies, but not well represented. I think that at least half the books I read must have been by women. I was a voracious reader and I naturally moved towards books by women. Because I had so little experience with the world to bring to the things I was reading, at least a woman's sensibility would be speaking to me. My brother was in the other room, and, you know, we had the sexist country at our house. He was over there reading the Hardy Boys and I was reading Nancy Drew. We thought that was okay.

Humphreys: I actually read a lot of boys' books when I was young. I read the Hardy Boys and not Nancy Drew. I just didn't have Nancy Drew. I think that was the only reason. But I also read every single Louisa May Alcott book, and those books were extremely important to me. It's about a family of girls, which is what I lived in. And the oldest girl, who was a writer, was named Jo.

Shivers: I think it's terribly unfair that you actually got to be named Jo.

Humphreys: I used to do the things that she did. She would take apples up into the garret and write. I didn't like apples but I took them up there, in an attic where no one had been for hundreds of years. It was 93 degrees up there and I wrote. It was an amazing influence on my life to do that. I think if a child reads something with a character with his name, it's really power-ful. It would be nice if we could find one for everyone else.

Barbara Hardy: You were lucky because that's one of these androgy-nous names.

Humphreys: Oh, yes. I realized that also from an early age. I was sort of a tomboy. I thought my parents wanted a boy rather than a girl. I didn't have any brothers, but it took me a while to realize that it was okay to be a girl. I read Pearl Buck at a later age and Edna St. Vincent Millay as well. But I didn't really notice which books were written by women and which were by men.

Gilchrist: It never occurred to me. The only reason I wanted to know the names of authors was so I could get the rest of their books. I had no curios-ity whatsoever about the author.

Hardy: I also read a lot of boys' books and boys' magazines, but I also read an awful lot of tripe, or trash. I had a wonderful aunt who was the least academic of her family, and she once said when I picked up one of her women's magazines, "Well, I'll say this for Barbara, she'll read anything." She was very pleased.

Shivers: Other than Louisa May Alcott—at least I almost got Louisa—my favorite book was *The Secret Garden.* I still love it so much. And also around the house there was a copy of *Pride and Prejudice,* which my mother had left over from her days at Meredith College. I read it over and over and over. I loved it.

Darcy was so wonderful. But I always read whatever, too. Just whatever was there. In fact, my first learning about sex was from my brother's Boy Scout manual. One other thing that was a big, big influence on me. I remember exactly the moment when a teacher came in and read "Patterns" by Amy Lowell.

Hardy: I read a lot of books that, like the books by Louisa May Alcott, were about America. All the *Anne of Green Gables* and so on. I didn't realize for a long time that they were about America.

Humphreys: I thought they were British.

Gilchrist: I could never read *Anne of Green Gables* or any woman who would allow herself to be a victim in literature, or really even the Alcott books. They would begin to bore me. I fought for a living. I fought with my brothers for excitement and fun. It was my greatest pleasure in life. And I could not understand anyone being in a position where they couldn't fight. So I didn't understand why they didn't. Or else I would be empathizing so much. To this day in a film if someone is going to be struck or hit I'll leave the theater. I have never been able to see the middle part of *Fanny and Alexander* when that child was beaten. I literally can't face it.

Questioner: It seems that not much writing by women is included in the established canon. Just a little sprinkling here and there. Would you like to voice an opinion about why?

Hardy: Publishers are doing a lot about it. There are good presses, and women's presses have been introducing a lot of new stuff. Feminist critics have been attacking the exclusiveness of the great tradition, and I would have thought things were moving.

Humphreys: I think in the last ten years or so there has been a renewed interest in some of the nineteenth-century and early twentieth-century women writers. But it is still sort of grudging. I mean it's for women. These women writers are being dug up for women to read. It's not like they're being restored. The reason I think that women writers are not part of the grand tradition and graduate school work is that graduate school teachers don't like to give much value to domestic fiction, to stories of the family. Immediately there is a reaction against that subject matter. And they won't come out and say so; they use the term "limited palette."

Questioner: Don't you feel that women will read what are considered to be male books on male topics while men will not read about domestic issues? I will read *Sports Illustrated* or *The Right Stuff* or some football book my husband has, but he would never turn around and read my book.

Gilchrist: You've just got this bigger palette.

Hardy: It's also because women's liberation has outstripped men's liberation.

Questioner: I hate to be the devil's advocate here, but my husband just read *Hot Flashes* and loved it.

Gilchrist: Well-married! We have got to stop a minute here, because it is one thing to talk about fiction, but I am more interested in the poets of the past. I have always felt like women poets—women poets in America—are well represented in anthologies. They dominate to some extent. My God, Emily Dickinson dominates the century practically.

Hardy: There's something very interesting about this. It is possible to write a history of English poetry, of the whole of the canon up to the end of the nineteenth century mentioning only one woman poet, Emily Bronte. I am speaking now not about American poetry, though you haven't got many in the nineteenth century you need to mention. But you could not write a history of English fiction and leave out women. And I think women's experience has allowed women to write novels, but it has been very much more difficult for women, whose emotional range has been very, very restricted, to write poetry. I do think there is a big genre difference here. You've got Emily Dickinson in the nineteenth century and we've got our Emily.

Gilchrist: In the late fifties all of a sudden we've got Sylvia Plath and Anne Sexton. We've got this burgeoning of incredibly powerful women poets in the United States; and all the women in the United States including myself that aspired to write began to write poetry in the shadow of Sexton, primarily Sexton, and then all of the ones after.

Humphreys: I think Virginia Woolf said that fiction had attracted in the past more women than any other art. And she said the reason is that it is the easiest. But I like to think that what she meant was that it's the most accessible. Women have been able to do it in secret without anyone knowing—you know, hiding their work and working at it in spurts. I did that myself, so I know you can hide it. And I think that's one reason that we may have gravitated towards it. I don't know exactly why poetry also couldn't be clandestine.

Questioner: Given what you've just been discussing, would each of you comment on the way writing has affected your everyday lives?

Humphreys: My everyday life has been totally transformed by writing because I have come to think and see in a totally different way. My normal life before I started writing, which was happy and healthy, is now neither one of those things. I am constantly questioning things. I have gone from being very conservative in most things to what I consider extremely radical. Because writing questions things. You fall into that frame of mind. And my everyday life, more or less, has disintegrated. I can go to the grocery store now, and I can cook food. So there are a few things I can still manage to function in, but I'm on the edge of it. I'm always looking through things and looking through experiences and people to try to figure out what the answer is. And I don't think that's a normal everyday life. I think in the long run it can be very disturbing. And the more I write the more I become like that. It's a kind of circular process.

Shivers: I will have to say it's affected me in entirely the opposite way. I was never healthy and happy because I was always trying to find that missing thing. I never was able to fit in. I never found people to talk to, so that kept me unhealthy and unhappy. This may be us finding it at different ages or many other reasons too.

Hardy: One very obvious thing—the reason I think a lot of women have not written is that women leading a conventional, domestic life tend not to have solitude. And you have to have solitude.

Questioner: Mrs. Humphreys, would you say you are losing your identity through this?

Humphreys: No. The opposite. I am gaining my identity, but I'm losing the capacity to find an identity that doesn't include writing. Writing—it's like a fungus—it has taken hold and taken control.

Hardy: One of the most outstanding little examples of writing in everyday life is Jane Austen, who didn't have a study. She used to have a blotter and as soon as visitors came—she couldn't get away from the visitors so she would slide her manuscript under the blotter. The amazing thing is that she wrote anything at all. She had to do it in this crowded world over which she had absolutely no control. She couldn't say, "Oh, I'll go upstairs now. I'll go and write."

Gilchrist: You can't ever tell when all of a sudden you're going to need long periods of solitude. And I don't mean all afternoon or all weekend. It may take three or four months. You may need to get in the car and go somewhere for three or four months. It's very difficult—you can't explain this to young children. Though maybe if the children grew up with it like Jo's have grown up with Jo writing, maybe they think it's well she's out of their hair. My children love to think that I am on a piece of work because they know I won't call them up at 8 o'clock in the morning and give them some advice.

Questioner: Nineteenth-century novels tend to end in marriage. It seems like recent novels begin in divorce. What's happening to the American family in novels?

Hardy: Some nineteenth-century novels, because they didn't have the possibility of ending in divorce, ended in death. I think family life has always been rightly suspected. It's always been looked at as suspiciously comic or tragic—nineteenth and twentieth century.

Shivers: I think we are all trying to deal with that, in the books we are doing. I had to kill a couple of men off in my first book. In the second one you have a divorce, but you also have a marriage. We are trying to figure all that out.

Questioner: Yesterday Ms. Shivers said she wrote for herself. I took that to mean that it was her standard that was important, not the standard of the *New York Times*. But how important to you is publication? And who is that dear reader in your mind when you write?

Shivers: That goes back to what I just said in answer to the other question. I am trying to figure it all out. I am trying to figure myself out. And so, therefore, I am writing for myself. I think the thing about publishing is that that's the way to do two very important things. By being published and being acknowledged you get a little money and a little respect. Somebody knows that you are doing something. Before you are published, people just don't take you seriously. The other thing that publishing does is that it's given me friends. I have had a chance to meet other people who are writing and I didn't have that chance before. Until you publish you don't usually have that chance.

Questioner: Who do you think your audience is? Would each of you please answer that?

Humphreys: I have two audiences in mind. One is a very vague, general bunch of people that I can't identify but who are probably a lot like me. In that sense I am writing for myself. But I also frequently have in mind real people whom I want to win. The first one happened to be someone who was no longer alive, which made it an odd undertaking. I have specific people in mind. I want them to like it.

Questioner: I was struck by what Louise Shivers said about the importance of making friends through her publications—that is, friends who are also writers. I would be curious to hear what the members of the panel might say about what role other writers, currently writing writers, play in their lives as writers. What do you get from them?

Shivers: Knowing that when you are sitting in that room by yourself, and it's just as painful as it has ever been, you are not by yourself. Next week we will be back wherever we all are. I will be back home; I'll know that Gloria is back. But I'll hear that hurricane that she read about, and I'll think. . . . "Well, she's lonesome too." I remember one day, about a year and a half ago—maybe I shouldn't tell this—but Jo and I were really feeling in the pits about the books that we were writing. I either called her or she called me and we just talked to each other. She said, "God, this young adult novel I'm writing!" And I said, "Well, I'm writing this stupid romance novel." It helped just to know she was there. We didn't have to see each other or talk that much. It just helps to have somebody to say it to—to know that you've got other people out there who care.

Hardy: For people starting out who may not have met writers, it's very important to know that literature isn't written by gods and goddesses and doesn't come out in printed form. It is written by people with arms and legs, and written with pens and on typewriters. I think it is very important to get the ordinariness.

Humphreys: It's also nice to realize that essentially literature is not competitive—though that's easy to forget in the system we have today. I like to know that there are other writers with whom I am not racing and that we like each other's work. That we are in some ways working toward the same end.

Sharp: I thought what Ms. Hardy said underscored the impetus for having this symposium. It's important that we hear the voices of writers. It's also important to see that they really have arms and legs and hair and everything, and to identify with the person behind the printed page. I think it has been a great experience. I want to thank them. They have been incredibly giving of themselves.

Evaluating the Eighties

Robert MacNeil / 1989

From *The MacNeil/Lehrer NewsHour*, December 29, 1989. Copyright NewsHour Productions, LLC. Printed by permission.

Robert MacNeil: Next tonight, we continue our look at the decade just ending, different perspectives of what made the 1980s memorable. Tonight the views of six leading writers and artists. Wendy Wasserstein is a playwright and essayist whose play, *The Heidi Chronicles*, won a Tony Award and a Pulitzer Prize in 1989. She's currently compiling a collection of her essays for a book called *Bachelor Girls*. Isaac Stern, the violinist, has just completed an international tour. In recent years, he led the effort to save New York's Carnegie Hall from demolition. He will be performing with the San Francisco Symphony and the Philadelphia Orchestra in the coming months. Robert Stone is a novelist whose book, *Dog Soldiers*, won a National Book Award in 1975. He is now working on his fifth novel, called *Outer Bridge Reach*. August Wilson is a playwright whose recent play, *Fences*, won a Pulitzer Prize and a Tony Award as well as a Drama Critic Circle Award.

Wilson is in New York now rehearsing his play, *The Piano Lesson*. Sam Gilliam is an abstract artist whose works appear in major museums throughout the country. He's won several honors, including a fellowship from the Guggenheim Memorial Foundation. Ellen Gilchrist is an author whose latest short story collection is *The Anna Papers*. An earlier collection of stories titled *Victory over Japan* won her an American Book Award in 1984. She joins us tonight from Dallas. Ms. Gilchrist, what will be memorable to you about the eighties?

Ellen Gilchrist: Oh, so many things. So many things, Robert. But the events that began when the people of Estonia began to sing for their freedom and have now spread all the way down to Romania, this is amazing. I can't leave my television set. In 1980, I didn't even own a television set and now I can't quit watching it.

McNeil: Mr. Wilson, for you, the eighties.

August Wilson: I think in order to determine it you have to get into the nineties to see what was significant and what was memorable about the eighties to see what happened the past ten years that had an impact. I think the last month or so in the eighties is going to wipe out everything that happened prior to that. I think in Black American culture, for me the emergence of rap is a very vibrant expression of the culture and the emergence of the Black director is personified by Spike Lee I think were two important developments in Black American culture.

McNeil: Mr. Stern, the eighties for you, the most memorable happenings in the eighties.

Isaac Stern: The most memorable. I think that has already been touched upon by the others and also by the people you had on your science group yesterday, the impact of television on all the arts, the changing pace of acceptance of patience to accept the time to pay attention to the inner values of the arts, and I think to a marked difference in the eighties which will see its effect in the nineties is the breakdown of encouragement in private support for the arts without a balancing effort for support from the government all leading to an educational lack which I think is the root of all of the problems facing all of us as artists. I do believe that education, the education of educators as well as young people is the most singly important priority that we have, youth.

McNeil: Mr. Gilliam, what do you think most significant about the eighties?

Sam Gilliam: I think the rise in distribution of minorities within the arts and the defeat of Senator Helms around the obscenity proposals.

McNeil: You mean the case of the National Endowment for the Arts and its funding of the Mapplethorpe photographic exhibition, that issue?

Gilliam: Yes, I do.

McNeil: How do you feel, Ms. Wasserstein, about the eighties? What is, do you think, most important about them?

Wendy Wasserstein: Just before coming on here, I heard that Vaclav Havel was made president of Czechoslovakia, and I thought any decade that ends with a playwright becoming president of Czechoslovakia has come out all right actually. And I think I agree with Mr. Wilson in terms of a broadening of perspective, especially in the arts in terms of women writers, women artists, Black writers, Black artists, in terms of what is a point of view has seemed to become much broader and I hope into the nineties will become even more broad.

McNeil: As a mere white male, Mr. Stone, how do the eighties strike you?

Robert Stone: I think in American fiction the eighties were the time during which the old competition between realism and fiction and the modes of fiction that just set out to replace it were obviated by the question just being resolved more or less by itself. I think the best work that was done in the eighties demonstrated that a documentary or downright style of narrative did not have any more of a handle on reality than a narrative style that was more associative and indirect and poetic, and on the other hand, that a style of addressing reality that was more poetic, that the elusive nature of reality could be pursued just as effectively indirectly and through evocation as by modes that were deliberately and heavily realistic. I think the question just resolved itself.

McNeil: An escape from realism, you mean, or an escape from the fetters of realism in the eighties, is—

Stone: I think really that we were, both sides in this controversy were deluding themselves. I mean, those who argued in favor of realism I think felt that there was some special relationship that could be forged between a simple narrative and things themselves, and I don't think that's true. I mean, there's no one narrative style that exists in a closer relationship to things than another. I mean, reality is here and language is here, and I mean, the most simple descriptive writing can evoke the most complicated and elusive aspects of reality in life.

McNeil: Do you have a comment on that, Ms. Gilchrist?

Gilchrist: I don't like to think about writing in those terms. I just know what I like and I know what I want to do and I do that and I know what I like to read and I read that, and I don't think abstractly about it. I just react to work.

McNeil: Mr. Gilliam, you are an abstractionist. Is there a symbol that you can think of, a visual symbol or is there something that symbolizes the eighties that you will remember as being characteristic of the 1980s?

Gilliam: Yes, the event of commodities, this is commodities within the visual arts, this is the use of TV and the public media, which is present now.

McNeil: Who else has a symbol for the 1980s?

Wilson: What best I remember I think that characterizes [the] eighties is seeing someone step over a person lying on a sidewalk to go into a store to purchase a $2,000 watch. I think for me that says a lot about where we are as a culture and if culture is how you live and morality is what it means, then I think we have to question what is the meaning of our lives. We're talking about the National Endowment of the Arts. If we endow the arts for $153 million and we endow the military with $530 million to build one airplane, you see, one is creative, the arts is creative, the other is destructive, and I think that we as a culture have to ask what is the meaning of our lives, and is this the culture in which we want to live and is this the culture which we want to pass on to our kids? You see, I would rather, and I understand the importance of defending the shores of America from foreign invasion, but can we do it with $100 million bombers, and $530 million for that, because the arts are going to help to define the culture by presenting ideas that can possibly change and alter the way that we live.

McNeil: Ms. Wasserstein, do you want to comment on that, or do you have a symbol of your own for the eighties, something that sums up the eighties for you?

Wasserstein: Gosh, I remember this picture of Nancy Reagan sitting on Mr. T's lap at Christmas, and somehow at one point that summed up the down side of the eighties to me and sort of commercialism of the eighties and the arts, I often thought what was wrong with there seemed to be in a sense formed not over content but just form became the content. It didn't matter what was the morality, the ethics or what it was about, just as long as it looked pretty good or it seemed good, and I find what's interesting in terms of writing, as we get to the end of the decade, at least play writing is, there is, in fact, a coming back to storytelling, a coming back to reflecting what is going on in this society, a coming back to what is the content here, and it's not just the veneer or the sheen, and I find that very exciting going into the nineties.

McNeil: Form over content in the eighties, Mr. Stern?

Stern: Again, back to television, which has been the catalyst of so much political change in these dizzying weeks that we've gone through, I remember this program when I first heard of a somewhat unknown prelate many years giving an interview to you in Paris, his name was Ayatollah Khomeini. Now he used the media to create another revolution and nothing in the arts is untouched by the social revolts that go on in our time. What troubles me is the same thing, the images that you all bring up, is how to bring images to those young people whom I think are always gifted. I think there is no young child without talent, but I do believe deeply that we have failed them with bad teaching, bad schooling, and that now today that we read that libraries will close and be unavailable to young people on Saturdays in this city of all cities is I think outrageous in terms of priorities. The whole idea, everything that we write about, whether it's writing, theater, the plastic arts, thought, any kind, music, itself, is an evocation of all the arts. It's the most natural form because it doesn't, it's not limited by words or images.

Each one can have his own or her own image, but there is a wonderment between one note and another, one sound and another, which you have to take time, a little time to understand, not be shouted at, not be screamed at, not be repeated, just to listen, and how do you say *ah ha*, or *ha ah*, or *ha ha*, or *ha ah*, same words, but how do you get there? The in-between, the same thing we try in all our forms is how we get from one small idea to another.

McNeil: And you think the mass media are discouraging or not providing the opportunities or the time to listen?

Stern: Well, they have exploded in many ways. In the first place, this camera, which is the most all seeing eye that we have, we're all subject to it. For opera, for ballet, it works wonderfully. For music, which is much less a moving thing, the greatest thing the camera does for example are professional football games, that's the greatest use of television cameras we see today, they're wonderful. But when you have to show an idea, then the person behind the camera also has to use the camera as an artistic instrument. How do you show the evolution of an idea or make people want to hear the next word you're going to say?

McNeil: It depends who's saying them, I guess. Do you have a symbol for the 1980s, Mr. Stone?

Stone: I don't know if there's one symbol. One thing that's interesting about the eighties in terms of style as opposed to content is the disappearance of bohemia, as far as I can tell. I mean, the bohemian style among artists, at least among writers, seems to have just disappeared. When I was younger, I mean, we had to externalize our sacred mission and we lived in holy poverty and the girls wore black and now it seems as though writers and politicians and gangsters and stock brokers are all in the same restaurants and they're all pursuing the same style of life.

McNeil: Ms. Gilchrist, you say what, Ms. Gilchrist?

Gilchrist: I have on black. [*Laughs*] Mr. Stone should come to Fayetteville, Arkansas. We still have bohemians there.

McNeil: Bohemian is the need to proclaim a separate identity and to differentiate yourself from ordinary people and you say artists aren't doing that anymore.

Stone: It doesn't seem to me that they are.

Wilson: I think rap artists are doing it. I think the whole thing with rap is they are defining themselves and they are working out among themselves without any help from us and I was going to respond to Mr. Stern, we have failed in educating them so the rappers are educating themselves. They are working out what their social relationships are. They are working out their definition of themselves, the relations to the society they live in. They're working out their own sexual codes of conduct, and all this stuff is happening, and I think that Robert was saying earlier about bohemia, they've just evolved into something else that you and I no longer recognize. And I think it is important to keep up with what's happening with the younger people because they are moving without us.

Stern: Oh, there are a lot of bohemians still among the artists. They have their own version of bohemia today which they follow and they are influencing a lot of younger people. There is more activity in some ways among young people. As we speak tonight, there is going to be a concert at Carnegie Hall, what they call the New York Symphony, it's what they call a Christmas Seminar with Alexander Schneider, a whole group of kids between the ages of fifteen and twenty-one. They play with a passion and a joy that is so communicative it demands the ear of the listener. We heard another group of young people between eleven and thirteen. There are young people, there are talents. There is a life out there that all it needs to do is to be encouraged and to be heard, but it does need the willing hand of authority and teachers. I'm reminded sometimes of what the Russians used to tell me, that they're never afraid of the minister of culture, only the culture of the minister. The new Russian cultural minister is really something very exciting.

McNeil: There's an idea that interests me and I'm wondering if you think there's an effect. Ellen Gilchrist, has the political conservatives of the 1980s affected the arts?

Gilchrist: I hope not. I don't, I don't really think about things affecting the arts. I think about the culture in general. I'm fifty-four years old and I think of the whole thing. If I get to see the images that have affected me, I guess I'll have to be the Pollyanna of this panel because I see those young people up in Alaska washing birds. Every time I see a bunch of kids in California or Alaska washing birds, I think that's more important than the fact that somebody was dumb enough to dump all that oil on the shores, because that's the future and that's what will give birth to the future. Also, I know most of the young people that I know carry cards in their pocket saying that if they die someone can have their eyes, their livers, their kidneys, their hands, their feet, these are the images of the eighties that have affected me.

McNeil: Who'd like to come in on this question of the conservative, the political conservatives in which so marked the eighties in public life? Have they leaked into the arts?

Wilson: I think it's part of the culture and I think they've tremendously affected the culture. We're talking about people dying. The death rate among young Blacks, kids in DC, murder victims because of the drugs, is astounding.

McNeil: But how's that connected with political conservatism?

Wilson: No, I think the conservative ideas have allowed for a certain cultural, a certain morality, certain meanings of life to foster and to grow. You cannot present a liberal idea. They are no longer fashionable. They were fashionable in the sixties. You know, this is the eighties. They are no longer fashionable. All of these things contribute to the climate in which we live our lives, the fact that we do spend $530 million on a bomber says something I think very crucial to who we are. We have to ask ourselves is this who we want to be? We know this is who we are, but is this the kind of culture that we want to pass on to our kids? If it is, then okay. If it's not, then I think that we should do something about. And we should be, those who want to change it have to be as ardent as those who are willing to accept it.

McNeil: Mr. Gilliam, do you find yourself painting in any way differently because there have been conservative administrations in Washington and the culture has been, that liberal ideas have gone out of fashion?

Gilliam: No, but maybe I should, meaning that if things had not changed this summer in terms of the obscenity amendment, I would have been, I would have been acting out. I think that one of the things that one thinks about that the conservatives has affected in the arts has been the lessening of private support in the arts and turning it more into cooperative support. So I mean that we titillate between different options now than we would fifteen years ago. So that there's not as broad a support, there's only a single source.

Stern: If I may, there is a little difference there that I think you should emphasize between the creative artist who either leads or mirrors ideas in society and the recreative art, the performer.

McNeil: The interpreter.

Stern: The interpreter who sees the possibility and carries the art form still further through his or her talent and then has to give it to a much larger audience, but the necessities, the platforms that the performing arts must of necessity have, have also been sharply affected by the eighties, again to a degree both by political conservatism in our support area, but also by the success, by the great success of pop music commercially. It has become a business as much as it is an art form, and it's not denigrating it when you say that, but it does create a business that is frighteningly successful for a short time for certain people. We look at the—

McNeil: Why is that frightening or worrying?

Stern: Because it makes other people think that art which does not earn its way is not good enough, and if they can earn it, why can't you? It's a completely different concept. It's the wrong, it's putting the emphasis in the wrong place. There is no way of equating the instant popularity, particularly in our decades, the decades of the eighties, the seventies and the eighties, that really exploded where the whole record industry changed, where television changed everything, where everything was available quickly, loudly for a short time. Now we've been going through political experiences of the most shattering kind. All of us are sitting here watching history being made before our eyes which we would have not expected a few weeks ago. But the fact is in music, which someone when asked about the rarefied atmosphere, I reared a little bit at that, because Mozart and Beethoven and Bach and Schubert and Brahms will go on despite the changes that are in history now and will five, ten, fifteen, twenty, fifty years from now also continue as they continued before the revolutions.

McNeil: Let me pick up with Mr. Stone on Mr. Stern's idea that in the eighties it became clearer that arts have to pay their way to be regarded as successful and viable.

Stone: Well, I think that was always clear and certainly it's made clear in every decade. Something else that's going on I think that may be political, now I'm oh-for-two so far. I started talking about the idea that realism and its opposites were coming together, and I was told that wasn't important, and then I said I thought that bohemia was disappearing and I was told that I was wrong about that. Now I'm going to try something else. I'm going to suggest that the avant-garde is as an artistic conception, as a concept in art, is disappearing. I think it was grafted from technology onto art and I think that as we come to the end of this century, we're really seeing the end of that forced association, and I think this is really political. I think there's a kind of coming to terms with the possible that is essentially political and in its artistic expression I think we see the withering away of the idea of an avant-garde in art, so I will now sit back and await correction.

McNeil: Has the avant-garde withered away?

Wasserstein: Oh, dear. I want to say yes, but I don't think so actually. But I think what's happened is because it is so difficult to be an artist in this society and to financially be one that what happens is you get involved with trying to make the avant-garde mainstream and a lot of corporate funding and how do you get that funding, and it becomes so in some ways maybe it has, but I think if you look at the Brooklyn Academy of Music and the vast success of that, I think what's happened is the avant-garde has in some ways become mainstream, so maybe in that case it's no longer avant-garde.

Wilson: Is that not going to create a new avant-garde—

McNeil: Isn't avant-garde simply what's newer than anything else, I mean, ahead of everything else? Or did it have to be self-consciously ahead of everything else?

Stone: Well, I think there was a real ideology of the necessity. I think the feeling was that it was a philosophical necessity to replace the obsolescent in art just as there was a technical necessity, a kind of impulse in the universe, a constant correction for the expanding of cognition and consciousness, that this was a serious, almost a Hegelian process, and I really think that the philosophical underpinnings of that attitude are being undermined.

McNeil: Mr. Stern mentioned the scientists we had on doing exactly this last evening, and one of them, the astrophysicist from Harvard, Margaret Geller, spoke of a decline of imagination, of national imagination in the 1980s. Does anybody pick up on that, do you think there's been a decline of imagination in this?

Stone: If that is actually going on, we are in big trouble. God, I certainly hope not. I don't think so.

McNeil: Ms. Gilchrist, do you have any comment on that?

Gilchrist: Oh, I don't think so. There's so many more people than there were in the world, and as long as there's a constant supply of people, of young people, there will be a constant supply of imagination. I think that we use it up—

McNeil: But collectively, as a nation, has the nation lost its imagination, its sense of reaching further and the possible—

Gilchrist: It's terrifying to me that we don't have the imagination as a culture to create a great educational system, but which scientist was it, was it Stephen Jay Gould last night who said that if you really want to change education, double the salaries of all the teachers in the United States and excellence will follow? I've carried that around with me all day.

Stern: That's very true. It's a perfect phrase. Bravo.

Wilson: I was going to say the imagination is the people and the culture is the people and the culture is an alive, organic, it changes every day, ever changing thing, and I think that as a people that we have been continually as Americans and also as Black Americans debating the character of our culture, but I don't see any lack of imagination as long as there are people.

McNeil: How about you, Mr. Gilliam?

Gilliam: I think the fact that attendance have increased greatly during the eighties is the sign that we have not lost our imagination, but the real test for the nineties will be whether or not the homeless, whether or not the persons who are victims of drug addiction and things like this will be saved because of America's imagination and the American population's imagination.

McNeil: Anyone want to come in on this?

Stern: Yes. I think there is a world of imagination out there, it's the support of imagination and the encouragement of imagination which is sometimes lacking. Really, the very essence of support for the arts is to get, to give the creative artist the right to fail, wouldn't you think?

Gilliam: Absolutely, it's certainly necessary.

Wasserstein: The problem is in terms of mass media, the decision by who's ever, you know, president of Paramount or whatever deciding *oh, yes, there's a common denominator and we must bring this down* or, *you know, this particular thing will be written by five different writers,* rather than an individual voice. But that doesn't have to do with the lack of imagination in terms of the artist. I think the artist will prevail. I know even in terms of why people continue to write for the theater, that's one of the reasons.

McNeil: You said at the beginning wasn't it exciting that Vaclav Havel had just been made president of Czechoslovakia. Do you come, as a play-wright yourself, do you come out of the 1980s feeling more involved with or interested in the governance of your own country or more detached from it, alienated it, whatever?

Wasserstein: I've become more interested in it definitely, and also more interested in the world. That's really what's happened in the past four months. It's a lack of isolation and a beginning to see what's happening other places and not focusing here. For myself, I hope that would be reflected in my plays and in other plays.

McNeil: Anybody else want to comment on that, a feeling as artists of your government and your connection with it and how the country is run being something that is directly relevant to you and—

Wilson: It's certainly been something I as a Black American have always been concerned with, because the government has never really been in my corner, so to speak. But I think that the Americans are perhaps among the people in the world that are the least politically sophisticated people and if the events in Eastern Europe over the past couple of months or as Wendy said, allowing us to look at the world, I think we need to keep the focus on our society, because we are seeing that it is possible to change the society, it is possible to change the way we live. We are responsible for the world that we find ourselves in and if we do not like that world, it is possible by accepting an individual responsibility to effect a change.

McNeil: Mr. Stone.

Stone: I think there is a responsibility that artists have to intrude their thoughts into politics. I think artists have a responsibility to their country in a way to try and serve it by thinking, by creating.

McNeil: Have the eighties made it easier or harder for you to do that?

Stone: I don't think there's been much of a change in terms of the effect of American artists on the body politic, I don't think things have changed very much. I don't think things are ever going to be with the way they are in Eastern Europe, and in a way we're lucky because we haven't really as a class, as intellectuals, had it that bad. On the other hand, Czechoslovakia, for example, is a small country where everybody knows everybody else in which intellectuals have always been very important people and that's not the case here.

McNeil: How do you feel, Ellen Gilchrist, about the government of your own country and your connection with it as a creative artist?

Gilchrist: I want to be Secretary of Education. No, I think that the artist's role is what it has always been, to hold a mirror up to the culture, to tell the truth as hard as we can and as well as we can about whatever little part of reality that we know and not get into politics, although I want to every day.

McNeil: Mr. Gilliam, you and government.

Gilliam: I feel very good. I think during the sixties and the seventies and possibly now in the eighties, I think that I've been able to with groups exercise a certain amount of free will over things that concern me.

McNeil: Well, I'd like to thank you all, Mr. Gilliam, Ms. Gilchrist, Mr. Stone, Mr. Stern, Mr. August Wilson, and Ms. Wasserstein, thank you very much all of you.

Interview with Ellen Gilchrist

James McKinley / 1991

From *New Letters on the Air*, May 1991. Host, Rebekah Presson. Interviewer, James McKinley. Printed by permission. Transcript by Tracy Carr.

Rebekah Presson: Welcome to *New Letters on the Air*. I'm Rebekah Presson. Our guest today is one of the most popular writers of Southern fiction, Ellen Gilchrist. Gilchrist is an American Book Award winner with four collections of short stories, two novels, and a book of poems to her credit. National Public Radio listeners remember her for her journal entries, which are also published. Gilchrist's most recent work is a collection of three novellas gathered under the title *I Cannot Get You Close Enough*. Ellen Gilchrist spoke about her work with the editor of *New Letters* magazine, James McKinley.

James McKinley: In the work at hand, *I Cannot Get You Close Enough*—and you're going to read from the third novella, the three in that volume—we meet a lot of characters. You love to bring characters back in your fiction, create them, and leave them alone and then bring them back. And some of them I'm particularly taken by. Anna Hand, now, she was a novelist, a poet, a translator, and she appeared in your book *The Anna Papers*—

Ellen Gilchrist: —Yeah, she's probably the most fully developed—emotionally—of any woman character that I've ever created. She's probably the wisest and the most highly evolved.

McKinley: And the one who comes to a tragic end.

Gilchrist: Right.

McKinley: And then another person we'll meet here is—

Gilchrist: —Well, it's not really a tragic end, because she just has cancer and she chooses her own way to die. Up until the moment of her death she's lived, you know, intelligently.

McKinley: And fully.

Gilchrist: Right, and so the rest of the characters are continually interested in her and [there's] all sorts of emotions and so they can't quit thinking about Anna. Anna can quit thinking about her relatives, but they can't quit thinking about her, and even after her death. And the three novellas in *I Cannot Get You Close Enough* are really a continuation of *The Anna Papers* because Anna's voice tells the first novella, which is the story of trying to get her niece Jessie away from her crazy mother, Sheila. And the second novella is about her illegitimate niece, Olivia de Havilland Hand, and how she brings this child into the family. And then, just to have a whole lot of fun, I wrote this third novella and brought all my characters up to Maine to be together, where they are spending the summer fighting over and looking for a packet of letters that Anna wrote to Noel Chatevin, whose house they're visiting. It's just a loony, crazy thing and why I wanted to create such a problem for myself, because over and over again in that novella, I have a lot of people in the room talking at once, and it's a very difficult thing to do. The easy thing to write is just one person talking to another person. You start bringing two or three people into the room, you set up a big, uh . . . but I like to do it.

McKinley: Well, now let's hear something from *I Cannot Get You Close Enough*.

[*Gilchrist reads from "A Summer in Maine"*]

Presson: That was Ellen Gilchrist reading from the last novella in her latest book, *I Cannot Get You Close Enough* on *New Letters on the Air*. Gilchrist visited Kansas City just after her birthday in February. In her interview with James McKinley, she says that while she does aspire to elegant, beautiful, and yet tough writing, she hopes to do even more.

Gilchrist: I think I probably am all of those things. [*Laughs*] What I'm trying to be is wise! Since it's two days after my fifty-sixth birthday. I sat around writing down theorems out of a book by Einstein on my birthday. All day long I wouldn't do anything stupid or crazy on my fifty-sixth birthday. I thought, now this is it, now you're really going to get after it here.

McKinley: Well, I'm about to celebrate a similar anniversary and *Victory over Japan*, there was a title that really spoke to me, as the stories did when I finally got to read them. But you've been through victory over Japan and victory over the Koreans and the loss at Vietnam, and many of your characters come out of that Vietnam generation.

Gilchrist: I've lived through a lot of history. To've lived through the last fifty-six years of life in a privileged position in the United States of America in good health is a big long panorama.

McKinley: Indeed—

Gilchrist: —It's amazing. And you've seen the same history. It's amazing what we've seen.

McKinley: Yeah, and I think that brings us back to the point of wisdom. You do get some perspective in your work, in fact, I'm going to rattle off some of the critical comments about your work.

Gilchrist: Well, I'm sort of awed and dazzled by the inventions and creations and things that have happened in my lifetime, the technology and the advances in medical science. Just an amazing thing. I mean, I lived in a time when they didn't have penicillin. I can remember when they first had penicillin and people no longer died.

McKinley: Or the polio vaccine—

Gilchrist: —I mean, people hardly die now compared to what they did in my youth. It's an amazing thing.

McKinley: Here's some things that critics have said about Ellen Gilchrist works. "Full of brutal realities." "They are strategies for survival." "They are home truths stylishly told." "They are elegant little tragedies, memorable and cruel." "It is great women's fiction." "They are stories of eccentricities and passion." That's just a few of the things from many different critics that have been said over the years. Do you agree with any of them? All of them?

Gilchrist: Well, I hope that I appreciate anything kind or good that anyone says about my work, especially when they phrase it beautifully, which they often do. But it just doesn't seem to have anything to do with me or the work I do. I just write the best books that I can and I'm never really satisfied. I'm occasionally satisfied with a poem. I've been completely satisfied with a few short stories. When I go back to them and I open them at any page, I can read any page and be completely satisfied with it, but I think that I always feel that I should've created a better structure. I feel like, the poet, I'm certain it was Randall Jarrell, and I'm forever telling this to friends of mine who are writers as they come to the end of a book, and Jarrell said that a poem is never finished, it is only abandoned in despair. But I think every writer feels that way about everything that they do. Every artist feels that way, except for the few things that are just a gift from the muse. So you're always pleased by people saying nice things about your work, but you always think, maybe they're being too kind. You never think they're being too mean. You think the mean ones are just crazy people with no taste.

McKinley: One other thing that critics often found in your work, and I had as well, is this tremendous ear, starting way back with *In the Land of Dreamy Dreams*, these agonized stories of adolescence, and catching those torments so perfectly. Is that the way you work? I don't mean to imply a kind of insanity here, but do you hear voices?

Gilchrist: No, but Vonnegut said once, in a book of essays about how he worked, he said when he's really cooking that he just types up the pages and tears them off and hands them to the editor. Now that's how I work when I'm really cooking. I mean, I don't even know I'm there! I'm just the typist. The story is being told to me by my unconscious mind, though I think now that I create characters and a scene. I create a milieu and the characters within it and a time and a place, and then I begin to mull it over, and I think that while I'm—I always work in the early morning—I think that while I'm sleeping, my unconscious imagination begins to work on these characters and this place and begins to make them move around. But the discovery, writing teachers call it the discovery, the discovery is in the writing. You can't, as Danielle Steel does, if you're talking about real writing, you can't decide what you're going to write and then write it. It doesn't work. Even someone who writes out the entire plot for a short story and tries to follow it will always be—the river does not run straight. You know, it goes off and it's just an exciting thing to do. Because I don't really know exactly what's going to happen until I begin to write the scenes. I only know what they begin to say to each other.

McKinley: And how they rub together and talk to one another—

Gilchrist: It's very useful to me to write the end of a piece of fiction so at least I know what the destination is. I mean, if the river starts in Minnesota, if the Mississippi rises in Minnesota, at least I know I'm going to New Orleans. Although, you know, ten years from now we may be going to Baton Rouge with that river.

McKinley: But so many of your stories echo that line in *I Cannot Get You Close Enough*, in the section you read, "It hurts to be alive." Lots of your work, the characters are hurting.

Gilchrist: Well, young people often are.

McKinley: But another part of that is—

Gilchrist: But they keep trying to stay on top of it. They keep trying to get ahead of it.

McKinley: Your characters persevere, though, even while hurting. I think one of your characters, I can't remember the story now, "I didn't become"—

Gilchrist: Traceleen's not in any pain.

McKinley: No, she's not.

Gilchrist: And Anna really isn't in any real sense. Anna is at least . . . [*trails off*] And I think more and more I see in my work the people that aren't in pain, like Andria, the half-Norwegian, half-Black girl in "A Summer in Maine," Andria's not in any pain. Andrea knows exactly where she's going. She just has to get up every morning and do her work and she's going to end up being a television newscaster, I mean, Andria knows exactly—people who do their work. . . . The really unhappy people in my fiction are people who have been ruined by their families having too much money.

McKinley: There's a theory today that all writing is autobiographical. Do you think that's so?

Gilchrist: Well, in the sense that it incorporates—all I can talk about is mine. One's writing, my writing, incorporates everything that I've experienced, been told, or read, but since I've been reading nonstop all my life—I mean, I read all the time, I've been doing it all my life! I can read and do other things. A long time ago, when I lived in a small town and there weren't many cars, I used to read while driving! Everybody, a lot of people used to do that. I love to tell that to people in the modern world because they don't understand that you could do it because you'd have to stop at the stoplight, you could read a few pages, and there weren't many cars and you could cruise down a half-empty street reading *The Catcher in the Rye*, which I remember vividly doing in my teens. So my work, the body of material from which I create my work, is not just my personal experience of life, but my personal experience of life and everything I've read. And I think that my books are—and I don't try to keep from doing it, no matter how much trouble it is to get the permissions. My books are larded, as it were, with lines from poems, pieces of poems.

McKinley: Epigraphs.

Gilchrist: Yeah, things that other people have said, because I consider those gifts to the world. Or if I can sneak in the name of a sonata or a symphony that somebody in Tahlequah, Oklahoma, maybe hadn't heard yet, and if they're my ideal reader, if, you know, they're the reader that I dream of, that I was, they'll go down to the library or the record store and find that music and listen to it.

McKinley: One of your enduring characters, or recurring characters I should say, is Rhoda, who appears in *Victory over Japan* and many other places and we kind of watch her grow from an extremely bright little girl who's curious about everything, particularly sex, we must say that, into a very lusty woman who enjoys sensual pleasures as well as intellectual pleasures. And some feminist critics have said, "Gee, Ellen Gilchrist is just great because she acknowledges our sexuality," but it doesn't seem to me that you do it in any didactic way. How do you react when people say, "Oh, she's great, her female characters like sex."

Gilchrist: Well, I'll quote a poem for you. A long time ago, about fifteen or twenty years, I can't remember who wrote them. Someone wrote these little things that became very popular for a while called groks. Do you remember groks? And my favorite grok was, "With everything either concave or convex, whatever we do will be something with sex."

Presson: Ellen Gilchrist spoke to *New Letters Magazine* editor James McKinley, at KCRU FM in Kansas City. Gilchrist's latest book is titled *I Cannot Get You Close Enough*. Some of her other titles include *In the Land of Dreamy Dreams, Victory over Japan, Drunk with Love,* and *The Anna Papers*. Copies of this and most *New Letters* programs are available for $8. If you'd like a list of titles, send us your name and address and the call numbers of the station you hear us on. Our address is *New Letters on the Air*, University of Missouri, Kansas City, Missouri 64110. Once again, that's *New Letters on the Air*, University of Missouri, Kansas City, Missouri 64110. *New Letters on the Air* is produced by the literary magazine *New Letters*. We had assistance this week from Janice Woollery and Don Harvey at KCRU FM. Gerald Kemner wrote our theme music. We receive financial assistance from the Missouri Arts Council. I'm Rebekah Presson.

Ellen Gilchrist: The Prize-Winning Short Story Writer Now Finds Novels Better Serve Her Vision

Wendy Smith / 1992

From *Publisher's Weekly* 239 (March 2, 1992): 46–47. Copyright PWxyz LLC. Reprinted by permission.

A creek runs through Ellen Gilchrist's front hallway. No, it's not the residue of some catastrophic flood; noted architect E. Fay Jones carved a channel for the site's groundwater when he designed the house in 1957. Nature is an honored participant in this serene structure, nestled in the hills of northwestern Arkansas, which admits the midwinter sunlight through floor-to-ceiling glass that constitutes much of the outer walls, and uses wood and stone to define its flowing interior space. "It's so Japanese!" approves the author, herself a student of Zen.

Although she bought it only recently, the house suits Gilchrist perfectly. She has created a tranquil, productive life for herself in Fayetteville, Arkansas, after a childhood spent uneasily alternating between the Midwest and her parents' native South, followed by turbulent decades that included several marriages and three children born when she was very young—a personal history the general outlines of which she shares with Rhoda Manning, protagonist of many short stories in Gilchrist's American Book Award–winning collection *Victory over Japan* (1985) and of her newest novel, *Net of Jewels* (*Fiction Forecasts*, January 27), which Little, Brown will publish this month.

Gilchrist has lived in Fayetteville off and on since the mid-1970s and now seems firmly settled in this small university town. At lunch in the Old Post Office Restaurant, she knows half the people in the dining room and interrupts her meal at one point to give a big hug to a friend recently returned from Texas.

Human connections are important to the author. Her first story collection, *In the Land of Dreamy Dreams* (1981), contained four tales featuring Rhoda Manning, one of the group of interrelated characters who now, Gilchrist complains jokingly, "come over and demand a role whenever I think of a new dramatic situation." Rhoda's cousin Crystal and her Black housekeeper Traceleen made their first appearance in *Victory over Japan.* Another cousin, the writer Anna Hand, turned up in *Drunk with Love* (1987), her third collection of short fiction, and dominated Gilchrist's novel *The Anna Papers* (1988). A second generation of the Hand-Manning clan became prominent in the three novellas of her most recent book, *I Cannot Get You Close Enough* (1990).

As Gilchrist got more involved with this extended family, she found that short fiction was no longer a comfortable genre. "The thing about the short story form," she says, "is that in order to do a good job with it you've got to concentrate on no more than two characters; you've got to pretend that nobody has any children or parents, that only this moment in these two or three lives is of any real importance. I would corner off two people to write about, but I would immediately have to connect it to a bigger world to be satisfied with it. I think that in order to serve the vision I currently have of reality, I'm going to have to have at least five or six characters interplaying."

The author faced some problems of consistency and overlap when she wrote *Net of Jewels.* A harrowing scene in which Rhoda undergoes an abortion was lifted in large part from "1957, A Romance," found in *In the Land of Dreamy Dreams.* "There are certain pieces of my work where I know I got it right the first time," she comments, "and I just decided to use it the way it was." Gilchrist unabashedly rewrote Rhoda's history to make her a nineteen-year-old virgin at the beginning of *Net of Jewels*, although "Music" in *Victory over Japan* showed her having a sexual encounter at age fourteen. "At the time [of "Music"] I believed that a story has to have a dramatic ending, so I had her sleep with the boy even though it really violated my internal sense of Rhoda's personality. It works to get you out of the story, but it never seemed true to me; it was just a trick, like riding a bicycle with no hands.

"You can't go back to the easy fix you learn as a short story writer, where you kill somebody off or get somebody laid to create a climax. What I'm trying to do now is make a study of existence—that's the high ground, but I perceive it as that. I want it to be as true to what I know about human beings as it can be. When I was writing *Net of Jewels*, I thought: *The more I've written about Rhoda, the more I know about her, and I'm going to serve that knowledge in this book.* This is the difference between writing novels and writing short stories; there aren't any tricks."

Seated at her dining room table, casually dressed in a light brown wool turtleneck and a pleated navy skirt, her legs drawn up nonchalantly underneath her, the author seems as free from artifice as she hopes her work is. Chin-length, blunt-cut blond hair (showing gray at the temples) frames the pretty, apparently makeup-free face of a woman happy to be and look her age (fifty-seven)—so much so that in *Net of Jewels* she found it "really hard to revisit the mind of a twenty-year-old girl in the late 1950s."

It was a difficult book to write, she says, partly because there was little room for the humor that has always enlivened her work. "I would hope that I would always know what comedy is—if you can make people laugh, what else can anyone ask?—but I knew this novel would not be funny. I think what I've done here is written a little piece of history, a portrait of a time and place that is going to be, for young women reading it, like me reading Jane Austen, because young women really can't comprehend a world where if you got pregnant you *had* to have the baby; the only way you could get out was by putting your life in danger. I hope that I have recreated the intensity of the desperation of somebody who is pregnant and doesn't want to have the baby."

She also captured the slow, tentative transformation of a spoiled, self-absorbed young woman who begins to learn there is a world outside her family, a world whose moral challenges and dangers are incarnated for Rhoda in the civil rights movement. Gilchrist herself took part as an adult in the struggle to bring racial justice to the South, but she knew long before that there were a lot of things wrong with the privileged life her parents accepted as their birthright.

"I spent a lot of my formative years in public schools in Illinois and Indiana; a big part of me is an old Harrisburg, Illinois, cheerleader from a town that was a real democracy. I didn't have the words 'racism' and 'sexism,' but I was fighting against them all my life, because I was fighting to be free. I was one of the lucky ones, because I'm a reader; I had the literature of the world and the library as my backup staffs. You teach someone to read and they're not going to be encapsulated; they're going to find like minds. I always knew there were other places; I always wanted to go to them."

Yet, she acknowledges, she is unquestionably a Southern writer. "Both of my parents are from the Deep South, and everyone I knew growing up could speak proper, perfect English on formal occasions but could also speak a sort of mixture of English and the beautiful, inventive things that Black people had done and are still doing in the South with the language. I was taught to speak by people who take a long time to say things, and it's heavily voweled and full of adjectives—it's a Faulkner's language. When I first read Eudora Welty and Faulkner, I almost fainted; I couldn't believe that you could write things and have them published in this language that I spoke."

Gilchrist was nearly forty when she began writing seriously. "I had a newspaper column—in a real newspaper—when I was a sophomore in high school. But after I started getting married and having babies, I stopped. I was raised in a world in which you didn't have ambitions after you had children; the moment you had a baby in your arms, the ambitions were transferred to your child. When the boys were young I studied with Miss Welty for a year [in the mid-1960s at Millsaps College], and I had written a lot of poetry and been reasonably successful in publishing it. But then I got married again and forgot all about it."

When she was in her late thirties, a close friend took up writing poetry and asked for her help; editing the poems, Gilchrist says, "I was jealous of what she was doing." Just how remote writing had become from her life became apparent a few days later when another friend casually referred to the excitement of meeting a poet, and Gilchrist realized that "my best friend in New Orleans didn't even know I had ever been a poet." Long-suppressed feelings were stirred up; shortly thereafter, reading Anne Sexton's *45 Mercy Street* in a public place, she found herself weeping uncontrollably.

"I began to have this recurrent dream of being in my house in New Orleans and opening a door to find all these rooms that I didn't know were there, full of chests with the drawers full of treasures. Nothing had been touched in a long, long time, and I had this feeling that I wanted to get other people in the house and show them these rooms. So I began to write. I was going on a vacation with my husband, scuba diving with some friends. We were out the door, walking down the steps to the car, and I walked back in the house, opened up a coat closet in the hall, got out a Royal portable typewriter I hadn't touched in about seven years, and took it with me to the islands. I don't think I ever went in the ocean."

Poetry got her up to Fayetteville; her friend Jim Whitehead, director of the University of Arkansas writing program, told her that she needed to be in a community of writers. Bill Harrison's short story course convinced her to try a new form, and a National Endowment for the Arts grant helped her complete *In the Land of Dreamy Dreams*, which the University of Arkansas Press published in 1981. That brought her to her agent, Don Congdon, and her editor, Little, Brown's Roger Donald.

"A young man in the writing program here was working as Don's assistant; he read *Dreamy Dreams* and gave it to Don, who called me up and asked if he could be my agent. He told me all the people he'd represented, which included most of my favorite American writers, and we talked for about an hour. I didn't know anything about agents; I said, 'Do we have a contract?' and he said, 'No, we just trust each other. If you get sick of me, you can quit.'"

A number of New York editors wanted to sign Gilchrist, but she was most attracted by Roger Donald's offer of a contract for a novel and a collection of short stories. She has worked with both men ever since. "Don reads the manuscripts, too; he's a very fine editor. Roger and I don't mince words with each other; he doesn't tiptoe around my feelings, and I don't tiptoe around his. My strength as a writer is that I can accept criticism and learn from it. I don't think what I've written is etched in stone; I know it's a draft, and I feel free to write that draft because I know that Roger and Don or both will tell me what part of it is bullshit and where the story really begins."

The first draft currently occupying Gilchrist is of a new novel and Olivia, the illegitimate, half-Native American daughter of Anna Hand's brother. "A friend of mine told me that the government is now giving scientific grants based on the security of the computer systems, so everyone decided to code scientific information into computer in Navaho. The big idea for a book is always kind of like a vision, and as soon as I heard this I knew exactly who was going to get this information and exactly what she was going to do. Because Olivia's on the make; she has to find a place in the world, and she wants a job. So it takes place in Tahlequah, Oklahoma, in the summer of 1991, when Olivia goes back to learn the old Indian languages."

Although Gilchrist is "really looking forward to writing a book set in 1991 after this long morass of the 1950s," she didn't deliberately set out to give herself a change of period. "You can't really plan fiction," she says. "You just turn it loose. Whatever the muse gives me, I serve that. I can't afford to care whether it's the right thing to do—it's just what I'm doing next."

Voice of Rhoda Instructs Authors

Beth Macy / 1993

From the *Roanoke Times*, October 5, 1993. Reprinted by permission.

People ask writer Ellen Gilchrist all the time, "Are you Rhoda?"—referring to the inimitable Rhoda Manning, the extravagantly funny and mixed-up character who appears and reappears in several of Gilchrist's books, including the American Book Award–winning *Victory over Japan* and her latest novel, *Net of Jewels.*

"I say I'm Rhoda as much as I am a binary neutron star," Gilchrist said Saturday at the ninth annual Blue Ridge Writers Conference. "You might create a character based on your mother, but in three weeks you're not even gonna recognize your mother in that character anymore."

It was definitely Rhoda—and by extension, Gilchrist herself—for whom 150 area writers turned out Saturday at the daylong conference featuring a Gilchrist reading and discussion, as well as advice from other professionals, including Highland County writer Donald McCaig and Gilchrist's agent, Don Congdon.

The fifty-eight-year-old Gilchrist, who's just as outspoken as her wacky Rhoda Manning character, read her hilarious (and somewhat controversial) recent short story, "A Statue of Aphrodite," featuring a fifty-eight-year-old Rhoda—"who still hasn't learned very much." She also discussed her own writing process in a talk called "Muse of Fire."

"The poet Randall Jarrell said a poet stands out in storms all his life and once or twice gets struck by lightning," Gilchrist said. "You have to be out there writing so you can be a container for when the muse strikes."

The early, prepublishing years are the hardest for a writer, she said. It's hard to get that first break because publishers are only interested in new writers who are already successful.

That's where tenacity comes in. "At first you need to publish wherever you can—journals, newspapers, magazines. And then hopefully you'll find some niche. Like [newspaper columnist] Molly Ivins. She didn't find a hole and fill it. She made her own hole, her own niche, and filled it."

Gilchrist herself didn't begin writing until she was nearly forty, although as a fourteen-year-old she did write a weekly newspaper column called "Chit 'n' Chat 'Bout This 'n' That."

"I had a lotta children and got married a lotta times," said Gilchrist, who was born in the Mississippi Delta but now lives in Fayetteville, Arkansas. "I wasn't interested in hanging out with my three little boys and breaking up the fights, so I read all the time."

When her children were in their teens—"leading the revolution of the seventies," she said—the family had to fly all over the US getting them out of jail. "I thought, if they're not going to use the genes, I'm going to."

Gilchrist said "voice"—the style or sound of the narrator or writer, "the imprint of the mind driving the hand"—is the most important tool a writer can use. "Voice is what makes us absolutely fall in love with certain books."

The only way to establish the voice of a character is by writing. "Sometimes it just comes. Sometimes you hear a scrap of conversation and you can tell a whole story in that one little bit of voice you just heard. Or you read something and you hear a voice."

Southern language provides Gilchrist with the most melodic voices, she said. "The further South you go, it's like music. We've turned language into song in the South."

"I was twenty-six when I read Faulkner and Miss Welty. And I was amazed. I thought, 'I can write the way we talk?'"

Gilchrist—who has the phrase "Goodbye, Sequential Thought" taped to her television set—said she fears the melody of language has become lost in the dominating culture of America: television.

She and her friends meet every Tuesday night to read the plays of William Shakespeare aloud. "He constantly talks about the imagination," she said. "Back then they were as excited about language as our culture is today about TV."

"Never take language for granted," she told her audience. "It's an amazing thing to be able to tell a person you saw a horse and they know immediately what you're talking about."

And don't let the goal of writing get lost in the hard, hard work it is to get published, she added. Wanting to be writers, "You're asking to be in a priestly caste."

The key to discovering the joy in the creative process of writing is to keep on doing it—to be there when the muse strikes.

"No psychologist can ever figure [the muse] out, either—no matter how many brain smears they take," she said. "And when it does strike, I always think it'll never happen again."

The joy of writing more than makes up for the struggle every writer faces, she said. "Don't let anybody talk you out of it, if you really wanna write— because it's so much fun, the creative act of writing."

Poking yet more fun at the television culture, she added, "Our time will come. The electricity will go off one day and they'll all beg us to come over and read."

Most of the conference attendees—English professors, playwrights, freelance writers, desktop publishers and journalists—were inspired by Gilchrist's reading and talks, though not all.

"We had five or six born-again Christians who were extremely upset" by Gilchrist's reading, conference president Liz Jones said. Gilchrist's story did contain a certain four-letter word, in addition to Rhoda's rantings about sex—specifically, her lack of it.

Asked what Gilchrist thought of the controversy, Jones said, "She loved it. She hopes they ban her books at Liberty University."

Interview with Ellen Gilchrist

Rebecca Newth / 1994

From *Ozarks at Large*, April 23, 1994. KUAF Radio. Printed by permission. Transcript by Tracy Carr.

Rebecca Newth: Good morning, this is *Ozarks at Large*. Readers and fans of writer Ellen Gilchrist know what to expect from one of her novels: a collection of wonderfully eccentric, very interesting characters. Her books include the National Book Award winner *Victory over Japan*, the collection of short stories *In the Land of Dreamy Dreams*, and the novel *Net of Jewels*. She has written poetry and collected journals. She was a regular commentator for *Morning Edition* on National Public Radio in the 1980s. Her latest book, *Starcarbon*, is now on bookstore shelves. This week, she talked with *Ozarks at Large*'s Rebecca Newth about her latest work, the writing process, and about writing in so many different forms: poetry, essays, short stories, and novels.

Ellen Gilchrist: I don't think analytically about literature, about reading it or writing it. I just don't think in those terms. I've been reading constantly since I was four or five years old. Since before I could actually read, I was reading. I mean, I was always reading. When I made the leap from pretending to read a book to actually reading a book, I don't know. But I was satisfied with what I was doing even when I could only read half the words in a sentence. This is so much a part of my life that I don't—and I never separate the forms of writing into genres. Although I know if I've been reading a lot of one thing—I know that I was thinking when I was going to do this interview with you today, I thought, you know, I wrote that book a year ago, I finished that book a year ago. I should go through and make sure I know the names of all the characters and I thought, *oh, well, there's always the cast*—because I read Shakespearean plays all the time—I was thinking that I could open up my own book and that there'd be, you know, there'd be a cast of characters, and I thought, *oh, no, that's right, that's Shakespeare.* So I don't know. The forms all get, are all one thing to me. I know how to write in the different forms, but when I'm inspired, the form that the inspiration should take always comes with the inspiration. I mean, if I'm going to write something, it's either a poem or a novel or a short story or an essay. It just comes all of a piece.

Newth: Do you ever—

Gilchrist: But that's because I've read all those things, so my mind has these little containers that it can fit an inspiration into. Well, we all do. It's not just mine. I ply my trade.

Newth: Do you write in restaurants?

Gilchrist: Sometimes I do. Occasionally I do, and it's an utterly charming thing to do.

Newth: In longhand, to be able to just sit somewhere.

Gilchrist: I don't think there's much difference between writing in a restaurant and reading in bed and eating cookies at the same time. I have always loved to eat sugar and literature at the same time. To eat sugar and either read or write literature at the same time.

Newth: Well, you mentioned your cast of characters and I wondered, I was fascinated with the names of these people, and I know other novels have had these people in them, but is there a story with that?

Gilchrist: No, just that when I conceive a character, then I name them. Not always simultaneously, but the name, the naming of the character is a part of the creation of the character. And I think that we all have a sense of someone's name fitting them, but if our parents name us, our parents know who we are as soon as they see us. Where are we coming from? Out of their gene pool. They know which one of all those possibilities an infant is most like. All mothers know that. When a child's grown, a mother looks at it and it's the same person you saw when it was an infant. So. Well, that's getting too complicated.

Newth: I was wondering if we could begin with that part about Olivia de Haviland Hand, then, which is on page 17.

Gilchrist: All right, I see.

Newth: Because there are some good names in there.

Gilchrist: Where would you like me to begin?

Newth: With "This Olivia"?

Gilchrist: Oh yes. [*Reads from* Starcarbon]

Newth: And that so perfectly gives a sense of her whole dilemma, it seems, which you really catch so well.

Gilchrist: I'm not sure which genes would be good for that.

Newth: In a sense, are your books kind of a homecoming? Because when you write about New Orleans, I sort of sense that, and then Fayetteville is in this book, too. Is there a sense that you kind of have a chance to go home each time?

Gilchrist: That's a really wonderful question, Rebecca, because I've been thinking about that a lot. It's a very strange thing if you work as an artist, as a writer or a painter or a musician, or a playwright, or whatever. You learn by doing and you're always turning around every few years filled with wonder that you even could have done this with the little knowledge you had four years ago or five years ago. And then there's another kind of epiphany. You begin to understand your work in its relation to your life and you begin to see what it was you were doing and how the two forces played, or helped each other, played against each other, played off of each other, and used each other, and fed upon each other, and I think, you know, only, because I've been writing almost constantly since 1976, which is seventeen years. This is closing in on twenty years I've been doing this, and I'm beginning to understand that I have to experience a place and a time and a people for a long time before I naturally wish to write about it because I don't understand it. I don't have enough deep knowledge of it to write about it. And I lived in New Orleans for twelve years and visited there all my life before that, before I wrote about the culture, the part of New Orleans with which I had interacted all those years. And the same thing I think is true of this world, of this world, of Fayetteville and Tahlequah. You see, now, everybody has their own Fayetteville, everybody has the part of the Ozarks that they think—mine is, you know, from the headwaters of the Buffalo River to Tahlequah, to Tulsa, all that part. I never go up toward Kansas City, for example, and I don't really go down toward Fort Smith. It's just up here, this area that's just my stomping grounds, as it were. And I'm just now beginning to have that deep enough into my psyche so that I get tears in my eyes when I hear that song, that corny song that PBS goes off the air with every night. I was thinking one night, "I want them to play that at my funeral." [*Laughs*] "Arkansas, You Run Deep in Me," you know, that feeling. I'm beginning, after all these years, I think I always loved this place and had a feeling for it and *The Annunciation*, the first novel that I wrote was set in Fayetteville, but that book was character-driven. I think that more and more when I write about this part of the country, the place, the place invades the work like a spirit, and so I guess whenever I write about someplace that I used to be, like the Mississippi Delta, it's just like being there, to write about it. It's just, I'm just traveling there in my mind. I guess I always write about the Delta in the summer. Either Christmas or the summer because most of my life, I was just there in the summer and at Christmas. It's just like being there. I can feel the air, and I can almost feel like I should reach up and start swatting all those little bugs that would come up from the bayou. People don't think about that but a long time ago in the country, bugs were always everywhere. Swarms of little gnats. Children didn't pay any attention to them, you just beat 'em out of the way with your hands and went on down to the store. So it is, I guess, a homecoming always. I got lonely for New Orleans late last spring and wrote a short story set there and sold it to *The Atlantic*, but they haven't published it yet.

Newth: Well, sometimes when I read your work I think it's as if you've got a different perspective, and a different, almost like a lens, in which you look at these things, as if a person who was maybe at first a playwright and who saw everything visually suddenly said, "Well, I'll write a short story." But it still had that other difference to it, you know? Are you—would you be able to define that or—there's a seasoning or something.

Gilchrist: No, what I see in my mind when I'm writing is a play—except I'm involved in it from all the angles. It just wears me out sometimes. Even if I'm writing something that's funny, I'll just be exhausted. But Rebecca— this is the only example that I know that I always use—if you're driving a car down the highway, and a rabbit or a dog runs in front of the car, your whole body—the chemistry of your body in a microsecond completely changes. That's an adrenaline rush, I suppose, but it's more complicated than that, physiologically. Actually, you haven't hit the dog. It's just the idea that you might hit the dog that's done this chemically to your body. So if I'm writing something that's exciting I'll be experiencing all the physiological changes in my body and the excitement, and this and that and the other.

Newth: You're saying to not think too much editorially, but just to get into it, just to experience it again.

Gilchrist: Well, certainly for the first draft. You can't be looking over your shoulder. Which is what I was trying to tell those children down at the Governor's School in 1984 or whenever it was when I got accused of telling the children of Arkansas to ignore their parents.[1] I thought I was talking to the young writers and I was telling them how not to be blocked by having their imaginary parents looking over their shoulder when they're doing creative work! You know, your parents, even the most wonderful parents in the world, which I had, are your first and most severest critics and what they create in your mind and leave in your mind is a Jiminy Cricket who's always saying, "Well, that's stupid" or "That's not good enough" or "What are you doing that for?" and your real parents probably wouldn't even say anything. They'd probably say, "Oh, my darling, that's wonderful." But somehow or other this creates a censor in your mind and in order to do creative work, you've got to be able to *figuratively* shut the door and keep those parental voices from judging your work. You can go in a week later or the next day and edit and work critically on your own work, and you learn how to do that, but you can't do it in the first creation. The first creation has to be completely free. Of course, our culture knows that now; we talk about that all the time. We try desperately to incorporate that into the way we educate our children.

Newth: Well, we wish you well and we thank you so much for coming over here and talking with us, Ellen Gilchrist.

Gilchrist: Thank you.

Voice: Writer Ellen Gilchrist. Her latest novel, *Starcarbon*, has just been published. She talked with Rebecca Newth this weekend at the *Ozarks at Large* studio. Rebecca's "Arkansas Voices" is a regular feature of *Ozarks at Large*.

Note

1. In 1985, Gilchrist addressed the class of the Arkansas Governor's School and said, "I ask you to start ignoring your parents. Be really nice to them, and forget them. At the age you are now, it's time to start using your stuff, your real stuff" ("Author Draws More Criticism for Her Comments to Students," *Batesville Guard*, July 25, 1985).

A Conversation with Ellen Gilchrist

Martha Wilson and Gwendolyn Sell / 1995

From the *Arkansas Review* 5, nos. 1–2 (August 1996), 156–64. Reprinted by permission.

Following a lecture series sponsored by the Honors Program at Macon College on February 8 and 9, 1995, Ellen Gilchrist spoke with Macon College professors Martha Wilson and Gwen Sell. Gilchrist has received critical acclaim for numerous novels and collections of short stories. She lives and works in Fayetteville, Arkansas.

Question: You mentioned in your lecture that you don't have a favorite writer, but which author do you consider to have had the greatest influence on you?

Ellen Gilchrist: I don't know because it's always changing. I don't feel that there's any one great influence so much as that at different times of my writing life, different pieces of work have been certainly influenced by different people. But I'm always fighting to keep anyone else's voice from leaking into the voice that I write with, and I think I've gotten better and better. Probably the early stories were more influenced by Eudora Welty and Flannery O'Connor and Faulkner and all those people I thought they were at the time. I couldn't help but be influenced, but I think my own voice has gotten clearer and clearer, so I don't think the voice is ever influenced. The real influences to me as a writer are other things. I read Shakespeare every Tuesday night or Monday night with a group of my friends. Well, sometimes it ends up being more like two or three times a month or maybe even two times a month, but we do it a lot and we've been doing it for years. I won't be influenced so much as I'll be enthused, and I'll be led to believe that anything is possible because for William Shakespeare anything was possible. If I'm going to be influenced by anybody, it's going to be by the best writer in the world. I want to be influenced by people who, over time, created a real body of work that is vast and encompassing and it's more than I could possibly ever dream of doing. I was influenced once one winter—I mean I don't know how I could call this an influence—I reread John Fowles, and I remembered how big and how rich and how luxuriant a novel could be and also how mysterious. I don't know. . . . Influences are something that a young writer is subject to.

But after you've been writing enough, you are more than likely and more in danger of being influenced by your own early work than you are by another writer's voice. Because if you've used your voice enough, it's yours. I could safely read Faulkner while writing fiction now, but that wasn't true seven or eight years ago. If I read Faulkner, I had to quit writing for four or five days while I aired it out—mostly because it's a mirror of language that I heard all my life.

Question: You mention O'Connor, Eudora Welty and their works very often.

Gilchrist: Really just one story of Flannery O'Connor's. I like "A Good Man Is Hard to Find." I don't like any of the dark things.

Question: Do you see any common threads between your work and O'Connor's and Welty's?

Gilchrist: No. Ms. Welty is a practicing Methodist; Ms. O'Connor is a practicing Roman Catholic; I'm atheist—always have been. I have a scientific mind. I think the relationship between my work and other Southern writers is that the English language as we use it in the South is a dialect like that of Ireland. Of course, the thing you love Eudora for is the humor. If you're like me, you like the funny stories, but I also like the story called "First Love," I think, about a young girl who is alone in a house. Well, maybe she's not mistreated, but she's certainly lonely and it's the biggest house in town, and the poor boy who catches fish every day walks by her house carrying the strings of silver fish. And God, the story is so sexual and the imagery is so deep and so Freudian and so beautiful, so Victorian. You can't put that interpretation in print because, you know, they [writers like Welty] are among my mother's generation, and God knows, I'm cloned out of the generation— just cloned out. People in my generation were raised in extremely Victorian backgrounds. Everything was beautiful. The world was made beautiful, and I love it. I don't disavow it. I like it. I'm sorry it's gone. When my mother and the last of these women are gone, it'll never be in the world again.

Question: You mentioned that you didn't feel that you were influenced by the women writing in America today and that you didn't want to be influenced by them. Why do you think that is?

Gilchrist: Well, because their themes would be the same as mine. I don't want to be influenced by anyone whose themes are the same as mine. I don't want to be influenced by anybody, period. I just want to read for pleasure, and it doesn't interest me to read other people who are exploring the same thematic material that I am.

Question: Why do you think so much critical attention has been given to Southern women writers—such as Lee Smith and Gail Godwin—since 1970?

Gilchrist: Well, they were women who had the time and the mental freedom to write. You can't write if you're afraid to write. You certainly can't write if you've got a house full of children and have to sweep the floors every day. You know, it's a jealous obsession—it's like being a concert pianist. You can't run a house and do it in your spare time. You can't be involved in the lives of a bunch of children who take up all your mental space and energy. I mean, that's how it's arranged. That's how nature has arranged it. If you'll notice, Ms. Welty didn't have any children, and I don't think Flannery did either.

Question: Neither were they married.

Gilchrist: No. I just think it's natural. I don't think it's just Southern. I think it's just a natural progression of women gaining economic freedom and not just that—but the freedom to say what they damn well please and not care whether their aunts and uncles threw their hands up in dismay. I mean, mine certainly would have thrown their hands up in dismay, but I don't care, except for one or two who just deeply love me and did anyway. They always thought I was funny and just have striven, have striven to understand what it is I'm doing. They're all kind of coming around to me. I just removed myself from the scene so I didn't have to listen to any of it, and I think you have to do that. Artists have always had to do that. You can't stay in the bourgeoisie and be an artist. Bourgeoisie—no artists allowed. I love the bourgeoisie, and about every five or six to ten years I have to go back in for a while just to make sure I can get back in. I've got to make sure I can get back in a country club if I want to. It's only in retrospect that I see this.

Question: Do you think that your family was so shocked that you were an artist or that you were a woman being an artist?

Gilchrist: They weren't shocked by any of that. I've always been a writer, and I've always shocked them in one way or the other. But there have always been writers in my family. They were shocked by the language. I mean I was writing down things that they wouldn't even say, and I've always said those things—ever since I heard the words—because I love language. I love language, and when I was a child, if I would hear anyone using great strings of profanity, I would love it. It was so passionate, so full of energy. I mean, I liked any kind of language. I like big words and odd words and profane words, and God, you know, if there's a middle child—if he could learn some words that got their attention, he definitely was throwing those down the stairs whenever he wanted to. But mostly I was trying to write what I'd heard. I was trying to write the language that people actually speak. Of course, we have about three realms of discourse in the United States. We have a realm of public discourse in all the newspapers and magazines which is all so guarded and so careful that we don't hurt one another's feelings. Then we have our private conversations with one another, and then we have intellectual discourse which is yet another thing. That's all interesting. The theater is the best place to watch that happen. Someone like Albee who will just put characters up on the stage and they just say exactly what we have been saying all day. And we are all going—ahh, ahh, ahh, ahh, fraught with meaning, and secrets, and secrets, secrets we are always keeping. If we all said what we were thinking all the time, we would all be fighting all the time.

Question: Many of your characters are women searching for personal freedom.

Gilchrist: I believe in freedom, men, women, and children. I don't even have dogs tied up in the yard. I've always had freedom. I declared my freedom when I was about four years old, and my father thought it was funny. You know, I've always been able to get my own freedom, so even to this day it is very, very difficult for me to imagine someone who would allow themselves to be enslaved in any form or fashion. You know, the sort of slavery that many, many women still live in [in] the United States. You know, they have to please their mother, their daddy, their in-laws, and their husbands. And they call that being unselfish. They call that being unselfish, and then they go down to the church and the preacher tells them they did good, and they get these little rewards and they hope their children are going to turn out all right. Maybe that'll reward them, but they don't have any freedom. I could never imagine anyone that wouldn't just rise up out of bed every morning and fight to be free. That's my Irish blood. I work as an individualist, my style, my life.

Question: Your sense of humor seems important in relation to your work.

Gilchrist: A sense of humor is a sense of balance. It's just a sense of balance. I've always been around a lot of people that thought everything was funny.

Question: Is that a form of salvation—to see the cosmic humor?

Gilchrist: Well, only human beings can do it, and really it's the mark of our superiority over the other species. No other creature really laughs; no other species knows how to laugh. We laugh at ourselves.

Question: Kevin Calder is a protegee of yours. How did that relationship develop, and are there other young writers you work with?

Gilchrist: Kevin is just my friend. He wrote to me, and the letter was so charming and so amusing that I wrote him back. Then he wrote me and asked me about writing programs in the United States. And I said, "Well, I don't know anything about any of the rest of them, but I know that Jim Whitehead is a great man and is a great teacher." So the next thing I knew, Kevin had come up to Fayetteville to be in the program, and that's just how it started. I used to have a number of young poets in New Orleans whose work I worked on. But the more you write and the better writer you become in the sense of the more technically skilled you become, the less good teacher you are for anybody. Now I would not know how to tell them what their voice is because I'm so used to taking any piece of writing and trying to make it into my voice. One of my sons is a journalist. Since he was ten years old, he wouldn't let me see a paper that he turned in. I can't help it, because I'm going to definitely overedit anything that I touch. I think the best writing teacher is an English teacher. I don't think that highly accomplished writers are good teachers for everybody. They are good teachers for someone who comes along that has a voice that is similar to theirs anyway, but if someone comes along with an entirely different kind of voice, what could they do? It's just a gift. It's just a gift—some people are gifted teachers. They can help some other person find their own voice, which is all you can do, I think.

Question: One of the things you spoke about in your meeting with students is the advice that you would give to people aspiring to be writers. I think your first principle was to read. Are there others?

Gilchrist: I don't know. I think people who want to learn to write start doing it when they are really young. Nothing can stop them. They are driven to it—they pick up forms and create their own forms and—the worst thing that you can do, and I see this every now and then in the United States— the worst thing that a parent can do is to take it too seriously and start going around telling people their child is a writer, or putting them in classes, or talking about it in front of them. And I just shudder. If my parents had done that, well, I would have been furious with them because writing was something that belonged to me—like my own room or my own clothes. If I wanted them to notice that I had written something, I would go tell them about it. They always left me alone. Nobody ever would bother me if I was reading. Nobody would ever bother me if I was writing. They wouldn't say anything about it, and neither would they bother me. And many, many a night, if my father was away, we could just run all over our mother and do anything to her we wanted. I'd be sitting in the living room reading a book, and my mother and two brothers would be having a formal dinner. If my daddy wasn't there, she wouldn't make me stop—because I could not stand to stop in the middle of a chapter or something. When I'd get to a stopping place, I'd march into the dining room. I couldn't have done that if I was doing anything but reading a book, but somehow very early they knew that this was part of my life and they just let me have it for myself.

Question: So they didn't prohibit certain books? You were free to choose what you wanted?

Gilchrist: Well, if you remember—you probably don't—but the libraries did that.

Question: Oh, I do remember, I do remember it very well.

Gilchrist: I used to go into the adult section and read the books. I'd just sit in between the stacks and read, but you couldn't take the books home with you. I don't know how librarians got them separated. My mother got all kinds of books from the Literary Guild and the Book of the Month club, and my grandmother had a huge library and I read all their books. But I read so much and so fast, that I'd just throw one down and pick up another one. I read a lot of biographies, and I read a lot of history. I read all the Thomas Costain books, and things like that. I believed Thomas Costain[1]—I'll never be able to believe any other version of English history. Talk about an influence.

Question: What are you working on now?

Gilchrist: I'm writing two novellas about Nora Jane—I guess they are set in 1994.

Question: You have mentioned that the novel seems like a great demon to you.

Gilchrist: It's not a demon, it's a dinosaur—it's this huge thing that should have died years ago, and it's always gnawing at your back. A publisher will give you three times as much money for a novel as a book of short stories, and besides that—it just—all of a sudden something starts turning into a novel and you think, "No—down—down!" God, what I hate is putting them together—when they get almost to the end and you've got all these chapters and things, and it takes up a whole room just to have the whole sets of papers sitting all over the place. You can't leave town because if the house burns down, there are no copies.

Question: It just seems that a short story would be so very difficult to write because of the condensation.

Gilchrist: No. The short story form is natural to me because I wrote poetry for so long. It's a very, very natural thing for me to write the beginning, the middle, and the end of a short story—a little collapsed piece of time. Sometimes I violate the purest—the best. The best short stories are very pure—the form feels really pure while I'm working in it. All of this makes perfect sense, and then other ones will be just slightly too long— slightly too far outside of the ideal form. But everybody knows that. It was what I was telling the students. You know, you have to do the work, you have to do whatever work your imagination gives you, and you don't know when one of those moments or inspirations are going to turn into the really fine and unforgettable story that you can sell immediately, that will immediately be put in anthologies and that everybody will talk about for years and want you to read to them. That one is maybe the first one, or the third one, or the tenth one. You have to write all of them to get to that. Every painter knows that; every composer knows that.

Question: Do you know when you have written that *one*?

Gilchrist: Yes, I do. Nearly always—I nearly always know. Mostly because it was so easy to write—the best stories are so easy to write, they write themselves. Or, as Vonnegut said, those moments when you just type up the pages and hand them to the editor, you know. It's what we call a muse. But you don't have the container to hold that gift in unless you are working all the time on the form. It's just like any other art form; you learn it by doing it. The more you do, you know. If you don't, you can't. The sad thing to me is that people wish they were writers but then become discouraged or disillusioned because on the two-week vacation they can't get a real start on a novel. Of course, they can't. Every now and then someone does, and that leads the others to believe it is not only possible but that they should be able to do it.

Question: Thank you for taking time to talk with us.

Gilchrist: You're welcome. Those were good questions.

Note

1. Thomas Costain was a journalist, editor, and historical fiction novelist.

Conversation with Ellen Gilchrist

Kyle Kellams / 1998

From *Ozarks at Large*, September 1998 (aired September 1, 2016). Printed by permission. Transcript by Tracy Carr.

Eighteen years ago this week, Ellen Gilchrist came to our studio, which was then on Dickson Street. Her latest book, *Sarah Conley*, had just been published and it marked a bit of a departure for the writer. Many of us became familiar with Gilchrist and became devoted fans through her short stories. Her collection *Victory over Japan* earned her a National Book Award. When she was at our studio in September 1998, she explained why her then-new book was a novel and this excerpt from that conversation is this week's Thursday archive.

Ellen Gilchrist: I think that the beginning impetus was that I wanted to write a novel—one of my readers or one of my friends kept talking about it, and I said, "*Why* aren't you satisfied with the collections of stories? Why do you want a novel?" And she said, "Because I want to be able to take a book with me to bed and have it there night after night. I don't want it to be finished in one night." And I kept thinking about that, and I thought, "You know, that's the best argument I've ever heard for why I should want to write a novel." But a novel is a huge investment in time and energy and hope—it's an investment in hope and self-confidence. I mean, you've got to really lay a lot of stuff out on the table, put a lot on the line to write a novel. You have to keep believing in yourself for a very, very long time. It's not difficult to believe in the world you're creating, in the characters, or it isn't for me. Once I create the characters and I set them in motion and the plot and the characters come to me as a whole, and once I know the world I'm creating, I want to keep writing the book because I won't ever know the end of the story. I mean, I may think I know what happens, but I don't know how it—just because you know that Princess Diana died doesn't mean that we aren't still just insanely, absurdly curious about the details. And I feel that way about a fantasy world that I create. So that's why I wrote a novel.

Kyle Kellams: Do you have an idea when you start putting these people's lives in motion how much of their past do you know and how much of their past reveals itself to you as you're writing?

Gilchrist: I used to believe—and I'm in a very rational mood so I'll say things, I'll introduce this with "I used to believe," I don't know if I believe it anymore—but when I was closer to being a poet, I believed that I knew it all and that the act of writing was the act of discovering something that I already knew, because always, when I'd finish part of it, most of the parts of a book, sometimes you'd make a mistake, but you'd finish a part of it and I'd say to myself, or I'd get the feeling, "That's right, that's what happened." So that the act of discovery was more like memory than like creating something out of nothing. And so I always felt, of course, I *believe*, I believe on my rational and irrational days, that the mind is so much huger than we know, that our memory encompasses so much more. Hell, for all we know, we could have the memory in our genes of everything up to the moment of conception of all of our ancestors. We do have those patterns, surely we have those patterns. I conceived that idea or thought it up and ran it through a young friend who was studying psychiatry at the time when I was fourteen when I first had that thought, about the age Sarah Conley is. If the mind is incomprehensible in its breadth and depth to our five paltry senses, then why wouldn't it be possible to think of a whole story? Especially, I mean, I'm sixty-two years old, look at the memory store that I have just from my own life. If the only conscious memory store I have is only my own life because, and I used to be interested in the idea, I guess I still will be if I start talking about it, that our peripheral vision and our peripheral hearing, that we are really taking in so much more data from such a wider field than the conscious mind could bear.

Ellen Gilchrist in the *Ozarks at Large* studio this week in 1998, when her novel *Sarah Conley* had just been published. We dig into our show's twenty-seven-plus years of archives on most Thursdays. Ellen Gilchrist, by the way, has a new book released just this summer. The collection of nonfiction essays is titled *Things Like the Truth: Out of My Later Years.* Published by the University Press of Mississippi, and it's available now. She teaches creative writing at the University of Arkansas.

Author Uses Her Imagination

Lori Herring / 2000

From the *Clarion-Ledger*, May 28, 2000. Copyright Lori Herring—USA TODAY NETWORK. Reprinted by permission.

Ellen Gilchrist will tell you that writing fiction is as easy as coming up with a character's name.

"You could do it," she says reassuringly by phone from Fayetteville, Arkansas. "All you have to do is just write down a name. Pretty soon, you will have imagined an entire history for them. You'll know who their grandparents were. You'll know everything."

This is from a woman whose imagination is so strong and independent that her imaginary friend from childhood, Jimmy, appeared to her not too long ago as she attended her ailing mother.

"Whenever people are very ill or dying around me, Jimmy will pop up," she says casually, the way one might mention a visit from a neighbor.

"And the other day, I was at the gym on some torturous machine supposed to make your waist more flexible, and Jimmy was standing there saying, 'Do you have to do this?' He was standing there in a black suit—a black tie and a white shirt."

Silence on the phone.

"I'm just telling you how I create a character," Gilchrist says, laughing. "I call Jimmy to mind the way you tell yourself a private joke."

Should've guessed.

Vicksburg native Gilchrist has nothing to her credit if not a charming, sharp, quirky sense of humor. She also, of course, has three novels and ten story collections, including *Victory over Japan* (1983), winner of the 1984 National Book Award, *In the Land of Dreamy Dreams* (1981), *Drunk with Love* (1986) and *Light Can Be Both Wave and Particle* (1989).

Oh, and better not leave out her newest, *The Cabal and Other Stories* (2000).

Gilchrist was writing another novella when she came up for the idea for "The Cabal," which is about what happens when a psychiatrist in Jackson goes mad and starts telling everyone's secrets.

"It wasn't just a better idea. It has the possibility for real irony and real humor," says Gilchrist, her lilting voice a honeypot of Southern charm and grace, tinged with enough fun to let you know she never takes herself too seriously, that she herself is a character worth remembering.

"So," she continues, "I put the other aside and wrote this one in a real big hurry."

Gilchrist managed to salvage that second novella by turning it into *The Sanguine Blood of Men*, the script that Caroline, a main character throughout "The Cabal" and the proceeding stories, has written.

"I think this book is a lot of fun," she says. "It was a lot of fun to write it."

It's not hard to imagine that Gilchrist's stance in life is necessarily fun and by nature funny; that this boundless aptitude for humor comes out in her work regardless.

"There's a gift that working really hard for a long time gives you," says the sixty-five-year-old author, who didn't start writing seriously until she was forty, though she says she's always been an "omnivorous" reader.

"You can't deliberately start writing funny. If it's funny, it will be funny. You can't make it funny."

Incidentally—just because "The Cabal" is set in Jackson sure as heck doesn't mean the characters are based on anyone here, dead or living.

"Give me some credit for my imagination," she says. "There's not a single true historical fact about a single person I've ever known in that book.

"I've always wanted to set a book in Jackson," she continues.

"Especially if you're going to write a book about talented people. There's so much talent in Mississippi that I thought it'd be more believable in Jackson."

Gilchrist changes the subject, talks of a book she "splurged on" about ancient paintings discovered in a cave in the gorges of the Ardeche River in France.

"They found that cave and they knew what it was," she says of the people who happened upon a thirty-foot-long wall of painted horses and other animals from 30,000 years ago. "When they went back to that room, they could hardly breathe for excitement."

Also, there were two handprints in the bottom of the wall.

"These people were reproducing the reality they knew, and that is the most wonderful thing in the world," she says. "People want to reproduce the beauty and wonder of the world around them. We all do it in different ways. Writing is one of them."

Ellen Gilchrist Discusses "Rich," Theme, Imagery, and Learning from *Huckleberry Finn*

Paul Mandelbaum / 2004

From *12 Short Stories and Their Making*, edited by Paul Mandelbaum (Persea Books, 2005). Reprinted by permission.

Ellen Gilchrist: This was the first real, finished, serious short story that I ever wrote. It was 1976 probably, or '77. I had a dinner party one night and Jim Whitehead and Bill Harrison, the directors of the [University of Arkansas] writing program at the time, were there. I had been in the writing program for about six months. I was working as a poet. At the dinner party they were asking me about New Orleans, and I remember thinking: How could anyone explain that complicated, multilayered old city to anyone who hadn't lived there?

I'd not only lived there, I'd been visiting my relatives there—my uncle was the editor of *The Times-Picayune* since I could remember. It's just part of my life. But how could I explain it to him? Especially uptown New Orleans, the part where I lived. Because during the years when I lived there, I was married, I lived in a world where everyone was very rich. There was just so much money and so many beautiful European things. So many beautiful fabrics and clothes and things like that. I was *shocked* by the excess, in a way. I mean I *liked* it. I wanted some of all that stuff, too.

The excesses of a wealthy urban culture are all tied up in the story. And people were *mean* to each other in a way that I'd never seen. At cocktail parties, after they'd had a few drinks, people would say things to one another that nobody I knew in Mississippi would ever have been graceless enough to say. And it read to me like *meanness.*

Paul Mandelbaum: One of the themes "Rich" seems to grapple with is how unnerving the desire to be socially accepted can be. That seems universally true.

EG: I would have found this if I'd been on the Upper East Side of New York City, probably. In any big city I would have found the same thing, it's just that I happened to encounter it in New Orleans. Read that fabulous new translation of *Anna Karenina*—good *God*, it's the same thing I was writing about.

PM: This need to be accepted can turn very self-destructive.

EG: There had been a number of really terrible suicides within the circle of people in which we moved. They weren't our close friends, but they were people we knew and had been to parties with. There were three or four, and I think they were all men who had done things like jump off the Mississippi River Bridge. This unbelievably handsome man, married to a woman who was so beautiful—they were like the beautiful couple—shot himself. And one man had shot his dog before he shot himself. A wealthy man who was married to probably the smartest woman I ever got to talk to in New Orleans. Someone I admired greatly for her brilliance.

And so all of these suicides—I mean how could people who have everything in the world, all the money that they need—I couldn't understand how these people could kill themselves, because at the time I didn't know enough about clinical depression. And how clinical depression is exacerbated by drinking—I had kind of figured that out, which is why I let that lead up to it. Different sorts of clinical depression and suicide are caused by drugs and alcohol. That's what happened to Tom.

PM: Maybe those are important clinical reasons, but the most interesting poetic reason the story seems to suggest is that he just gives up believing he can maintain the illusion of belonging to this social world.

EG: Absolutely. Absolutely. It's falling apart for him. He came down there with all his natural skills and beauty and promise and got eaten alive by the culture. If he'd stayed in a small town in Tennessee he'd be all right. I'm sorry to say that, but I probably believe that.

PM: It feels thematically significant that the neighbors see a physical resemblance between Tom and Helen, because Helen is an outsider.

EG: Like Tom. The outside; she's that.

PM: You've got that pitiful moment on page 306 when Helen's eyes are "shining," at the prospect of Lisa wanting to come home after school with her. It's heartbreaking. Helen is not the most likable child in the world, but in that moment it's—

EG: You don't have to be chubby and dyslexic to have that happen to you.

PM: Sure. Anybody can identify with that longing.

EG: And here's Lisa, who has, compared to Helen, nothing in the world. And yet she's got some sort of charismatic power that makes other people let her decide, you know—she's got the stuff.

PM: And Helen wants to be near that.

EG: Helen wants a friend.

PM: On page 303, you have this simple transition: "At about the same time Helen came to be the Wilsons' little girl, Tom grew interested in raising Labrador retrievers." Which I always found wonderfully ironic, since the Wilsons are mystified about Helen's pedigree. Tom seems to be compensating.

EG: I wasn't thinking that when I was writing it. I was just making up a story.

PM: Let's talk about the side story about the drowned fraternity pledge.

EG: That's a true story. All the little side stories like that are true stories. And I had thousands to choose from. I chose the ones that really shocked me.

PM: He's an outsider, as well, trying too hard to belong.

EG: Well, if I was thinking in those terms, and I probably wasn't, I was thinking: What would drive Tom to Letty? Just because she was wealthy, that wouldn't be enough. Because he'd have his pick. It was because she liked him and because she was quiet and because it seemed peaceful. And the good part of Tom, the good things about him are why he turned his back on that world.

PM: That scene where Letty's saying, "Let go of it, it wasn't your fault," reflects better on him than it does on her. He's more troubled by the drowning. He suffers more moral confusion over it.

EG: He's smarter than she is. He's just plain old smarter than she is. She's been very, very sheltered and she's simple.

PM: The scene also established Tom as—if this story has a main character, it's Tom.

EG: A lot of my work is character-driven, in the deepest, truest sense. But this is really about a time and a place.

PM: The thing that's always struck me about "Rich" is the way it operates as both a short story and a satire. As a satire, society is its main subject, but at the same time you've gone to a lot of trouble to characterize Tom—with his tragic, human flaws—as a protagonist.

EG: Well, I always get involved with my characters. As soon as I name them I believe them. I believe them, just like they're real people. So I can't help making things character driven because I believe the products of my own imagination.

PM: Religion seems to be one of the social conventions the story seems to be satirizing. For these characters at any rate, religion seems to have less to do with spirituality than it does with social appearance.

EG: I didn't mean that. I've never really been religious. I respect religions much more than I ever did when I was young. The older I get the more I respect the good things about religions and what they bring.

PM: Helen is the only one in the story who more or less prays—when she's hiding under the bed and dreaming the dream of the heavy clouds.

EG: Those are my own childhood memories, when something would go wrong. My dogs were always getting run over. During the Second World War we had to live all over Indiana and Illinois while my father built the airports and my grandfather would send me little fox terriers, because he raised hunting dogs on his plantation. I'd come home from school and my mother'd be standing there: "Another fox terrier got run over." And I'd crawl under the bed and hold onto the bedsprings for hours. I don't know whether I was just being a drama queen or what. I used to pray when my dogs would die, or when I'd lose something, I'd pray like crazy, but the rest of the time, I didn't care a thing about God.

PM: I wanted to talk about some of the images in the story—a couple in particular. The baby's blood spreading out like a ruby lake—

EG: I remember writing that. Bill Harrison had told me that every story should have at least one really memorable simile. And I thought, shoot, I've been a poet for years, I can do that.

PM: That metaphor of Helen's brain flinging its roses forth—

EG: Well, I think that's a little over the top. I'd edit that out now.

PM: Both of those images seem especially fresh because you're describing something horrible by comparing it to something beautiful.

EG: I know it. Because I'm not a horror writer.

PM: Is that a conscious choice, to search for imagery in the opposite direction?

EG: It's not a conscious choice. That's not how poets work. Not really how writers work, I don't think. Or didn't for me. I just think something up and write it down. That's really the truth. I don't go looking for something except the titles.

PM: Don't you discard things? Keep thinking until you get to something you like?

EG: Nope. I don't do that either. I throw away big sections of things, and I take extraneous words out. But I don't go think, *Oh, well, that's not good,*

I could—I don't go get one thing and then replace it with another thing. Either the whole thing works or it doesn't. See, I got *into* this story when I was writing it. Like I do with anything I'm writing, the only way I could find out what happened next was to keep on writing it.

Bill Harrison challenged me, because he was helping me and I was talking to him when I was writing, and I don't know how much of it he read or didn't read, but he said, "In the first place, it's got to have a really dramatic ending, and you've set it up that somebody's got to die." So I wrote the last three or four paragraphs, because I was fascinated with that idea.

Oh, *that's* how the labs got in the story, because I was thinking about that man who shot his dog and then shot himself. And I was thinking about how everybody always talked about how much those dogs cost. How much they were sold for and all that, which I thought was just ridiculous. I'd pay four thousand dollars not to have a lab locked up in my backyard. It bothered me that in New Orleans all these yards were full of all these penned-up dogs, these great big beautiful working dogs all penned up in yards, and maybe once a week they'd take them out and let them pretend to work. I mean who am I to have all these judgments about what other people are doing, but the Labrador Retriever thing in New Orleans just blew me away.

So I wrote that ending, and I wrote the rest of the story to justify the ending that I'd written. Does that make sense? I used to do that a lot.

PM: Do you remember what Bill Harrison was referring to when he said you've set it up that somebody has to die? Maybe he was talking about the fraternity drowning, because that does seem to—

EG: Foreshadow it?

PM: Yes.

EG: I may just think he said something like that. Anyway, he said, "You know, I want to see you write a really dynamite ending for this story." He was just trying to show how to write a short story. Trying to show me the process. Or *a* process by which you could write one.

PM: How have readers reacted to this story?

EG: They've liked it, except young women with small children were horrified by it. People who are readers of my stories and love my work were horrified by the fact that I'd let someone kill someone. Because that's really not like me. It was just an exercise to show Bill that I could write something horrible if I wanted to. I don't like having written somebody shooting somebody, especially a child and a dog. It's really not the way I look at the world. That's why I left it out of my *Collected Stories*. I had to leave out something, so I just decided to take out all the stories that had a murder or a suicide. Because I have thirteen grandchildren. I kept thinking, "Oh, I'm their grandmother, I don't want them to read that stuff."

But the good writing in it—you know, that's good writing in it.

Rereading it, the stuff I like are the things that I think are funny. Well, not funny, I guess *irony* would be a better word. "He was rich in being satisfied to sleep with his own wife." "She took her committees seriously and actually believed that the work she did made a difference in the lives of other people." [*Laughs*] "Letty became the first girl in her crowd to break the laws of God and the Napoleonic Code by indulging in oral intercourse."

PM: Would you please read a couple of paragraphs out loud on pages 316 to 317, starting with Tom in the silent marsh while meanwhile Letty's reading a bedtime story about the chicken guillotine from a *Madeleine* book?

EG: [*Reading*] ". . . She had decided that God was just trying to make up to her for Jennifer."

Isn't the human spirit wonderful? To live in a world where people behead chickens all day long? And don't invite each other to cocktail parties? And then on the other hand, well, easy come, easy go with the babies!

PM: Those two scenes seem wonderfully juxtaposed against each other: Letty surrounded by the confirmation teacups, reading that gruesome story, while Tom is river-boating into the heart of darkness. And the story's moving into this very primal, brutal place, where Tom finally allows himself to wonder that unbearable epiphany: that he can be known utterly.

EG: It's scary country down there. All my cousins, people who hunt down there, like those swamps. There are alligators in those swamps, and people go out in those little flat-bottom boats? What would they want to do that for? To kill some ducks? It takes all day to make duck taste good.

This is the end of the story: I love this. And I remember writing it: [*Reading*] "A pair of deputies from the Plaquemines Parish sheriff's office found the bodies. . . . And no one, not even the district attorney of New Orleans, wanted to believe a man would shoot a three-thousand-dollar Labrador Retriever sired by Super Chief out of Prestidigitation." Those are real dogs' names; my cousin had those dogs.

PM: Great name, Prestidigitation—

EG: It means sleight of hand.

PM: Very suitable for Tom, the lifelong illusionist. What I find most striking about the end is the brutal order of it: how it implies people might comprehend the child being killed before they could understand the dog.

EG: Right. Why shoot the dog? I remember when that horrible suicide happened, people would say when they'd hear about it, "He shot the *dog*?"

PM: What does that say about people?

EG: [*Laughs*] Right.

PM: By the way, when the story says, no one believed that a man would kill his own illegitimate dyslexic daughter, I've always read that as just the—

EG: Everyone had decided that she was really his, but it's not the case. That's the kind of rumors that get started and people believe them because they want to.

PM: I wanted to ask you about the special challenges or writing about race and racism.

EG: It's a challenge for every Southern writer. But I try just to write what I saw the way I saw it, as Faulkner did. The main thing, as Faulkner knew, is that the narrator, voice of the author, must be a voice of respect and reason. But when you're writing dialogue, dialogue has to sound like what it sounded like—

PM: Or a character's thoughts—

EG: Or else we can just give up writing. Writing literature is not public discourse. I don't think it's the same thing as being on a talk show.

PM: I recall hearing somewhere that you consider yourself more a short story writer by temperament than a novelist. Is that true?

EG: Yes, I think so. I like the shorter forms. Having read and written poetry most of my life.

PM: It's been said the short story has more in common with poetry than with the novel.

EG: I believe it's true. You're always trying to pack as much as you can into a small space, because it'll have more power that way. The laws of physics. "Rich" is a poet's short story if there ever was one. It flows from paragraph to paragraph and it's beautiful language, full of surprises, I think, but I wasn't trying to do that, I was just trying to find out how to write a short story. Now obviously four pages of it wasn't going to be enough, and then I wrote an ending. And I was going to see how I was going to find my way toward the ending, and the only model that I was, I'd just open up *Huckleberry Finn* to any page and find out anything I wanted to know. Any question.

I remember getting up from the dining room table one night and saying, "Freddy,"[1] I said, "I don't know how to get them from one room to the next." So I remember I opened up *Huckleberry Finn* to the chapter where Huck is locked up in the cabin and his daddy—his father's left to go get some more whiskey—and he goes through a series of actions to free himself, and then he gets out of the cabin and gets in the boat and leaves. He kills a pig and leaves blood all over the place so people will think he died. Remember that? But it's after Pap leaves and it's everything he does to get out of the cabin. That is just textbook. What could anyone tell you about how to move characters around that would be as meaningful as that? I remember thinking: "Oh! Well, that's all there is to it! These are the steps that it took for him to get out of there: he did this and this and this and this and then he opened the door, and then he left the blood trail, and then he threw the pig away and then he got in the skiff and then he was on the Mississippi River." And because it was such a logical sequence of events, you believed this highly illogical stuff! Have you ever been on the Mississippi River, even in a big boat? It's completely illogical that anyone could get into a skiff and push out and get into the currents of the Mississippi River. Don't go trying it.

PM: How long have you been teaching now?

EG: This will be my fifth year. I love it. I've learned so much from my students; I like them so much. I've been teaching long enough to see their work come to fruition, and they've had some success. One of my students won the *Playboy* fiction contest last year. One of them sold two stories at once to *The Atlantic*. For three years my students have won the undergraduate fiction award, and this year won the undergraduate fiction award *and* the undergraduate poetry award. I don't know what it is. I'm not probably as good a teacher as some of the other teachers, but I'm able to inspire some of the students, and that thrills me.

Note

1. Freddy Kullman, Gilchrist's husband from 1968 to 1981.

Arkansas Memories Project: Ellen Gilchrist Interview

Scott Lunsford / 2010

Selections from the David and Barbara Pryor Center for Arkansas Oral and Visual History, University of Arkansas, Arkansas Memories Project, Ellen Gilchrist Interview, July 13, 2010. Transcript by the Pryor Center; their transcript methodology is "to produce a transcript that represents the characteristics and unique qualities of the interviewee's speech pattern, style of speech, regional dialect, and personality. For the first twenty minutes of the interview, we attempt to transcribe verbatim all words and utterances that are spoken, such as uhs and ahs, false starts, and repetitions." Three asterisks (***) indicate a new section of the interview. Printed by permission.

Scott Lunsford: Take us—um—take us through one of your grandparents' homes. Just kinda walk us through. What—what were they like?

Ellen Gilchrist: Well, Granny—my grandmother's house in Courtland[1] was kind of wonderful because she re—was a—she read all the time. She'd gone to college. I mean, in a time when women didn't go to college, but people in her family did—in the Clark family—in the governor's family. And—uh—she didn't get married till she was twenty-six, which was shocking enough.

SL: Mh-hmm.

EG: But she—after my grandfather died, she began to line the walls. Every room in the house—every room in the house was just bookshelves, and they were filled with all these wonderful books. And I liked to go stay with her 'cause you could just read all day. And I don't remember—she didn't know how to cook. We would just live on toasted biscuits and tea, [*SL laughs*] and I don't know what we lived on, but the only thing I remember eating there were toasted biscuits and tea. [*SL laughs*] But we just rea— Coca-Colas—and we read books.

She'd be back in her room readin', and I'd be out on the porch reading, or up in the tree house reading, or somewhere reading, reading, reading.

SL: So now . . .

EG: Historical novels.

SL: Uh-huh.

EG: So I'm not a good student of history because my vision of history is warped by historical novels. [*Laughs*]

SL: By the characters found in the novels. Um—so—when—um—was the—was the house mansion-like? Was it a large, two-story, columned . . .

EG: No, no, no. No, no, this was a—this was a frame house on the main street of Courtland. . . .

SL: Uh-huh.

EG: . . . when I visited there after my grandfather died. There was a—a beautiful house out in the country, which my uncle and his wife later restored and lived in after he retired from the air corps. But—um—I don't like great big, mansion houses. I like frame houses full of books.

SL: Mh-hmm.

EG: But this house—this Fay Jones house I live in reminds me of Hopedale Plantation, which was—which my grandfather—my Alford grandfather built, which was a long, flat house with wings on it, and a kitchen, which was out back, that later got incorporated into the house. But they also had—m—m—my Alford kinfolks had lots and lots and lots of books, but they had been Greek and Roman scholars and lawyers, and so they're the classics. They didn't have a lot of novels and Book of the Month club books like Granny did. They had—uh—I re—the first thing I remember reading in my life was a book of Bacon's essays. . . .

SL: Mh-hmm.

EG: . . . Francis Bacon's essays, and I—I could—I was beginnin', and I—I didn't learn to read. I just learned how to read by seein' words and pickin' things up. A lot of children did that.

SL: Mh-hmm.

EG: I knew that word—I knew it said Bacon, and it was very small, just the right size for a little five-year-old girl, and I carried it around 'cause it said Bacon, which was my favorite food, and they'd only give me [*SL laughs*]—they wouldn't let me eat as much of it. I mean, you know, I was—would have lived on the most fattening foods in the world all day long and been obese [*SL laughs*] except people didn't let children do that back then. They monitored what they ate. But—um—finally, I opened it up, and I read part of an essay by Francis Bacon in which he says, "A person who has children has given hostages to fortune." And every time one of my progeny gets pregnant [*SL laughs*]—I mean, they're all male, so it's mostly the women—they get pregnant, and I think, "Hostages to fortune." [*Makes clicking sound*] [*SL laughs*] And I don't think that—we've been so lucky so far. They've all been healthy. . . .

SL: Mh-hmm.

EG: . . . they've all been strong; they've all been funny; and they're pretty.

***

SL: When did you start having this voracious appetite for reading?

EG: All my life. All my life.

SL: As soon as . . .

EG: I could read long before I went to school. From the time I was carrying Bacon around with me. And children are that way. Some of 'em just—you know, look at the Chinese. Look at the number of figures that they learn by a very young age. You don't have to teach—real readers don't have to learn phonics or anything. They recognize a word, and then they don't forget it.

They're just like collections of things you like—all these words. But I was a—always been a fast reader. If I came to anything I didn't understand, you know, I'd just skip over it. I knew I'd figure it out later. But if it was really an interesting word, I'd look—we always had big dictionaries. No matter how many times we had to move durin' the Second World War, this great, huge, very heavy dictionary would go with us. And I just loved to read, so you know, if it came to somethin' like memorizing somethin' or a catechism— my brother—my older brother has a photographic memory. I mean, he really can remember any page of an encyclopedia that he turns the pages of. And I don't know how he—it makes him so mad if you say that because he says it's an inferior form of intelligence to just remembering it. And I said, "Well, you know, it's true." [*Laughter*] But I loved any kind of test that had to do with words or memorizin' a catechism 'cause I knew I'd be the first one to do it and do it the fastest.

SL: You know . . .

EG: You know what, maybe it's because I knew I could. Maybe it's because the grown people all around me were readin' and writin' all the time, and it was just a way of bein' grown. Maybe the reason children aren't good at takin' tests is 'cause they're afraid. I wasn't afraid of anything to do with words and books. It was my forte. [*Laughs*]

SL: Yeah, it's different now. It's very different now. I mean . . .

EG: I think children are bored to death in school, but we probably shouldn't put this in the thing—we don't want to hurt teachers' feelings 'cause it's not their fault. It comes from above. There are edicts coming from above, but . . .

SL: Well, and also technology changes things. There's all—it's a different . . .

EG: I have a friend . . .

SL: . . . it's a different set of tools now.

EG: . . . I have a friend in Fayetteville named Ed White, who's a really wonderful psychologist—psychiatrist. And he told me a story once of a young—he'd—they'd brought him this little seven- or eight-year-old girl, and she was supposed to be so smart, and she was so smart. And she was doin' so poorly in school, and she wasn't doing anything—they—and so he was trying to figure out what was wrong, and he said, you know, "So explain it to me." And she said, "Well, you go in there, and you take the book, which you've already read." And she said, "And then they start reading, and you sit there and wait for 'em to turn the page." And I thought, "There it is."

SL: That's it.

EG: The ones who can turn the page faster oughta be in another group.

SL: Mh-hmm. Well, it sounds like to me that you immediately started emulating those that were around you that . . .

EG: Right.

SL: . . . everyone was so well read, and there was such a wealth, a treasure trove, of material.

EG: No, what they were doin' in their spare time was reading. My great-grandmother and my great-aunts—they were reading all these magazines. My grandfather was readin' the *Progressive Farmer*. But they were always reading, but especially Granny in Courtland. She was deep into big, real books. From the Book of the Month club [*Laughter*] and the literary guild.

SL: Well, they—you know, I have to say, this is fairly unique. I mean, you probably—did you have any inkling at all that your circumstances were different or much different than a normal growing-up period? I mean, did you—what about—you were moving around so much, did you ever have—were you able to connect with kids . . .

EG: My mother . . .

SL: . . . your age in different communities?

EG: My father would find me a best friend before I got there. Before I got there, he'd've found me a best friend, and there she'd be. And . . .

SL: So friendships were arranged for you.

EG: [*Laughter*] Right. No, I mean, you know, I make friends really easily and real deeply.

SL: But did you find that your friends were experiencing the same kind of values growing up of—was everyone that you knew, all your friends, were they locked into reading and were just reading . . .

EG: No. No, they had the same kind of mothers and fathers. One—my best friend from the fifth grade to about the eighth grade, when we moved away from there, was a woman named Cynthia Hancock. She's still my best friend. We write to each other all the time. She named her oldest daughter after me as she promised she would, but I never had any daughters. But I wanna name one of these grandchildren Cynthia soon—or great-grand-children. Maybe we can get that new one in New Orleans named Cynthia. Anyway, Cynthia's father was a judge. He was the, I guess, the circuit judge. He didn't have to run for it, whatever it was, but he tried cases. And he read all the time, and he had a wonderful library. And Cynthia's daddy and I, the judge and I, talked to each other all the time. But Cynthia was a cheerleader and the drum majorette. She had many other things to do. She could twirl batons—you wouldn't believe. I always considered—I mean, I knew this thing that I did all the time—reading and writing and everything. And—but not everybody—not—my friends didn't do that much. And then all of a sud-den, I'd have some wonderful friend, like a gay architect who became my friend in Alabama who loved books and loved the same books that I did—as much—or a doctor that I later knew, and people like that, and I—but I didn't need to talk about books to anybody. I just read 'em. And my mother was a—my mother read the kinda books that I liked.

SL: So back in—when—you just don't remember much of your infant childhood in Mississippi at all. You—you're tellin' me that the first mem . . .

EG: Oh yeah, I do because my cousins were—because I had an older cousin, Bunky. I remember goin' into Hopedale in the snow at Christmas and havin' Bunky standin' there waitin' for me, and he was four. And so I couldn't have been more than one. But I have vivid pictorial mem—but it's all about people—you know, it's about cousins.

SL: Mh-hmm. You know, it's interesting. Your father came back to build the levees there. After that flood, there was a tremendous flight of African Americans northward. I mean . . .

EG: When they started goin' to Chicago.

SL: Yeah . . .

EG: When Black people in Mississippi . . .

SL: Because, you know, the . . .

EG: . . . started goin' to Chicago.

SL: Uh-huh.

EG: Right.

SL: So . . .

EG: Where they had wonderful lives—some of 'em.

SL: You were brought into the world after that flight, and I don't know what—you know, you were—there were some—I guess what I'm rolling around to—do you remember much of the segregation and the—and . . .

EG: Yeah, because at Hopedale Plantation, my family—my mother's family were horrified by a man named Bilbo,[2] who was a racist and a seg-regationist. And they wouldn't—my grandmother wouldn't have his name said in the house. I mean, if people were sittin' out there and they were talkin' about somethin' that was in the newspaper, my mother wouldn't—grandmother wouldn't let his name be said in the house. They were religious people. They just didn't—but everything was so insular then. I mean, we all got newspapers, and we read 'em every day, but I didn't read the newspaper. I was readin' books, you know.

SL: Was there ever any—did this Bilbo guy just stir up trouble all the time?

EG: He was a governor that—I've forgotten. I don't know historically—since my grandmother wouldn't let his name be said, [*SL laughs*] I never have studied him. I [*unclear word*] should go read up on Governor Bilbo. I know that it—that they were annoyed by hatred or prejudiced or anything like that. There were wonderful, wonderful African American people on Hopedale.

SL: Mh-hmm. Well now . . .

EG: And they were very tall, so I think these people must have been Watusi because they were that tall. Man, the overseer—my grandfather's overseer and a woman named Diddy, who was the mother and grandmother of the people that would be in the house—they were very haughty. And when I see pictures of Watusi in Africa, I think that's where those people came from.

SL: Well, did you have any relationships with African Americans grow-ing up?

EG: Sure . . .

SL: Did you . . .

EG: I played with 'em. And that's who I had for playmates when I was little when I'd go down there.

SL: Yeah, I . . .

EG: Diddy would send her grandchildren over there. They'd get bored with me after the cookies were all eaten. [*SL laughs*] I'd be doin' stuff like makin' doll furniture out of cardboard, and I could amuse 'em for—I could keep 'em around for about an hour, and then they'd go scatterin' back home.

SL: You did that . . .

EG: I didn't like . . .

SL: . . . on the porch just off the kitchen, right?

EG: Yeah. No, I think out front on the front porch steps . . .

SL: Oh. Uh-huh.

EG: . . . is where we used to play.

SL: And your mom would have . . .

EG: The people at . . .

SL: . . . cookies made or sheet cake or somethin'.

EG: Oh, there were al—there was—there were always—there was always lots of food in the kitchen. But I think the cookies came from the store. I think they were things like gingersnaps out of boxes.

SL: [*Laughs*] I member reading that you would—that they would stick around and play with you for a while, and then they just kinda disappeared, and you used to go look for them.

EG: [*Laughs*] Right. Or I'd go over to Diddy's. I liked to go over to Diddy's house and just talk to her. I have no idea what we talked about. She was the matriarch of the Afro American families.

SL: Mh-hmm. Now . . .

EG: But she—I liked it—I just liked her bein' so tall and so haughty. She was really haughty. Hard to please.

SL: Mh-hmm. [*Laughter*] Well, she probably had to be that way. . . .

EG: But everybody was nice to me because my mother, whose nickname was "Bodie"—they loved Bodie. Everybody that ever knew her loved her, and if I was her daughter, they'd be nice to me, even if I was a lot of trouble.

SL: Well now, you were kinda trouble, weren't you, growin' up?

EG: I was pretty busy.

SL: Seems like I 'member you felt like your mother really never had her heart in disciplining you, that . . .

EG: That woman could not dis—my—that woman could not discipline a child. She didn't really want to. She thought we were funny. My brothers loved her so much. They did what she told 'em to do, but she thought I was funny. I amused her. I could make her laugh. She would giggle at stuff I did.

SL: You remember going to a funeral, don't you? There was a funeral early in your life that you—somehow or another . . .

EG: When that little boy died in the first grade and they brought the whole first grade out to—his father ran over him in the driveway. When cars—audience, you don't know this—when cars first came into being and we had sloping driveways and towns with hills, there were—for a lot—a lot of children were killed by a car running over 'em because the rearview mirrors weren't good. Or there were a lot of reasons, all of which have been fixed now, hopefully. People don't back over their children in the driveway anymore. Anyway, he backed over a little boy in the first grade, and they had the child laid out in a coffin on the dining room table, and they brought the first grade down there to march around and tell him goodbye. That was my first funeral that I remember. [*Laughs*] This was not good.

SL: Did they have—did they have ice around him? Do you remember?

EG: No.

SL: Sometimes if they were gonna be there for a couple of days . . .

EG: We didn't stay long.

SL: If they're . . .

EG: I think maybe they gave us a cupcake or somethin', but then we marched back out and went home or back to school—one or the other. Oh my gosh, can you imagine that happening now?

SL: Hm-mm. Wouldn't. It wouldn't happen now.

EG: Takin' the first grade to [*laughs*] view of the corpse of one of the kids.

SL: Wow. So you were—you started reading very early, before you ever went to school. Let's talk about your early elementary school days. What—it seems like I remem . . .

EG: I liked goin' to school. I liked the teachers. Occasionally I'd get a teacher that I didn't like, but I liked teachers. I was hopeful. I was bored all afternoon. I was—I take naps in the afternoon. I have since I was very young. And I would just kinda—"Oh God, will it ever be three thirty?" or however long we'd have to stay in school.

SL: Do you remember a favorite teacher early on?

EG: I remember a second-grade teacher who had the wisdom to read us a continued story at three thirty, or somethin' like that, in the afternoon right before we'd leave. And all day long, you could look forward to it. She was pretty, and she was reading us, I suppose, a book. And she would read us a chapter in the afternoons. That was wonderful. But you never could tell what you were gonna learn. And besides, there were all those people where you could, you know, interact with 'em. Even if you couldn't talk, you could always be looking at 'em—passin' 'em a note. [*Laughs*]

***

SL: What were some of the earliest conversations you remember having with your father?

EG: Teachin' me to tie my shoes; teachin' me to play ball; teachin' me to roller-skate—I re—teachin' me to ride bicycles; teachin' me to ride horses; teachin' me to swim. I mean, he had my brothers, but I mean, he didn't leave me out. My father taught us to do things. He taught us to drive long before we could actually drive. I guess that's why Dan-Dan let me drive into Rolling Fork in her Buick. But he just taught—he taught us things. How things worked. I have—I remember what he loved were post-hole diggers. [*SL laughs*] And to this day—I love it. He loved watchin' people build fences or—and he'd get into it. He'd be doin' it himself, and it was a wonderful thing to me—the invention of this thing that would go down in there, and [*makes crunching noise*] [*moves hands up and down*] and then put it over there, and then you could get that post in there, and you could build a fence—keep the horses from runnin' away.

SL: So he was a pretty physical guy. He liked the physical work.

EG: Yeah. He loved sports. You know, he—but I could never learn to play baseball because I would not pick up the grounders.

SL: [*Laughs*] Why is that?

EG: Somebody wants to throw me high balls and let me pretend like, you know, I'm puttin' somebody out, that's one thing. But gettin' down—kneelin' down and pickin' up the grounders—no way.

SL: You didn't want to do that?

EG: No!

SL: Why?

EG: Throw me some high ones. [*Laughter*] Throw me somethin' I can catch.

SL: It's too much work to stoop down and kneel down on one knee and put the glove in front of it and . . .

EG: Not my brothers. [*Laughs*] They'd do it. See, you love it. You think it's great.

SL: Mh-hmm. Mh-hmm. That's funny. That's funny. Well, so let's see now. Dooley—what was Dooley's real name?

EG: William Garth Gilchrist III.

SL: And he was your older brother.

EG: Mh-hmm.

SL: Were both your brothers older than you?

EG: No. My other brother is eight years younger than I was.

SL: Wow.

EG: He was born in the middle of the Second World War in Seymour, Indiana. And I couldn't believe—why did my mother do that to herself? And then we had this wonderful, little, fat, blond boy. He was just irresistible.

SL: My parents would call that kind of a fall and spring crop. [*EG laughs*] You know.

EG: My mother liked him so much 'cause he grew up—he di—he did, and he really looked like her—very blonde, very blue-eyed. And he grew up to look exactly like her father. And he acts like her father.

SL: Well, let's talk a little bit about her father.

EG: Her father—Big Daddy. He was six feet four or five inches tall and . . .

SL: Wow.

EG: . . . he was strong and beautiful man.

SL: And y'all called him Big Daddy?

EG: Mh-hmm. As opposed to my little daddy. My—and we had sandwiches. If it did two pieces of bread, it was a Big Daddy, but one piece, it was a little daddy. No, it just . . .

SL: Now tell me again, what was it that her father did?

EG: He came to—he came from Madison, Mississippi, where his father was a lawyer and a schoolteacher. He would drive around in a buggy and pick up the children and take 'em to the schoolhouse and teach 'em. He was a lawyer. But his son, my grandfather, Stewart Floyd Alford, came to the Delta and was an overseer on a plantation called Esperanza, which is the Spanish word for hope, and then he bought the adjoining land and turned it—and cleared the land and turned it into Hopedale Plantation. And he had brothers and cousins—I mean, you know, there were—it was a family of men. There—my grandfather was not the only per—he wore a s—a coat and tie all the time. And then my grandmo—then he married my grandmother, and then my grandmother's sister married a doctor from New Orleans, and they became fast friends. There are all these pictures of 'em together doin' things like figurin' out rural electricity or wells. I rem—I always associated him with wells—artesian wells, which you could dig in the Delta near the river. Just beautiful, wonderful water. There's water in the Arkansas Delta that tastes like the water in the Mississippi Delta. It's full of sulfur. I love the way it smells and tastes. [*SL laughs*] And if you take a bath in it, it's like the most luxurious bath salts in the world have been added to the water.

SL: I've never heard anyone say that they love the sulfur water.

EG: I love—see, it's just the smell of bein'—I was at Hopedale. Where there's—you know, nothin' never stopped happenin' there. In a house with just your mother and your father and your brothers—although we had company all the time—you know, we had our friends over all—but at any moment, things could keep happening. But in a house full of people runnin' a plantation, there is somethin' goin' on every minute. [*Laughs*]

SL: Now there was an African American named Eli. Is that right?

EG: Eli Nailor.

SL: Nailor. You know, most of the photographs that I've seen of him, he has his head down. He's looking at you or one of the children or picking up—I never got a really clear . . .

EG: Nailor was the same age as my great-grandmother, and my great-great-grandmother adopted him. After—there was an epidemic, either of smallpox or measles or some flu. But I think that it was something like—there was a horrible epidemic in the Delta, and Eli—and Nailor's parents were killed in it, and he was the only person left. And with five or six other orphans—a man drove a wagon full of orphaned African American children around asking people if they could live with them, and my great-great-grandmother, who was a devout Catholic—the one I'm named for—took him. He was about six or seven years old. Think how scared he was.

SL: Yeah.

EG: But she was such a beautiful, gentle woman. And he was the same age as my great-grandmother. And they grew up together, and they ran the kitchen together, and they argued. [*SL laughs*] I bet they've been arguin' since they were six years old. They argued about every detail of everything they were cookin.' And it was real quiet, real low-key. No voices were ever raised. And he'd laugh at her. [*Laughter*]

SL: They loved it, didn't they?

EG: They cooked.

SL: They cooked.

EG: And he just spoiled me rotten.

SL: Give me an example.

EG: Well, the thing I—what I really liked to eat—there were two things that I liked to eat above everything else. Well, I liked French fries and fried chicken and mashed potatoes. But what I really loved to eat was pot liquor, which is the juice off of black-eyed peas. And I wanted pot liquor, and then I'd put buttered corn bread in that and kinda stir it up for a long, long time until it was sort of a—I don't know what it was like. [*Laughs*] Delta pasta. And then I'd eat it.

SL: I get that still . . .

EG: He'd always get me pot liquor and cornbread.

SL: So pot liquor is just the juice from the black-eyed peas.

EG: Mh-hmm.

SL: Well, I experienced that New Year's Day. You know, we always had—Mama always said, "You have to have this for good luck." I don't know if—that you ever came . . .

EG: I don't know if the juice—I mean, I guess you probably have to actually eat the peas to get good luck.

***

EG: Yeah, 'cause I guess I graduated from high school in [19]51 or [19]52. And then I went to Vanderbilt, and I pretty much made straight As, and I loved it, and I studied Shakespeare. But then I went home to spend the summer, and Mother and Daddy had moved home to Decatur, Alabama, and all my cousins and people were goin' to the University of Alabama. So by the time the summer was over, I said, "Daddy"—and they told me there was a great writing teacher at the University of Alabama named Hudson Strode and that I should leave Vanderbilt for a year [*SL laughs*] and go to study with Hudson Strode. So Daddy gave me a car, and I drove down to Tuscaloosa and checked into school and went over to the Chi O house and told 'em I was a Chi O transfer, and I moved into the Chi O house, and it was, like, a couple of weeks before I found out that Hudson Strode was on sabbatical. [*Laughter*]

SL: The whole reason for you being there . . .

EG: I know it.

SL: . . . was on sabbatical. So did you . . .

EG: And by then I'd fallen in love with a boy at Georgia Tech.

SL: Uh-oh.

EG: And so the next semester, Daddy said, "Sister, if you're gonna go to school in Alabama, for God's sake, why can't it be Auburn?" which is where all of his family go to school and where he'd graduated. And I thought, "Auburn is really near to Atlanta." And so then I went and spent a semester at Auburn, and the next summer, Marshall and I ran away and got married. We ran away to the north Georgia hills and then went over to North Carolina or South Carolina—one of the Carolinas—where you could get married without a waiting period or somethin' like that. We got a wedding license and got married. And then I went to live with him in Atlanta, and we started havin' babies. [*Laughs*]

SL: Okay . . .

EG: And then I spent about, you know, ten years bein' a mother of all these beautiful little boys. Never did get to meet Hudson Strode.

SL: How did you choose Vanderbilt?

EG: My brother had gone to school there. My older brother was there.

SL: And you just kind of . . .

EG: But my daddy's cousins had always gone to school in Nashville—to a girls' school there called—not Agnes Scott—somethin' like that. Agnes Scott's in Atlanta, but the co—you know, people in Daddy's family had always gone to Nashville to school.

SL: And what was it about Vanderbilt that you loved so much?

EG: I loved the first semester, which was broken into three trimesters. The first trimester of school you studied Shakespeare, and I had a great lecturer, and then I had a younger—a graduate student who taught—you know, you'd have the lecture one day of the week. But mostly, you know, I could already read. [*Laughs*] So I was introduced to Shakespeare. It was enough.

SL: Yeah.

EG: Actually, I used to teach Shakespeare at night. I would, you know, I would teach it to groups of Kappa Sigs and their girlfriends in the basement of the Kappa Sig house. My brother had been a Kappa Sig. I would teach what I was reading [*SL laughs*] because they weren't reading it. And so I was already teachin' Shakespeare, which I'm gonna do in the spring of next year.

SL: So as a freshman, you were basically tutoring . . .

EG: And I think I made 'em love Shakespeare.

SL: Yeah.

EG: They all would keep comin' to the classes.

SL: Well, I mean, this was—I mean, were you . . .

EG: It's an odd thing when someone's gettin' an education. They're not interested in everything they're studyin'.

SL: Right.

EG: I mean, you know, I went to biology and biology lab. I was interested in it. Later, after my children were four and five and two or six and seven—however—when I went back to school at Millsaps to get my de—finish my degree, then I really, really became interested in everything that I was studyin'. But at the time—you know, eighteen- and nineteen-year-olds are interested in one another . . .

SL: Sure.

EG: . . . and in love.

SL: Absolutely.

EG: And the unbelievable power and energy that they have. If you can get 'em vial—vitally interested in one thing like Shakespeare, you've done a good job.

SL: Well, didn't you—I mean, what about boys growing up before you went away to college? I mean . . .

EG: I had a boyfriend mornin', night, noon, every day of my life.

SL: Well, there you go. Let's talk about that a little bit.

EG: Cynthia Jane would give me all of her old ones. [*SL laughs*] And I had my brother's basketball and football teams and—but I always had—I always ended up havin' a close male friend who was not my boyfriend but was my intellectual peer. He'd be what kids call a goop now, I guess, but you know, but respected and loved by other people, but he'd be a, you know, a bookish, interesting person like that. They would always be—and sometimes—no, they would never take me to dances.

SL: The boyfriends would not?

EG: Not the ones that were my close friends.

SL: Oh. Right.

EG: I'd go off to dances with, you know . . .

SL: Well . . .

EG: . . . the cornerback or somethin'.

SL: [*Laughs*] I . . .

EG: My older brother . . .

SL: I was a football player.

EG: My older brother was very, very protective of me . . .

SL: Well, I was gonna ask . . .

EG: . . . and my family were very old-fashioned.

SL: I was gonna ask . . .

EG: The chances of anyone, you know, makin' a move on me or anything while Dooley Gilchrist was in the world were zero. I was so safe.

SL: [*Laughs*] I member Ronnie Hawkins tellin' me that he was terrified of my father. [*Laughs*] So . . .

EG: You would've been terrified of mine. I mean, not that he—he was just funny and kind and generous and all this stuff, but you wouldn't . . .

SL: You wouldn't cross him.

EG: Hm-mm. A boy at Vanderbilt tried to rape me . . .

SL: Uh-oh.

EG: . . . one of my brother's friends at a house party in Florida. My mother was chaperoning it, and we were alone on the beach, and he was drunk. And he was a very, very nice—and is a very, very nice person. And he was tryin' to rape me, and I remember turnin' around—finally—you know, 'cause I was real physically strong—I was fightin' him off and everything, and finally I said, "Okay, so-and-so, you know that Dooley Gilchrist will kill you." Everything stopped.

SL: [*Laughs*] Excitement level went down pretty quick . . .

EG: People didn't have intercourse with one another until they got married in the world in which I lived. Occasionally, they did. But not popular girls—not girls from nice families. I mean—well, that's not true. I'm sure that—it wasn't common. I think the boys were as frightened of it as girls. We all believed that the moment you had intercourse you'd get pregnant, and you did. So if I'm thinkin' about boys when I'm that age, I'm thinkin' about who should I marry. I don't think about who am I gonna have for a boyfriend, or who am I gonna hook up with or somethin'. I'm thinkin' who should I marry. Do I like their last name—all that.

SL: Those—all the sex stuff was really never discussed or talked about was it?

EG: We did—we couldn't tal—we didn't know anything to talk about. Every now and then—I had a cousin from up in Tennessee that had some information that was very, very, very interesting, but I didn't believe it—about things people do to one another . . .

SL: Mh-hmm.

EG: . . . other than normal intercourse.

SL: Uh-huh.

EG: I really wish she'd never told me that. [*SL laughs*] It's just too horrible to imagine, you know.

SL: Well, it seems like I remember you writing about how the adults would kinda shelter the children from some of the real things that were going on in life. I mean, the—in particular, relationships that people had, and they kind of . . .

EG: Well, my mother was very nonjudgmental. If she was talkin' about somethin' that happened to somebody, she'd be, you know, tellin' you all the reasons why the poor thing—you know, that happened because of this or that or the other. It just wasn't—that wasn't the thrust of our lives. We were ambitious. I wasn't—I mean, I was ambitious, but my close friends were *ambitious*.

SL: This group that . . .

EG: They wanted . . .

SL: Go ahead.

EG: People wanted to do—well, you know, and I had this intellectual friend in Kentucky the year we lived there, and I was writing an article for the real newspaper once a week, and when I went away to sou—when I would go down to the Delta in the summer or when I went to Southern Seminary, I'd have him—he was my intellectual friend—I'd have him write the stories for me when I couldn't be there. And then later—about fifteen years ago, I went to Louisville, Kentucky, to give a speech, and he's the president of the National Bar Association. Of course he is! [*SL laughs*] And has grown into this absolutely gorgeous, powerful, movie-star-lookin' man [*SL laughs*]—nothing like the gawky, young boy that—whose verbal skills were good enough to write my column for me when I was gone. That was so pleasant to me to have that happen. I hope that students—I hope that kids are still as ambitious as we were.

SL: Well, I think some are. I think some of that still—there's some great ambition and inspiration. . . .

EG: I hope so.

SL: . . . and belief that you can do things, and it does matter. I think there's still some of that.

EG: And that there're things that are in the—within your reach. My father's first cousin was the chief justice of the Fifth Circuit Court of Appeals. My mother was marr—my mother's sister was married to a newspaper editor. I thought you could do anything you thought up, and it never occurred to me—I didn't need Germaine Greer—it never occurred to me to think that bein' a woman or bein' a girl limited me in any way. It never entered my mind.

SL: That's interesting because that was so atypical that a strong woman could be that confident at that time because they were—I mean, for the most part . . .

EG: Well, the kind of things . . .

SL: . . . I mean, the stereotype is that . . .

EG: What did I ever want to do? I wanted to be a writer. But I wanted to be a poet, and I wanted to—and I wanted, maybe, to be a journalist. But the things that I wanted—the things that I was ambitious for were within my reach because I could do 'em easily. You know, it wasn't like I was tryin' to be the senator or somethin'.

SL: In this traveling group that your father kind of had dominion over during the war, were all the kids kind of—I mean, were they all readers, I mean, or . . .

EG: No.

SL: No, it was . . .

EG: Neither were my close friends.

SL: Really?

EG: I just read books, and I'd sit up all night at slumber parties tellin' 'em the stories of 'em. Or I'd write their book reports for 'em. I did that all my life.

SL: Really?

EG: I'd feel so sorry for 'em. They're all sittin' there cryin' 'cause they can't get their book report written. I could write it for 'em in five minutes if I had the jacket cover. Wouldn't even have to read the book. [*Laughter*]

SL: It was probably a book you'd already read anyway.

EG: Yeah, it was probably a book I'd already read anyway.

SL: [*Laughs*] Well, and they probably got great grades, didn't they?

EG: I don't know.

SL: [*Laughs*] Well, was . . .

EG: I know the father of my children, the man at Georgia Tech that I—the young man at Georgia Tech that I fell in love with—one of the first things I did for him before we ran away and got married was I wrote him a book report on Dorothy Parker. I loved Dorothy Parker. I knew all her work by heart. And his probably gay professor kept him in after class—this big, strapping, athletic KA—and said, "Oh, Mr. Walker, I would never, never have thought you were a fan of Dorothy Parker. This is just wonderful. Made my semester." And he gave him an A on it. [*Laughter*] God knows I'd give anything to have a copy of it.

***

SL: Tell me about your running off and getting married. Where was it—you went to the Carolinas.

EG: Oh, I planned it, of course. I'm the imagination, right?

SL: Okay.

EG: All we're doin' is at a fa—we're just—one night at a place—a famous place in Atlanta where people from Georgia Tech used to go to get these footlong hotdogs—except I wouldn't eat anything that big, but they had all this gross stuff on top of 'em. Marshall loved 'em. And I think we're discussing the fact that we wanna go to bed together. But people really didn't do that. They just didn't do that. And so we were sittin' there, and we—and I said, "I'll sign up for the second semester at Emory, and I'll come up here," or the f—whatever it was. Must've been the first semester. And then some close friends of ours—one of his fraternity brothers and a girl we loved named Happy—her name was Happy—Happy Chandler—had run away and gotten married in South Carolina. And other people had done it. We knew where to go. And so then I came to Atlanta, and I went out the afternoon before, and I went down to this great big, famous department store and bought a white—long, white piqué dress with the little pearl buttons all down the front and lace on the collar and some white shoes. And then I went down to the bookstore part and bought a book on how to have sexual intercourse. This is true. Or I bought whatever there was. It still didn't tell you what to do or anything like that. But it was mostly about contraception, I guess. But it was a very disappointing book, actually. [*Laughter*] And I don't know what else I bought, and then I went back home, and he came and got me in the morning, and we drove up to North Carolina and got mar—got a license and got married by a sheriff with the sheriff and his wife as the deputies in a little court-house in some tiny, small town.

SL: You don't remember the name of the town or . . .

EG: Hm-mm.

SL: That wasn't important, was it?

EG: I must've known it at some point. It was South Carolina.

SL: Yeah.

EG: It was a famous place to run away and get married in.

***

SL: We are gonna skip over your other two husbands . . .

EG: We're gonna skip 'em because it's too complicated.

SL: Okay.

EG: And then we're gonna get me to New Orleans, Louisiana, with my wonderful—well, actually he was my fourth husband 'cause I married the father of my children twice. But I'm promising you, this is all too compli-cated for an interview.

SL: [*Laughs*] Okay.

EG: And I was all—and I was very young, and it all happened in a short period of time. And then I'm in New Orleans, and I'm running miles every day, and I'm playing tennis constantly, which in New Orleans, you can play tennis all day. I mean, if it—wh—it rains, but it doesn't rain very long, and the court's dry. And my children are turnin' into teenagers right in the mid-dle of the revolution. And Audubon Park is full of hippies. And the first love-in happens. And what else? What else?

SL: [*Laughs*] Okay, now wait . . .

EG: No hurricanes and oil spills—we just got parks full of hippies, and all the children goin' to join 'em as quick as us draggin' 'em back, hopefully.

SL: Make love, not war.

EG: Right.

SL: So . . .

EG: And so then I got drunk one night—the last time I ever had a drink, I think. I may've had a few drinks since then, but that was years ago—more than thirty, thirty-five years, somethin' like that. And I fell down a flight of stairs and had a brain concussion.

SL: Oh my gosh.

EG: Please, a brain concussion and was in the hospital. And they gave me Valium, and then I got addicted to Valium. All this is happenin' in about a week. And my mother is there, and she's all goin' crazy, and everybody's goin' crazy. And we were plannin'—we owned a sailboat in the British Virgin

Islands that we kept at a place called the Moorings on Tortola. And we had a trip planned, a scuba diving trip, two weeks—about three weeks after I fell down the stairs, and so I went to a psychiatrist to talk to him to make sure my brain was all right before I went on a sailboat. And he said yes, that I could go on the sailing trip if I'd wear a football helmet. But then he started laughin' and he giggled, and we knew he wasn't really true, and [*SL laughs*] he said, "But I want to talk to you, you know, four times a week until you leave." So I said, "Okay." So maybe the next time I went to see him, I had just discovered Gabriel García Márquez, and I gave him a copy of *One Hundred Years of Solitude*. And I didn't know at the time, or I hadn't paid any attention—his—he was from Brazil. I mean, he spoke Portuguese, as well as Spanish. So he read it in English and in Spanish before I saw him again, and he told me how much funnier it was in Spanish, and I should try desperately to read it in Spanish 'cause I'm missin' all the great jokes. So I thought, "Oh, well, I can talk to this guy." And then I quit drinking. I just completely quit drinking 'cause I didn't want to have another brain concussion. And because I was in psychotherapy with a great Freudian—psychoanalysis with a great Freudian. And I called him the crying doctor. I would cry. I would go in there and just cry and cry and cry about things that I had never known bothered me, like leaving Harrisburg, Illinois, when I was thirteen years old—when I was a cheerleader and had just written a play for the whole school to do. You know, things that my parents, bein' so wonderful and strong and brave—and there bein' reasons for the fact that we were gonna leave. But I had always just—I've—and—but I'm still that way, and on my deathbed, I'm the queen of denial. I can deny—if a close, close friend of mine dies, I will not shed a tear. I will not shed a tear at Jim Whitehead's funeral. It will be over a long, long, long period of time of drivin' by that cemetery that I slowly but surely allow the finality and sadness of my best friend's death to invade me. But I don't let it get me. I don't know whether this is a strength or a weakness, but it's—I can't get a brain transplant—they don't give 'em to people at seventy-five. [*SL laughs*] So that's how I operate. And while I was talkin' to Gunther four days a week waitin' to go on the sailing trip, I began to write again. No, I didn't begin yet. When we left to go get on the sailboat, I was sorry that I was leavin' this brilliant Brazilian psychoanalyst that I'd been havin' so much fun talkin' to. Crying to. And then the tears would go away, and I'd be myself again. I'd go eat a donut on the way home. One of those great big donuts that are like a figure eight. . . .

SL: [*Laughs*] Twists. Cinnamon twists.

EG: You know—God, you know, I've just—you know, real, real release. What is—but I like things like psy—I'm a perfect person for psychoanalysis.

I like explorin' the brain. I like opening doors. I like all that kind of stuff, and I believe in it. Not for everybody. I guess it has to be someone like me. But overall I think a psychiatrist can help anybody, actually. But I—we were gettin' read—my husband was waitin' in the car. The couple we were goin' with that we owned the boat with were already out there. Everybody was ready— we were leaving. And I went back in the house and pulled my old Royal type—portable typewriter out of the hall closet and ran out of the house and took it with me to the islands. And as soon as we got there, I began to write. And the first poem that I wrote was about my oldest son. "Beautiful son, by your golden hair" and the somethin' that touches—"once more I am missing your birthday." I was gonna miss his birthday. He didn't care. He was out in the park with the hippies. Seven or eight of his girlfriends [*SL laughs*] and, God knows, probably drivin' my car while I was gone. But . . .

SL: How old were you now?

EG: I don't know. How old was I when I was—I have no idea. I don't even know how to pinpoint it. Except . . .

SL: Well, how . . .

EG: . . . maybe I was almost forty.

SL: Mh-hmm.

EG: I was almost forty. Because—and we had a wonderful diving trip, and nobody died. That—I don't think that's the time that Freddy ran out of air and I had to buddy breathe. I gave him the tank and swam to the top and swam ashore and climbed up a coral reef rather than buddy breathe with a smoker. [*SL laughs*] And that's the only bad thing I'll ever say about that wonderful man that I married that I deeply love. Because he smoked, he would always run out of air.

SL: Sure.

EG: [*Laughs*] Don't let your diving partner—if you're a jogger, you don't want your diving partner to be a smoker. You'll have to buddy breathe.

SL: Oh my gosh.

EG: When I got back to New Orleans, I continued to see Gunther four days a week for over a year. My insurance at my husband's law firm paid for me to see him. And I remember at one point he asked me, "Would you rather be anxious or depressed?" And I said, "Anxiety sounds more like me." And he said, "I would think so." So on the basis of the fact that I had anxiety complex, the insurance paid for it while I saw this—while I talked to this incredible mind. Not that he ever said a single word. He didn't. I talked. He listened. And all this time, I'm writin' unbelievable reams of really good poetry. And I'm publishing it. And a little newspaper in the French Quarter owned by Philip Carter—Hodding Carter's son . . .

SL: Hodding.

EG: . . . began to publish my poems, and then they asked me to be an editor. So now I'm a poet and a journalist. My dreams come true, right? I used to take my youngest son down to the Quarter with me when I'd have to go to the newspaper office. And he would spend all his time in the antique stores and the junk shops on a little street in the French Quarter while I was up in the office. He found some enormously wonderful things. He found for me once a scarf, and I don't know where it is, that was a—it was an air force pilot's scarf to wear in the Pacific Theater of the war, like my uncle would've worn—with the Pacific Theater of the war on white silk. Oh God, it was beautiful! Where is that? And I've been writing ever since. When I came to Fayetteville, it was because Jim Whitehead was here, and I wanted to learn how to publish my poetry. I was publishing it anywhere I sent it, practically, but I wanted to learn how to make a book out of it. I did not come up here to be a fiction writer. And then Bill Harrison got hold of me and said, "I'll show you how to publish that poetry. You'll just hide it inside the short stories." But I thought he meant that I would write a short story, and then I'd find a place to put the poem. No, he meant to use the poetic skills to write the short stories, [*laughs*] but I didn't know that. I just thought I was creatin' some little genres where I could put my poem in there. . . .

SL: Sure.

EG: . . . and get a bigger readership. Oh. And then—and so I've had a home here—whether I lived here all the time or not, I've had a home here ever since. So that's pretty much the story of how I got to be a writer.

❋ ❋ ❋

SL: So what was it—it was Jim Whitehead, but tell me how you came across Jim Whitehead.

EG: I don't know. I had met him. My good friend Tom Royals in Jackson was a close friend of Tom's, and—I mean, was a close friend of Jim's—and Tom—I'm gettin'—I'm talkin' too much. Tom is a close friend of mine, and Jim is a close friend of Tom's, and I had met him in Jackson, where my parents live and my brothers live. I had met him in Jackson, Mississippi, several times. And . . .

SL: Well, now . . .

EG: . . . was—I liked him enormously, and I was very impressed, and I knew the story of Gen[3] havin' the triplets, but I had never seen the Whitehead children. So when I decided that I wanted to go someplace just for a semester or for a few months to find out how to publish what I was writing, I sent a big box of poems to Jim, and he showed 'em to Miller and Bill, and he called me, and he said, "We need you to come up here." And I said, you know, "Why?" And he said, "'Cause this is wild and powerful stuff. You shouldn't be writin' this by yourself." [*SL laughs*] "You need other writers around."

SL: Yeah.

EG: And I said, "Right. Bingo." Although I knew all the poets in New Orleans, but they weren't like Jim. So I came up here that fall and rented an apartment and—near the campus. And I meant just to go home every weekend, and I did go home a lot.

SL: So what was goin' on with the kids?

EG: And I studied with Miller, too, a little bit. You know, Miller taught me a lot about gettin' rid of all the adjectives and adverbs, but in the end, I'd generally put 'em back in 'cause I don't use that many anyway. Pierre was in college at—down in Texas; Marshall was at Tulane; and Garth was in Alaska.

SL: So Garth sounds like the big adventurer.

EG: He is. He handed me a high school diploma, and he said, "Mother, that's the last time I'll ever sit behind a desk and let a man—a grown man boss me around as long as I live." And my daddy gave him a pickup truck. And his best friend was a forest ranger's son, and the two of them went up to Alaska. They drove the Alaska Highway in a pickup truck.

SL: What a great adventure.

EG: Yeah. We went up there and saw him a few times. He's always done things like that. And you know, I don't worry about my sons. I know how adept they are. I know how good they are at things. And I've never had any power over 'em. I have the same kind of power over my sons that my mother had over me. Zilch. [*Laughter*]

SL: Well, and you must've thought they were fun and funny. . . .

EG: I did.

SL: . . . too.

EG: And my daddy and my brothers and their father were all always, you know, bossin' 'em—tryin' to boss 'em around. Wasn't any reason for me to. It all turned out all right. They're all happy. They're successful. They've wonderful women. And they have all these babies! [*SL laughs*] Sometimes I have to remember to love them first.

SL: So you get to Fayetteville, Arkansas. Had you ever—you'd never been to Fayetteville before you came and . . .

EG: No . . .

SL: . . . met Whitehead . . .

EG: . . . I loved it from the moment I started—from the moment I got to below Fort Smith and I started climbin' into the hills, I just loved the country. It reminds me of north Alabama, where my father's family are from, but the hills there aren't this high. But I just loved it.

SL: So you start taking classes at . . .

EG: Yeah. Yeah, I was . . .

SL: You must be working on a master's degree now. Is that . . .

EG: Yeah. I went into the MFA program, and I did it all that year. And by then I'd started writin' short stories, and the first one had won some big award of the Associated Writing Program—that's the biggest thing you can win. It was the first choice of the publication of the nationwide Associated Writing Programs. And I don't know if—oh yeah, and then Bill Harrison came to me and said, "Ellen, this is a book—we—you know, I wanna take this to my agent." And I said, "No! I'm not gonna show this to someone I don't know in New York City." I said, you know, "Leave it alone. I don't want people judgin' my work." And he said, "But you know"—somethin'—he said, "I'll tell you what. Miller is starting a press—the Arkansas Press—and he wants a book of fiction. Will you let Miller publish it?" And I said, "Yeah, I'll let Miller publish it, but you're not goin' up to New York—talk to some strangers about my work." You know, I'm comin' around to feelin' that way about things again. And then Miller published *In the Land of Dreamy Dreams*, and it was this huge success and sold all the copies in about a week, and then he st—kept printin' 'em. He was printin' 'em as fast as he could, but they were bein' sold as fast as he printed 'em. And then someone who'd been in the program here took a copy of it to the agent that he worked for—Don Congdon, who represents some of the great names in American fiction for many, many years. And in European fiction. And he called me and asked to be my agent, and then after that, people started givin' me lots of money. Which is why I kept writin' fiction instead of goin' back to poetry. . . .

SL: To poetry. Yeah. Well, so this was a surprise to you—to have that kind of success right out of the shoot?

EG: Nope. I wish I could say it was. None of it's ever been a surprise to me. It's just interesting. It's interesting and exciting, but not surprising.

SL: So you knew . . .

EG: What is surprising is, you know, when you get up there and—well, I had a wonderful editor, who became, while he was my editor, the editor-in-chief of Little, Brown. I never had to argue with anyone. I never had to—you know, I never asked for anything that was outrageous, and he and my agent have been friends all their life, and everything was done with a telephone call. There was no, you know—and I never—after I published *Dreamy Dreams*, I never had to send anything to anyone. Since then, people have, you know, commissioned anything that I write. So if I'm writin' somethin', I know I'm gonna get paid for it. And I know how hard I work when I'm writing. And when it's funny, I know it's funny. So I know why people like it 'cause I think it's funny. And all I'm doin' is writin' down things that other people did and other people said. Half the funny stuff in *Falling Through Space* is stuff Jim Whitehead said to me, and I credited him with it, you know.

SL: [*Laughs*] So . . .

EG: So now I'm tryin' to teach . . .

SL: Well . . .

EG: . . . which is complicated and strange.

SL: You—how long was it after you got here that your first book came out?

EG: I don't know because I was—the first year I was here, I was just interested in—I was just mailin' poetry off to all the really fine poetry magazines, and I prob—I had the most publications of anybody. You know, I wrote the most; I sent the most poems out; and I had the most publications. And people get jealous when stuff like that happens—among the poets . . .

SL: Yes.

EG: . . . which surpri—that surprised me. But by then I was spendin' most of my time talkin' about poetry to Frank Stanford,[4] who helped me and loved my talent, or to Jim, who loved everything. He wanted success for me as much as he wanted it for himself, you know. I didn't have to deal with any of that. I just talked to my peers. Is that a terrible thing to say?

SL: No.

EG: And then I was—you know, I like—it's always been about the work. It's been about doin' the work.

SL: Well . . .

EG: It pleases me that other—that people like to read my books. It pleases me enormously. And when people write intelligent reviews about my work, I love that, too. But it's really just—there's something that happens when you're doin' creative work. I'm sure it happens to painters and to photographers, but certainly I know for sure it happens to writers. The process of writing—if you write for an hour or two every morning, the day is different than a day when you don't do that. And it's not all cathartic— well, neither is psychoanalysis. It's just—if you're writin' for an hour—couple hours every day, you're movin' toward a goal of creating a finished product of a short story or the beginning of a novel or somethin' or an essay. And I'm real sure of myself when—but it's not all good. I throw half of it away.

SL: I was gonna ask you, are—do . . .

EG: I throw novels away. I throw novels away every year. I'm more likely to get—to be pleased with what I've done, if I stay in the short forms. Then I get sucked into some insane idea, end up in a long novel, and then I . . .

SL: So, I guess, do you think of it at all as a continuing therapy for you when you're writing? I mean, does it . . .

EG: No.

SL: . . . it's just mechanics for you?

EG: No, no, it's not that. No, it's just makin' stuff up. [*SL laughs*] Makin' things up. Makin' somethin' out of nothing. That's what I tell my students: "Look, you're making somethin' out of nothing. It can be anything you want it to be."

SL: Let's talk a little bit about Jim Whitehead.

EG: I'd love to talk about Jim Whitehead. . . .

SL: Good.

EG: . . . the wonderful, marvelous, irreplaceable Jim Whitehead.

SL: Big guy. He was a big man.

EG: He was a big man in every way. I think I never noticed how big he was physically 'cause I'm too busy arguin' with his big ideas or talkin' to him about his big ideas or learnin' from his big ideas.

SL: One of the things that I remember having been said about him was that he did love to argue. That he would take a different point of view for the sake and for the fun and for the path that argument revealed.

EG: Who told you that? 'Cause I don't think it's true. I think Jim would never pretend to believe somethin' he didn't believe. Whatever he was believin' at the moment, he believed it with the power and force of a hurricane. [*Laughs*]

SL: Well, I mean, do—I mean, would he believe the same thing the next day or—I mean, it would seem li—I don't know.

EG: Well, his political views . . .

SL: Ah.

EG: Not about philosophy or science or literature. We usually agreed about those things. Or we could teach each other things about 'em. But oh, he had so much fun when Bill Clinton was elected to the presidency. After doubts—he may have had some doubts. I can't remember if he had any doubts or not, but that was fun. We all had so much fun doin' that.

SL: So usually these sessions were—didn't he have like a study . . .

EG: We—no, we talked about people. I mean, not that we gossiped, but we have a big group of friends—mostly writers or other artists or Ginny Stanford or someone like that. You know, we explored. We talked about our friends, and how they were, and if we could help, and did they need help, and how were they doing, and—Jim always knew everything that was goin' on with everybody in the literary world that touched both our lives. He knew if their children were sick. If somebody got cancer, he knew the exact technical details. When his daughter Kathleen—now this wonderful surgeon here—doctor and surgeon—when she was in medical school, we would argue. If we were gonna have—we would argue about what Kathleen's specialty should be. [*Laughter*] As if . . .

SL: You had any say in it at all.

EG: . . . as if either one of us—Jim probably had some power. And when she was going through her rotations, she would call me up, and she would get excited about each rotation. And I'd say, "I think she wants to be a psychoanalyst." He'd say, "Oh my God! You've got to be crazy. You didn't tell her to do that?" Or I'd say, "No, I think she's doin' internal medicine." He'd say, "No, I'm not sure that's right." [*SL laughs*] We'd talk about our children and what they should be doin', and we'd just talk about everything. Do you have a really good friend you just like to talk to?

SL: Sure.

EG: That's all we'd do is just talk about it. And not about the past. Always were talkin' about what was goin' on in the present, in the real world, to real people. And before I ta—I didn't teach at the university until after Jim left. And he would tell me about students that he had and problems he was havin' with 'em and problems they were having. He's just so involved—in so many lives, all at once.

SL: So he was a football player, wasn't he?

EG: Mh-hmm.

SL: At—was he at Ole Miss or . . .

EG: Hm-mm. At Vanderbilt.

SL: Vanderbilt, that's right. That's right. I'd forgotten that. I'd . . .

EG: I've forgotten what he—he was on the—he was a person—on the offensive line, I think. Person—no, the defensive line. Person that keeps the other people from makin' touchdowns.

SL: He—you know, stereotypically, you don't think of a big football player having the intellect that Jim had.

EG: No, or bein' a philosopher. Maybe it was scholarship money. He may've gone there—you know, it might've been his scholarship to Vanderbilt.

SL: Uh-huh. Did he ever talk about his football stuff with you? I guess not.

EG: I used to listen to him talk about football to—no, the only thing that ever interested me was the fact that he had injured his left shoulder so badly. I think it was his left shoulder. Might've been his right shoulder. [*Clears throat*] And he was just in pain for many years of his life from the shoulder—dislocated the rotator cuff or somethin' like that, and finally he had it operated on a few years before he died. But the surgery was helpful, but not that successful.

SL: Yeah.

EG: Maybe it was too late.

SL: Yeah. I know people that have had as many as three rotator cuff surgeries to—and it's never—it never is the same. I mean, I don't know of anyone that's had suc—a totally successful shoulder rotator cuff surgery. So . . .

EG: I liked to listen to him talk on the phone to people about football. 'Cause while we were talkin', people would call up if it was nearing time for the Arkansas-Ole Miss game or somethin'—people would be callin' from all over the United States.

SL: So there was Whitehead, and there was Harrison at the department when you came, and Miller Williams.

EG: Mh-hmm.

SL: Pretty—three pretty strong—not only personalities, but . . .

EG: Well, they'd created the program. It was theirs.

SL: Yeah. If you—so of those three, you were probably closest to Jim, you would say?

EG: Mh-hmm. Mh-hmm. I was all—you know, he was just always my best friend. But I love Bill and Miller, and I appreciate everything that they taught me and did for me, too.

SL: Mh-hmm. So how long were you in the MFA program?

EG: I stayed for that year, and then I went home for the summer. [*Clears throat*] And I had told them that I'd come back and teach—you know, have a teaching scholarship in the fall, but I couldn't do it. But I came back in the fall and stayed for about five weeks, and Bill Harrison showed me how to write the short story. And then I went back to New Orleans. But I always—but I bought a house up here, you know, and I was always coming back up here. I never really left Fayetteville. I just mostly lived in New Orleans for a while, and then I mostly lived here, and then I do like I do now. I live here most of the time, and I live down there because that's where all my family are. So I ha—now I have a main home here and a house down there. It's not big enough for all those babies.

***

SL: I still—I mean, I know that you have an infinite well of stories to tell or that you could tell because you tell them in your books. You . . .

EG: Well, I make some of 'em up.

SL: Yeah.

EG: Or I elaborate on somethin' that really happened, like goin' down to see those wild animals in Mexico with my brother and my cousin Bunky. I mean, they really took me down there, but I mean, you know, nobody broke their leg or any of that stuff, which is . . .

SL: Little drama.

EG: Yeah.

SL: A touch of drama. Seasoning. Throw in there. Well, when you—we did talk a little bit about how the best, for you—what works best for you is a pencil and a notebook—a pad . . .

EG: And a—no, it's got to be a yellow legal pad.

SL: A yell . . .

EG: Except I really like the white ones better now.

SL: Easier to see?

EG: Whitehead liked yellow legal—no, he began likin' white ones, too. But the typewriter's the best.

SL: Is it the pressure of the keys and the . . .

EG: Hm-mm.

SL: . . . the mechanical nature and the sound that it makes or . . .

EG: Hm-mm. Hm-mm.

SL: . . . what is it about a typewriter that . . .

EG: It's turnin' my thoughts into written prose 'cause if you're typin' on a typewriter, you can see what you're typing, you know. And it's—I like the way it looks. But I don't even know that—once I get started, I don't even know what I'm doing mechanically. There's nothin' that drives me crazier than havin' to stop and fix a ribbon. No, I don't let myself get upset. You know, this is my weapon that I choose to use it, and sometimes I have to put a new tape in it. [*Laughter*] That's . . .

SL: Ammo.

EG: . . . all there is to it. Only takes me a second, and I always have about a lifetime supply of 'em 'cause when I go buy 'em, I always think, "They're gonna quit makin' tapes for this typewriter at any given moment. I better buy all of 'em." [*Laughs*]

SL: Well, there's probably some truth to that.

EG: I know it.

SL: Eventually, they . . .

EG: Especially the eraser tapes. [*SL laughs*]

SL: So . . .

EG: I was gonna tell you about the good parts of bein' famous . . .

SL: Yes.

EG: . . . 'cause I could tell you about the bad parts in a heartbeat.

SL: Okay.

EG: The bad parts are havin' your work judged by other people. Even people who write very pleasant things about your work usually miss the point. Nobody knows what you wrote but yourself. But that's okay. The work belongs to the world; they can interpret it however they want to. But one—some wonderful things have happened to me because I became a famous writer that would nev—once, right after I won the National Book Award, Eudora Welty had told me four times that I should fly on the Concorde. And I said, "Oh, Eudora, there's no way I could—I don't want to fly at supersonic speeds. I don't even like to fly, you know, down to the coast. Why would I wanna fly?" But right after I won the National Book Award, my British publishers, Faber and Faber—I was so honored and pleased to have this great publishing company in Great Britain become my publisher, and they would publish the books right after they were bought. The list at Faber and Faber is just like Nobel Laureate after Nobel Laureate, so I wanted to do it. And they wanted me to come over there and meet 'em. And the National Book Award had an award of $10,000, which was thirty now—you know, at the time—it would be thirty now. So for—I don't know how I got myself to do it. Probably because I thought, "If Eudora could do this, as timid as Eudora is, I'll do it." [*SL laughs*] So I bought a ticket on the Concorde and flew to Great Britain on the Concorde, and I had on a long, white pleated skirt and a white—a soft, white blouse that came down. You know, it looked like a flapper dress. And I was so excited, and so I was probably very pretty because I was so excited. And we were in the lounge where you have to wait to get on the Concorde. It's a special lounge with all kinds of beautiful food and things. And there's a gray-haired gentleman sittin' there, and I think we spoke or exchanged newspapers or somethin', and when I got on the Concorde, I was sitting next to him. That's wh—at the beginning, the Concorde seats were this big. They became about the size of this chair, but at the very beginning, they were this big. [*Uses hands to suggest width*] And he introduced himself, and he was the president of Lloyd's of London, which insures the British Airways planes. It insures the Concorde. And I was telling him about my excitement. And he explained the plane to me and showed me the little clock, so you can see when it goes to Mach 1 and Mach 2. We have, you know, Mach 1, Mach 2, and Mach 3. We were gonna fly to London. I guess—I've forgotten—I think it takes three hours if the wind's right. And this incredible airplane was still very new. It takes off at seven hundred miles an hour, almost straight up, and then somethin' happens to the nose cone. It straight—and then it straightens out, and then within about fifteen or twenty minutes, you're at Mach 1. And you feel the plane go past the speed of sound. You know, you feel the plane pull like some giant has jerked it—so exciting. And he said, "Have you ever been to England before?" And I said, "No, I don't like to travel; I'm from the American South. You know, I don't even like to go to New York." Plus, I—well, I do like to go shoppin' in New York or to see the ballet but—and he said, "You've never been to England?" And he said, "Obviously, from your name, your ancestors came from the British Isles." And I said, "Did they ever! Every one of 'em from Scotland or from England." And he said, "Would you like to go up in the conco—in the cockpit?" And I said, "Of this airplane?" [*Laughter*] And he said, "Yes." And he got up, went up front, and right after we finished eatin' dinner, the pi—he came back with one of the pilots or the copilots. There were three officers in the cockpit. And they took me up to the cockpit of the Concorde. And there were four—pilot, copilot, third—second, third officer, and then there was a seat right here [*uses hands to suggest layout of cockpit*] near the door that went back into the main cabin. And I sat down in it and put the seat belt on, and I said, "This is—I cannot—I can't believe this. This is amazing. Thank you so much. I promise not to touch anything." And the pilot said, "Oh, it would be better if none of us touched anything." [*SL laughs*] And then the second officer said—the third officer said, "The plane is flown by computers." [*Laughter*] But I could see out the wide, wide front window. I could see the panorama of the British Isles come into view late in the afternoon—or we left New York around nine in the morning—three hours would be twelve, and then a time difference—it would've been six in the afternoon in a spring day. And there's—there are the British Isles looking just like they look in a children's map—you know, on a salt map, spread out. And from so high up that you could see everything all at once. You know, Scotland, Ireland, Wales, London, England. Too much. I don't know when I left the cockpit. Not until we were completely landed, I don't think.

SL: Is that right? That's the best seat in the house.

EG: That's the most amazing thing that ever happened to me in my life. And then I had lunch with the gentleman who'd let me do it later in London.

SL: What about—after you had success with your writing and—or it started and started to roll very well, did you meet other writers that you'd always . . .

EG: Well, I'd always—as soon as I began seriously writing and publishing poetry again after many years, I was in contact with other poets all over the United States—writing to 'em, telling 'em that I liked a poem that they'd published in *Poetry* magazine. They'd write back to me. And after my books became successful and after I was on National Public Radio—when I did that little stint for Bob Edwards and I made up the genre of the little personal essay, which God forbid is used by such corny people now. Most of the time I just shudder and want to turn the radio off. But I was, you know, invited to universities and colleges all over the United States. I gave addresses to the graduating medical school class at the University of California in San Francisco and to the University of Nevada. I just—it—where there're women, graduating students would beg to have me. And I flew all over the United States givin' lectures at—I had an agent out in San Francisco who was very good at all this. And I had a great time, and I met—you know, but by—I already just—if I really like a person's—a writer's work, then I want to be friends with that writer, and there's an instant rapport. I feel that way about Larry McMurtry.

SL: Okay.

EG: I love his work. He's said nice things about mine also. It's, you know, it's just an immediate and lifelong bond, if you really like their work and they really like yours. But it's impossible for a writer to be friends with another writer if you don't like their work 'cause it's hard to pretend that you like someone's work.

SL: It's not in you.

EG: Hm-mm.

SL: And it's not in them.

EG: Hm-mm.

SL: So . . .

EG: But I have—I don't keep up with all of 'em the way I used to. I used to—huge voluminous correspondence in those boxes and plastic bags between myself and other writers. Mostly about somethin' they're publishing; somethin' I'm publishing; somethin' they've read of mine.

SL: Well, did you—are there any that you ever got to spend some time with? Did you ever get to meet and . . .

EG: If I wanted to, but I don't like to leave home. [*SL laughs*] I mean . . .

SL: Do you . . .

EG: . . . and I'm busy writing. You know, I don't wanna . . .

SL: Mh-hmm. And it's probably true of them, too.

EG: Right. I have a lot of friends. You know, I kinda have enough friends. Busy people don't, you know, just go flyin' around to hang out like you do when you're young.

SL: Yeah. Well, let's talk a little bit about your NPR involve . . .

EG: The only time I ever did things like that were—one time I went up to see a famous movie producer—oh, in New England—and stay with he and his wife to talk about writing a screenplay for him—I've forgotten what it was about—really famous, powerful producer. God, what a dreary three days.

SL: Really?

EG: Walkin' around some Yankee producer's house up in upstate New York. Ugh, listening to his wife. Oh God, what a boring thing. It's better just to—and his ideas for what he wanted me to write were so far away from anything I was ever gonna do, but I couldn't find any way to truncate the weekend. I had to keep stayin' till I got to leave. [*SL laughs*]

***

SL: Okay, so let's—I was about to ask you about NPR and your time with NPR. What—how did that come about, and what was that like . . .

EG: The night that I won the National Book Award, a young man who had helped Bob—he and Bob Edwards had created *Morning Edition* together. We did not have an NPR station in Fayetteville. I was prayin' that we would get one. And as Woody Bassett told me later—I think it was Woody—the work was bein' done by lawyers in Washington, DC, [*SL laughs*] but I had no idea how you got NPR to be in your town so that you didn't have to be drivin' round California to get to hear it—the wonderful talk shows and things. And so there were hundreds of people tryin' to interview me that night, but I picked out the NPR person. What was that kid's name? He was just twenty-six years old, and he and Bob Edwards had created *Morning Edition* and were still creating it. And he interviewed me, and I said a lot of funny stuff. [*SL laughs*] And then the next day, Bob Edwards called me on the phone, and I knew who he was—how, I don't know, 'cause we didn't—maybe I just—'cause I'd been in New York listenin' to it—and asked me if I would be on *Morning Edition*. And I said, "Doin' what?" And he said, "Anything you want to. We just want your voice on the program." And I said, "Oh, but w—I don't know." So we talked for a while, and I said, "Okay." I said, "Look, I get all these fan letters constantly. And they're people askin' me, 'How do you—why are you who you are, why you instead of me?' or whatever. And I don't know how to answer these questions, and I never feel like I've answered 'em satisfactorily."

And I said, "You know what, I'll do—for a few weeks, I'll do a little diary for you, like journal entries." And he said, "We'll call it journal entries." And I said, "And I'll just tell you what I'm thinkin' on a weekly basis. What has captured my imagination. What book I'm reading that I'm involved in"— like a new biography of Einstein's, which led to Einstein's great biographer becomin' one of my closest friends in New York 'cause I reviewed his book. But—and not really a book review. And so I began to make those little pieces, some of which are in *Fallin' Through Space*. And they were just this huge success, and Bob would end the program with 'em. He'd open the program by tellin' 'em I was gonna be at the end of it, and he'd end the program. Which was good, because I never turn on media in the daytime, but I'd want to listen to myself. But I didn't want to spend a whole hour listenin' to myself, so if I could know what day it was on, I'd just turn it on at the end. And I had fun doin' it. Nobody ever edited it. I can't remember what that young—Jay Kernis, who's now a big producer on CBS or NBC. He's now a grown man and a happy man, and I've seen him three or four times down the years. We love each other. Jay never touched my stuff. Bob never touched my stuff. I'd go down to KUAF, and I mean, I'd type up three or four things, or I'd type up two or three of 'em, go down to KUAF, spend thirty minutes with the kids down there puttin' 'em on tape or whatever they used at the time to se— and they'd send 'em to New York, and they would go on the air exactly like I wrote 'em. And that went on for about a year and a half, and I was happy, and the audience was happy. And then NPR began to change, and they got all these young, Ivy League girls in there. Rabid feminists—you know, all the new wave and everything. Politically correct to the ninth power. And they'd call me up and say, "Are you sure you want to say this?" about somethin.' And I said, "Look. I'm doin' this for a hundred dollars a week as a public service to try to get NPR in Fayetteville, Arkansas. I'm not gonna—you're not gonna edit my work. Who are you?" And it—and then I got irritated with 'em. And then I started just makin' a tape every other week and, you know, and after a while, it just all kind of fizzled out. . . .

SL: Yeah.

EG: . . . 'cause I wasn't gonna put up with that. As long as it was just Jay Kernis, Bob Edwards, and me, and I'd write the things, and they'd put 'em on the air, okay. But if I got to go through the politically correct battalion to get there, it's not happening.

SL: That's neat though that you could just . . .

EG: All this time, my—good lawyers from Fayetteville were in Washington, DC, gettin' us an NPR station. [*SL laughs*] And my editor kept sayin,'

"Ellen, quit puttin' that silly stuff on the air. I don't know if you oughta be doin' that." And then my book sales started climbin', [*laughs*] and all of a sudden, Roger quit complainin' about me bein' on NPR.

SL: Well, that stuff was—was it hitting all the NPR stations all across the country?

EG: Oh yeah.

SL: What a great avenue. What a great venue.

EG: Well, I never thought of it as that, but I sure got a lot of wonderful fan mail. I used to try to answer it. Oh my God! It would take hours.

SL: You felt a responsibility to respond.

EG: Mh-hmm. Mh-hmm. [*SL laughs*] I'm sure that that's true, and I'm glad that I was there and got to experience it. The really good part—when Jay Kernis and Bob Edwards and I were havin' a really good time, the audience was laughin' its head off, and everybody was happy except my editor. But when the politically correct battalion started questioning every word that came out of my mouth—and that's what goes on now in media. That's why it's all so brainwashed. Videos are still—PBS still is pretty pure. I mean, they're allowed to—you can see some nice stuff on PBS, and you can see some nice stuff on video. But just the—you kn—I can see the lineup behind every word that gets spoken on television 'cause I've been there and had to put up with it. And the bleached-out language [*laughs*] with which they all lie to each other and pretend to be good buddies. . . .

SL: Yeah.

EG: . . . and they're not even in the same city—the two people who are allegedly talking to each other.

SL: I guess there's something wild and woolly and irreplaceable with early stuff.

EG: Oh, early NPR. Wasn't that fun? And I don't know who was pickin' out the music, but the musical segments that would go in between the little pieces on NPR were just brilliant. I learned a lotta great music from that. And I'd be callin' Washington sayin', "What in the hell was in between—what is that? I gotta have that!"

SL: [*Laughs*] Well, they really cared. They had the right priorities.

EG: Uh-huh.

SL: Keepin' stuff pure like that. Makes it more valuable. I was thinking of another question. Oh, now was it Dooley that had the radio that he built? Was that . . .

EG: No. No, no, no, that was one of my cousins in the Delta. And he was one—he was a fraternal twin. Laura and Bubba. [*SL laughs*] Except Bubba was Uncle Robert Finley's son, so—and I think his name—and it wasn't Robert 'cause his name w—I mean, I cannot remember Bubba's real name 'cause we all called him that. He was a genius. His father was a—was the only physician in three counties, and he had all this radio equipment down in the basement. And all durin' the Second World War, he talked to people all over the world, and he could get into—he was always—you know, what a wonderful person Bubba Finley was. And his sister, who was a gifted pianist, got married and has a daughter who wrote a symphony that was produced at the New Orleans Symphony recently and all kinds of—you know, the whole family are just wonderful. But Bubba Finley ended up livin' in Houston, Texas, and he was an inventor, and he invented things. What was it you were askin' about him?

SL: Well, I just remember one of the comments that you've written about the NPR thing—that you were comfortable being in the studio.

EG: Oh yeah, it was like Bubba's. [*Laughs*]

SL: Yeah. You had an affinity already f—you know, some people have a . . .

EG: Right. And I knew a newspaper editor's son later in Harrisburg, Illinois, who also had radio stuff, and he had, you know, he had egg cartons all over the wall and . . .

SL: [*Laughs*] It's funny how that early stuff makes you comfortable when it comes back around in a slightly different form or in ways that you wouldn't expect it to enter your life again. It's—you were so—I'm not sure . . .

EG: I get excited about things. I get excited about—I mean, you know, we have three or four sets of fraternal twins in our family, and the one—the girl is always the dominant twin. [*SL laughs*] Always. And the boy gets to do things like be a crazy inventor and never even has to pick up his hats and coats. She picks 'em up for him.

SL: [*Laughs*] The nutty professor.

EG: Right. They should all come with a girl fraternal twin. [*SL laughs*] Pick up after 'em all their life.

SL: Well, that's funny.

EG: I saw Bubba in Houston about fifteen years ago. It was so wonderful. People don't change. They're just like they always were when you finally get to see 'em again.

SL: That is interesting. I've always felt like the first five or six years of your life, the foundations are laid for what's—what you're going to be. I mean, you're gonna have influences and pressures and situations bring up different stuff, but who you are—the way you're raised before you can really remember much about it, I think, give[s] you the blocks that set who you are. And it's what you go back to. Unconsciously and willingly or unwillingly, it seems to me that the blocks are . . .

EG: Well, it's what you're drawn to.

SL: Yeah.

EG: But then, whatever your parents exposed you to is what they are interested in, so it's also genetic. I mean, you know, there are predispositions for things for sure.

SL: I love how—I love that story about how your father would seek out your friends for you whenever . . .

EG: Oh, I know. But I mean, he didn't want me to be lonely when I got there. He'd have—I mean, I don't know how—it would just—you know, if—he'd have to have a new lawyer and a new banker and a new—whatever people—real estate agent, and surely—and one of 'em would have a daughter my age, and she'd look like she was—as he'd say, "Just your speed, Sista."

SL: "Just your speed, Sister." [*Laughs*] That's fun.

EG: I think I found Cynthia on my own though. I think I found Cynthia at the swimmin' pool. Just my speed. [*Laughter*]

SL: Well, where do you wanna go now? What do you wanna talk about now?

EG: I think we've probably covered everything you need to make a program.

SL: Well, you know . . .

EG: I don't think we've left anything out, except that I'm not gonna talk at length about the four or five crazy years when I got married four times.

SL: [*Laughs*] Do you want to talk at short about it . . .

EG: I like . . .

SL: . . . other than it was just crazy?

EG: Yeah. No, I think that—a great writer once said, "I spit on the grave of my twenties." That's pretty good.

SL: Yeah.

EG: But you know, when you don't know what you're doing—but the thing is, I like what happened durin' those years. If I lived now and had birth control, you know, and was that same, young—would I be wise enough to have those three wonderful children who've given me this plethora of riches of grandchildren? N—probably not.

SL: Probably not.

EG: I'd been too s—how would you know, you know?

SL: Yeah.

EG: How would you know when to go do that? And yet people still do.

SL: It is interesting. The whole birth control thing really changed things, didn't it? I mean, you were talking about how people just didn't have intercourse until you were married. It just wasn't happening, but once birth control hit and was available for the masses, it did change things somehow.

EG: For good and for bad.

SL: Yeah. I always feel like those early twenties between . . .

EG: The thing is, I can't ever—I don't really feel any need to think about it or examine how those years in my life happened, I mean, because it's—what has happened—what happened because of all of that is exactly—I mean, I like it. I've always liked it. Ever since I got pregnant for the first time, I have loved the idea of havin' a child, and when I got the children, I loved 'em. They were exactly what I wanted. It's hard when you're a young mother if they get sick. It's difficult, and that's why I think that people should live near their families or near their mothers or their grandmothers or their aunts or someone. You know, not just a good friend.

SL: Mh-hmm. A support system.

EG: Right.

SL: And backup. And more backup.

EG: I mean, the child's gonna get well by in the morning, but you don't know that when you're twenty years old. . . .

SL: That's right.

EG: Your baby's runnin' a temperature!

SL: Oh, I can remember waking up in the middle of the night just to see if they're breathing.

EG: Oh, right.

SL: Just, you know . . .

EG: Just go check on 'em. [*Laughs*]

SL: Sure. Well, they're at the foot of the bed—you know, sit up . . .

EG: I don't want 'em sleepin' on their stomachs either. Because—especially a tiny baby like this new three-and-a-half-month-old Josephine that we have—they sleep so still and so quiet, you're not sure they're breathing! You gotta get down close.

SL: That's right. [*Laughs*] That's right. Well, is there anything that you wanna say—anything more you wanna say about your children?

EG: No, just that . . .

SL: You've . . .

EG: . . . I've been so lucky. I've been lucky. They're all strong and happy, and—we lost a pair of identical twins at birth. They would've been my second and third grandchildren. Beautiful little girls. Aside from that, we just get 'em. [*Laughter*]

SL: They just keep comin'.

EG: I know, and they're pretty, and they're strong.

SL: Well, okay. If you're comfortable, I—we can stop. I . . .

EG: I think you'll have a wonderful piece. I think havin' it be long . . .

SL: Well, you know, we don't really . . .

EG: . . . I think havin' it be long won't make it any better.

SL: Well, it's interesting. You know . . .

EG: I think it's like those novels I try to write. I think we oughta stop while we're ahead.

Notes

1. Courtland, Alabama.

2. Theodore Bilbo, governor of Mississippi (1916–1920, 1928–1932), US Senator (1935–1947), segregationist, and white supremacist.

3. Guendaline Graeber Whitehead.

4. Frank Stanford (1938–1978) was a prolific American poet and the founder of Lost Roads Press, which published Gilchrist's *The Land Surveyor's Daughter* in 1979.

The Last Southern Writer?
An Interview with Ellen Gilchrist

Luke Lampton and Scott Anderson / 2013

From *China Grove* 1 (Fall 2013), 38–62. Reprinted by permission.

It is now more than fifty years since James Meredith entered Ole Miss. The South, the United States, and the world as a whole are a very different place than they were then. There are Walmarts and McDonald's within driving distance of almost anywhere. Family ties are stretched and broken.

Television, Internet access, and twenty-four-hour news cycles have battered down and eroded the differences that created regional identities. There is no question that there will continue to be writers from the Southern states, but are there any more Southern writers?

There is one. Her name is Ellen Gilchrist. A poet turned author in the tradition of Robert Penn Warren. Her densely woven fabric of interrelated characters and plot lines flows as life's blood through her works to create a world as rich and durable as Yoknapatawpha yet as current as the latest skirmish in the Middle East.

China Grove editors Luke Lampton and Scott Anderson sat down with Gilchrist at her home in Ocean Springs, Mississippi to discuss the story "Toccata and Fugue in D Minor" and how we got to this point in her ongoing narrative.

Luke Lampton: I wanted to start with you. Anybody who's familiar with you, familiar with your career, can see the breadth and variety of your writing. Scott and I are convinced that you are one of the nation's most accomplished women of letters. You are a woman of letters. To call you a novelist is to minimalize your accomplishments.

Ellen Gilchrist: That sounds good.

Scott Anderson: Like Robert Penn Warren, that's the example we used in the car. He was a man of letters. He wasn't necessarily one thing or another.

Gilchrist: I studied philosophy. That was my major. I didn't want English teachers telling me what to think about pieces of literature.

Lampton: What do you perceive yourself as, what writing medium claims you? You've done novels, novellas, poetry, short stories, essays, which one is closest to your heart?

Gilchrist: Although I don't write poetry anymore, I get . . . the other morning I woke up and opened up this fantastic translation of Rilke, the works, not new, of course. It's the translation by Stephen Mitchell. It's fantastic. Have you seen it? [*She finds a copy of the book and shows it to us both.*]

Lampton: I have, I love it.

Gilchrist: I opened up to a part I'd never read, well I don't think I'd ever read them, *Sonnets to Orpheus*, I just started to read them and suddenly it was an hour or two later and I thought . . . my God, my God . . . so I love poetry. But I also love writing nonfiction, and I like writing fiction now that I've learned to hide the poems inside the story. And I like it that people enjoy the stories. [*The book stays in her hand, not an inanimate object, but like a living thing. Like a small bird she is holding, ever so gently. It moves constantly.*]

Lampton: You just said you like to hide the poem inside the story?

Gilchrist: Well, that's how Bill Harrison talked me into taking short story writing seriously. He said, "God damn, nobody's going to give you any money to write poetry. Nobody makes any money writing poetry. You can always hide your poems in the stories." I thought that he meant . . . and I did this for about three years . . . have one of your characters reading a poem or quoting poetry in the dialogue. So, I would put all of these poems inside my books. Seamus Heaney let me use two of his, before he'd even published them himself.

Anderson: I will say, *In the Land of Dreamy Dreams* is such lyrical poetry.

Gilchrist: That's because, before I did that book I'd never written anything else. All I'd written was poetry. I'm always thinking, I wonder if I could get back to the purity of language I had then. I only knew and read and wrote poetry.

Lampton: What Scott was noticing was your first two books, *The Land Surveyor's Daughter*, a book of poetry and your second book *In the Land of Dreamy Dreams* is short stories. *In the Land of Dreamy Dreams* was a transition for you from the more direct poem to the hidden poem you spoke of.

Gilchrist: [*Pauses momentarily to think*] I don't know, it's all a process, just a process.

Lampton: So, you spoke of Rilke, poetry is still very important to you.

Gilchrist: Not just Rilke, but all poetry. I see it in my life everywhere. It's like being at my cousin Bunky's funeral and all I can possibly think is Shakespeare.

Our revels now are ended. These our actors
As I foretold you, were all spirits and
Are melted into air, into thin air:
And like the baseless fabric of this vision,
The cloud-capp'd towers, the gorgeous palaces,
The solemn temples, the great globe itself,
And, like this insubstantial pageant faded,
Leave not a rack behind.
We are such stuff
As dreams are made on, and our little life
Is rounded with a sleep.[1]

Lampton: Wow. You are now in your seventies . . .

Gilchrist: I'm almost eighty. I tell people all the time that I'm eighty, especially if I need them to do something for me. It's like giving them a twenty-dollar bill. I don't want to say I'm almost eighty, so I just go ahead and say I'm eighty.

Lampton: You still seem to be on poetic fire. You still seem to be writing and enjoying writing as much as you ever did. You still have a lot to say.

Gilchrist: I know it.

Anderson: You said to me on the phone the other day that at the funeral you were just filled with inspiration, so many things to write about.

Gilchrist: You think, *I've used up all the material.* But, my God, I haven't touched the material. I'm starting a new thing now, and they'll let me do it, I've talked to my whole family on Facebook and they all have agreed to let me do it, but I'm going to start telling stories using real names, and telling things we really did. I'm letting Miss Crystal and Traceleen tell a story together, a story we're all in. Miss Crystal is just the typist, that and she adds some detail. But Traceleen is having a horrible time. Her favorite grandson is the leader of a drug gang, and Miss Crystal has gone down to New Orleans to get her into tough love. Of course she can't go to AA in her own neighborhood, because everyone would know about it. So she's going to Trinity Episcopal Church.

Lampton: Before we leave *In the Land of Dreamy Dreams* I have to say that it may represent one of the finest collections of short stories ever written, by anyone. The poetic imagery is stunning. Both of us really liked the story "Rich" and we loved the ending, it's almost gothic in its violence in the way it ends and then the humor amidst the violence takes you aback. It was brilliant, and I loved . . .

Gilchrist: That was the first short story I ever seriously wrote in my life. Bill Harrison coaxed me into writing that ending. I said, I can write violence, so I did.

Lampton: Who was this?

Gilchrist: Bill was a screenwriter, he taught fiction writing at the University of Arkansas. I went up there and was in the program at first for one long winter semester. I stayed until school was over, then I went back in the fall for about six weeks and Bill showed me how to write a short story and it worked for me. It won all of the awards and was lead story in a magazine, and then I went back to New Orleans. Because Pierre [her youngest son] was still there. Freddy and my mother were taking care of him, but I had to go home. I begged him to come to Fayetteville but he wouldn't so I went home. I was flying home every weekend anyway.

Lampton: But where in the world did you get the inspiration for that ending?

Gilchrist: I had the inspiration from a friend, a wonderful, brilliant woman. Her stockbroker husband had killed himself. He shot his dog first. That story and image just stayed with me.

Lampton: In a strange way it is strongly related to *Anna Karenina*. The unshakable image that Tolstoy had of this woman who threw herself under a train. Trying to understand the desperate situation that person was in and trying to make sense of that. The power of your story is not only the aspect of shutting that off but the unexpected humor. That is one of the things that is so evident in what you do, not just the poetic beauty of the prose but the humor as well. The reflections of the district attorney at the end. . . . Did your family have pedigreed animals?

Gilchrist: Well, my cousin Bunky had been raising them all my life. The first lab I ever saw, my Uncle Floyd at Hopedale Plantation dragged me out into the yard one time. "Come on out here, Sister." They always called me Sister, or Shorty, or D. They dragged me down to the bayou where this man had these lab puppies, black lab puppies, I don't think they were three months old, and he was showing how they'd fetch anything from the bayou, and it was pretty fabulous.

Lampton: The other story I wanted to touch on from *In the Land of Dreamy Dreams* was the last story. It ends with Matille going to the bayou and looking into the muddy water and seeing her reflection there and the power of that ending, the poetic power . . .

Gilchrist: Well, my first cousin, Bunky's younger brother, died when we were about eight. We were the same age. His grandfather was an artist, he had portraits hanging in the White House and they all thought that my little cousin was going to be an artist. He was my playmate. He was always at Hopedale when I was there. And he died having an operation on his finger. He broke one of his fingers and they were afraid that the broken finger was going to ruin his artistic career, and he never woke up from the anesthesia. I guess it would have been ether back then.

Lampton: Probably . . . would have been.

Gilchrist: The whole thing just shattered our family. And my mother sent me down there all the time after that to stay with my family, Aunt Margaret and Uncle George and Bunky. They had never moved anything in his room. Everything was just the same as when he was alive. This was not some distant tragedy, it was personal, like the brothers and sisters of the children that were shot in Connecticut.[2]

Lampton: Let's talk about the new short story, "Toccata and Fugue in D Minor," what were you thinking when you wrote this story? You have a character in this story that appeared earlier in *A Dangerous Age*, Louise Hand.

Gilchrist: I used the *Toccata and Fugue in D Minor* in the title so that people would remember to play it at my funeral. I swear, that was definitely one of the reasons I wrote the story. I wrote that story six months before the airport bombing really happened, at Heathrow. Anyone with a mind was seeing terrorists everywhere. A friend's daughter was playing on a basketball team at the time and he got the obsessive idea that they were going to blow up a basketball gym. I thought that they were going to blow up the bridges over the Mississippi River. What did you think they were going to blow up?

Lampton: I thought transportation, bridges and trains. I thought that they would be easy targets. And then it didn't happen. Where are you going with this new book, *Acts of God*? Is it all short stories?

Gilchrist: Yes, it is. It has stories about Katrina. It has a story about some gay guys during Katrina. They're physicians assistants and they help the people in the city break into a drugstore, to help them get the things they need. They're down in New Orleans for a physician assistants' and nurse practitioners' meeting when Katrina hits. They end up helping in that hospital that got flooded, trying to take care of the patients. They saw people breaking into a drugstore so they helped them. Then they took the drugs they needed to the hospital in a rowboat. There's also a fantastic tornado story, it's something I read about in the newspaper that happened in northern Arkansas. A teenage boy found a baby, he was with one of those church groups that go to towns to help out after a tornado, and he finds a baby that the storm blew away.

Lampton: So oftentimes the short story starts with a little spark and the story grows around that?

Gilchrist: It will be a long time after I hear something that I write a story about it. It's something that imprints itself on my mind. So it's not just telling the story. [*To Scott*] So you're exactly on the right path. Writing your diamond book about Africa.

Anderson: It's already written. I just can't bring myself to publish it. Not yet. I don't know why I keep putting it off. I need to talk to Luke about that on the way home.

Gilchrist: You just have to go to the right funeral one day.

Lampton: Scott had said something interesting, in *A Dangerous Age* . . .

Gilchrist: The name of which is supposed to be *War*. W-A-R. I got talked out of it.

Lampton: So you got talked out of it?

Gilchrist: Yeah. I used to never let that kind of thing happen.

Lampton: We felt that that novel was going somewhere new. Somewhere we're not used to seeing you. Looking at world issues.

Gilchrist: Well, I'm a grown person now. . . . I'm slow to grow up. . . . It's a long process for people as spoiled as I am. We don't grow up fast.

Anderson: Poor Luke, he has been editing me for six years now, and back when I used to get edited more he had to put up with me calling him and I was always, "God damn it, somebody moved a comma in my story and changed the meaning of the whole thing."

Gilchrist: That's why I changed my life by leaving Little, Brown and going to Algonquin. I just don't want to be edited anymore.

Lampton: You started with Little, Brown?

Gilchrist: Well, I started with University of Arkansas Press, but then I went to Little, Brown. My editor was the editor-in-chief there. He and my agent would just talk on the phone. Everything we did was just a handshake. Just a phone conversation, and the three of us loved each other.

Lampton: Who was that?

Gilchrist: Roger Donald. He comes as a visiting lecturer to the university in Fayetteville. He sends the honorarium checks back to the program. The students just worship him.

Lampton: The relationship between a publisher, an editor, and a writer is often one that involves being best friends and at the same time being adversaries.

Gilchrist: We weren't adversaries.

Lampton: So that's not the way it ever was for you? You were connected to one another very early on.

Gilchrist: I would get mad at him because he would take so long to send the manuscript back, but that was all. He let me name a book *Light Can Be Both Wave and Particle*. They still put it in the science section of bookstores. He let me name a book *The Annunciation*. Christian bookstores called up and ordered hundreds of thousands of copies, and he had explain to them that they better read the book before they decided that they should put them on their bookshelves.

Light being both wave and particle still blows me away. I've been searching for first causes, every day of my life. Aren't you? The Episcopal Church with my mother, if they would just quit saying the "Holy Ghosts" and the Presbyterian Church with my father, where you were saved by stewardship sermons. Then literature, then poetry, then with science. . . . I thought theoretical physics, quantum physics that that's where it was. But I don't care how many universes you find: at the edge of the universe, you find what? Nothing . . . but nothing is something! Now I believe in DNA.

But my editor and I got together because my wonderful agent, Don Congdon, read that book [*points to* In the Land of Dreamy Dreams] then he called me up and said, "We have three publishers bidding on your next book, but the most enthusiastic is a guy called Roger Donald over at Little, Brown." So I said, "Okay, I'll come to New York and I'll meet these people." I was a poet, I didn't have any respect for what they were trying to do up there, reviews in *Time* and *Newsweek*. What did that mean to me. . . . I was a poet? This wasn't the world that I knew anything about, and I didn't need the money. But I flew up to New York and Jane Petty[3] was there for the opening of a play by a young woman from Mississippi. . . .

Lampton: Beth Henley?

Gilchrist: Yes, that was it, Beth Henley. Her mother was a friend of ours. Jane dressed me up to go meet Roger. She put a three hundred dollar blouse on me. I've always dressed just like this. [*Holds up arms*] Well, wearing a sweater like this is new to me. Everything I own is just alike: they all have collars. But I went to lunch with Don and Roger and I liked him so much. He made me laugh.

Lampton: Autobiography plays a big role in your heroines, your protagonists . . .

Gilchrist: Everything anybody writes is after all somewhat autobiographical, my mother's rose garden [for example].

Lampton: A lot of your protagonists have your spirit though. They are often spoiled, rebellious, precocious, and highly intelligent . . .

Gilchrist: Those are the kinds of people I like to be with. They're like the two of you. You show up fifteen minutes early to the restaurant for our lunch date because you don't want to miss anything.

Anderson: Okay, moving to this short story, Louise Hand . . .

Gilchrist: Yes, Anna Hand, her niece Louise.

Anderson: Louise is the new you. [*Ellen looks down and nods slightly.*] When I read this, I knew this was you. When I read *A Dangerous Age* I said, "This is to the new you." I know you're divided up in little bits and pieces in all of the other characters . . . in Traceleen obliquely, in Nora, in Rhoda, but this is most clearly the character that represents the new you. Anna's gone, Louise is running the show, she ran the whole book, even though it wasn't about her, in *A Dangerous Age*. So she's the new . . . [*has a small revelation*] and of course your middle name is Louise.

Gilchrist: Of course, so she's like Russell Scott. [*Scott and Ellen laugh.*] The you who isn't you?

[*Russell Scott is the pseudonym Scott wrote* Time Donors Wanted *under; Ellen had asked him why earlier at brunch, and he'd answered, "Well, I just took my first and middle name and stopped there." and Ellen had answered, "Of course you did. That's what I would have done too."*]

Lampton: Well, now I've lost my train of thought. [*Scott and Ellen laugh more.*]

Anderson: Okay, I'll shut up over here.

Lampton: No, actually I was going to expand on something you'd said. When you were writing, when you were fifty, and now at the age you are now.

Gilchrist: I was writing two books a year when I was fifty.

Lampton: The issues that concerned you when you were fifty, are they the same issues that concern you now? Or does a writer's vision change, as they get older?

Gilchrist: That's a hard question to answer. It's not that the ego shrinks . . . but the perspectives change. I don't have to keep the earth from ending in cold or fire, but I want there to be a world for my children and grandchildren to inhabit. I care what happens to the world.

Anderson: OK, so I'm going to go way off, speaking of the world, in a modern world that's so homogenized, can there still be regionally identifiable writers. Can there still be a "Southern" writer? I don't think that there can be any regionality. I'm afraid that you're the last Southern writer.

Gilchrist: This book . . . the book I'm writing now, is so politically incorrect. You can't be funny without it.

Anderson: We were talking about *Red* the other day [the stage play *Red* by John Logan]. I said that when I read that, that, that play. I think I just set a world record for using the word "that" in a sentence. Anyway, I saw you and Willie Morris, and Barry Hannah . . .

Gilchrist: Barry Hannah was a medical miracle that just refused to die.

Lampton: That's true, how did he not kill himself when he was younger . . .

Anderson: I knew him when he was at Alabama and he was stealing motorcycles and shooting arrows through people's front windows and all that stuff. And he was one of the professors in the English Department. I was one of the students there. Luke, you remember *The Ghost*, that piece I wrote about having a conversation with his ghost. Right after he died?

Gilchrist: I do believe he saw Jesus. I believe they had the exact conversation Barry says they did. It was during one of those times that we in the world thought he was going to die. Dean Faulkner Wells [writer, and niece of William Faulkner] was calling me up every afternoon. When he was really at the point of death, Jesus came to him and stood by the foot of his hospital bed. They were alone in the room. Barry looked at him and says, "Hello, sir, I haven't paid enough attention to you, have I?" And Jesus said, "Barry, there's still time."

Lampton: You were close to Barry?

Gilchrist: Yes, he liked me and I liked him. We didn't have to pretend we liked each other. We liked each other. He didn't like a lot of people, especially as he got older.

Lampton: And you and Willie Morris were very close?

Gilchrist: [*Raises both hands and crosses her fingers.*] We were like this. We were simpatico.

Lampton: When we were driving down, Scott said that sense of place is such a big thing in your writing. Not that you're a cheerleader for the South but that it forms such a part of your characters. Barry was the same way. As bizarre and unregional as some of his characters are they are all formed from the Southern clay. And we really do feel that you may be the last truly Southern writer.

Gilchrist: I would almost say I did it just to flaunt it. To flaunt it in the face of the people who tell lies and deliberately misrepresent the relationships we have in the South. The Alabama half of my family, the Gilchrists, were slaveholders, but my grandfather on my mother's side served in the Union army. They came down the river on flatboats and built a town, then they built the plantations all with the help of free Creoles, people of color from Natchez. There weren't any racists on Hopedale Plantation. The overseer was a Black man.

Lampton: There was a large population of free African Americans living in Natchez even before the Civil War. The South and Richard Ford, he doesn't consider himself a Southern writer. The generation after you has lost those kinds of ties to their past; they've lost a true regional flavor. Whether that was bad or good, or it was destined to be, I don't know, with a McDonald's in every town and television.

Gilchrist: They've all had television their whole lives. My students don't all come from the South. They come to the University of Arkansas, but a lot come from other places. When you give them something worth reading, good literature, they just soak it up. We were reading *Out of Africa* last semester and they couldn't put it down.

Lampton: What do you see in this new generation of writers, these young people who are coming to you to learn to write, what do you see in them?

Gilchrist: Most of them are single, most of them have no children, and they don't have any plans to have any children. Occasionally there will be one little baby, one little boy or girl. They are very kind to one another. I try to get them to read other things. Things outside of "great literature." I make them read geography and geology. For any given class I can't make a reading list until I see the whites of their eyes: you have to personalize it. I need to see who's there.

Anderson: [*Pulling* Red *out of his briefcase*] Let me just read this to you . . . [*reading in character*]:

ROTHKO: Hmmm, Pollock . . . always Pollock. Don't get me wrong, he was a great painter, we came up together. I knew him very well.

KEN: What was he like?

ROTHKO: You ever read Nietzsche? *The Birth of Tragedy*?

KEN: No.

ROTHKO: You call yourself an artist? One can't discuss Pollack without it. One can't discuss anything without it. What do they teach you in art school now?

KEN: I—

ROTHKO: You ever read Freud?

KEN: No.

ROTHKO: Jung?

KEN: No.

ROTHKO: Byron? Wordsworth? Aeschylus? Turgenev? Sophocles? Schopen-
hauer? Shakespeare? *Hamlet*? At least *Hamlet*, please God! Quote me
Hamlet. Right now!"

[*All laugh*]

Gilchrist: I could so do that, couldn't you? Play the role of Rothko. We
wouldn't even have to study. It's such a wonderful script.

Anderson: Alfred Molina is playing him in the New York production.
I've only seen video bits, but he does a wonderful job.

Lampton: So many writers find the academic environment to be anath-
ema. Willie did it for a while. Shelby Foote once told me he would wither
and die as a writer if he ever set foot in an academic environment, too many
distractions. Yet you've thrived.

Gilchrist: I'm only up there about eight hours a week and I'm not there
in any sense other than those eight hours. Sometimes I have a student I take
an interest in and want to get to know better, like my Bulgarian student
Miro Penkov. He was in medical school, for goodness sake, and now he's
given it up to become a writer. I said to him, "What are your parents going
to say to me? Here you were going to be a doctor and now you've given that
up to be a writer?" And he said to me, "Don't worry, they are very excited."
His first book is coming out by Farrar, Straus, and Giroux. I begged him not
to leave medical school, but he is such a talented writer.

Lampton: So when you're not teaching class you live in a glass house?
This is a special house. Tell us about your house.

Gilchrist: He was one of Frank Lloyd Wright's most talented acolytes.
His name was E. Fay Jones. He won the Gold Medal of the American Institute of Architecture.

Lampton: How old is this house?

Gilchrist: It's sixty years old. Roy Reed, he was an editor for the *New
York Times*, but he was an Arkansan and when he retired from the *Times* he
came back to teach in the journalism school in Fayetteville and E. Fay built
him a house; that's how I came to know E. Fay. So when one came up for
sale, one that had been completely torn up, well, I bought it. His ability to
site a house is just incredible. Mine has all east and west facing walls that are
all glass. The interior is made all out of California redwood.

Lampton: So you knew the architect?

Gilchrist: Oh yes, he was so much fun to hang around. I love geniuses. That's why I'm going to hang around with you two.

Lampton: Everyone has demons in their lives. What demons have you had to face to get here?

Gilchrist: No demons really. The only demon I ever faced was alcohol.

Lampton: Well, that may be what I'm talking about.

Gilchrist: Well I'd probably still be drinking if I didn't stop living in New Orleans. I drank way too much for about a year and a half. I ended up falling down a flight of stairs and having a concussion. So I had to go see a shrink, because of the concussion, to get permission to go live on a sailboat. I wanted to go and live on a sailboat off the British Virgin Islands. He said I could go, but only if I'd wear a football helmet.

Anderson: [*Laughs loudly*] I can just see you laying in the sun with a football helmet on your head.

Gilchrist: I took it with me and wore it for about an hour. Anyway, what's more important is that he was a child psychiatrist. He's still practicing. He was a Freudian. When I got back, I saw him four times a week for two or three years. A behaviorist had shown me how to quit drinking. During that whole time I wrote poetry all the time and later, as I began to be like, creepy famous, I saw this famous psychiatrist, Gunther Perdigao, he was half-German and half-Brazilian.

Lampton: So you got a lot of benefit from the psychiatry sessions?

Gilchrist: Well, yes, it opened up my subconscious.

Anderson: Were you writing poetry before the sessions began?

Gilchrist: Yes, of course, but I doubt if I was writing as well . . . maybe . . . or, yes I was . . .

Anderson: Poetry is so analytical, I wondered if what you'd gotten from writing poetry didn't open you to that? Or at least influence the outcome.

Gilchrist: I called him the crying teacher. Because all I'd do is weep. Weep for my teenage self, my childhood self, they were just the miseries that everyone goes through. My mother and father had been wonderful. It was unconditional love from both my mother and my father. I was the only female in the family; everyone else were boys.

It was difficult for me to move to so many schools as a child. It was during World War II. My father was building airstrips for the military, so I thought that everything we were doing was important to the war effort, and I was proud to do it. But it was still hard. It started to bother me when I was thirteen. I was a cheerleader and I had just written a school play that the seniors were going to put on, and here we had to move again. And lose my best friends.

Lampton: It's hard enough surviving adolescence without picking up and moving around everywhere. Do you think the psychotherapy helped you as a writer?

Gilchrist: Oh yeah, that's why when I left New Orleans and went to Fayetteville I went out and found the best thing that I could find to replace Gunther. He was a Jungian, but he had gone to Tulane, had trained in all the same places Gunther had trained. He was in the process of becoming a Zen Buddhist, his name was Ed White, he did become one while I watched. But it was very different though. He talked back. He entered in conversation with me. Gunther was a Freudian. He didn't talk. I spent four years on that couch four times a week just trying to find out what Gunther's middle name was. And all the time it was right there on the wall, on his diplomas. [*Laughter*]

Ed encouraged my writing. He was always introducing me to new writers, writers that I didn't know about. Gunther read too, when I first met him I had just finished reading *One Hundred Years of Solitude*, so I gave it to him when I went to live on the sailboat for a month. When I got back he'd read it in both English and Spanish. He said I was missing much of the humor not reading it in Spanish. People tell me that about my translation, that the humor is lost in them.

Lampton: You have been translated into a lot of languages.

Gilchrist: Lots of languages. My favorites were the Scandinavian languages. They would bring me over there.

Lampton: Would they understand the Southern meal of a mayonnaise sandwich and a Coca-Cola with a hole in the top?

Gilchrist: No, they'd call me up long distance and I have to explain it so they could translate it. Finally I would get to the point that I'd give them any answer because there was no way to really explain it.

Lampton: I wanted to get to your relationship with Eudora Welty, who takes on a fairy-tale aspect, at least the way it is talked about in Jackson. There was a relationship with her?

Gilchrist: The connection was more with her work than with her. To write the play I had to type huge portions of her work, *The Wide Net* especially. We didn't have copy machines. I had to retype almost all of the short stories in the book.

Lampton: How did that come about?

Gilchrist: We were trying to turn it into a screenplay.

Lampton: That was *Seasons of Dreams*. I think they still produce that play.

Gilchrist: Yeah, they do. Jane [*Jane Petty*, a staple at New Stage Theater] rewrote it recently, was busy at the time. I learned so much from that time. I call it, "casting my lot with the gypsies."

Lampton: So you and Patty Black met with Eudora to do a play based on her stories . . . to get her permission . . .

Gilchrist: No, Jane asked her, maybe Jane and Patty asked her. I didn't ask her. I was her student. I was writing short stories for class because she would ask me to. I didn't think I could write short stories, I was a poet. But I'd get the short stories back with notes all over them in Eudora's fluttery little hand, and I'd think, well, these are awful, she wrote things all over them. I still have one that I've kept. The rest I'd say, well these are no good, and throw them away.

Lampton: You were in Eudora's class, the only year she taught writing. What was that like? What was Eudora like as a writing teacher at Millsaps?

Gilchrist: That's where I met Jane, in Eudora's class. Eudora didn't presume to teach. She was a writer, not a teacher. She used a textbook she'd gotten at Wisconsin and she had us read the book. It was a wonderful book of short fiction.

Lampton: She was having to write then. Her mother was ill?

Gilchrist: She was trying to write *Losing Battles*. Her father and brother had died and her mother was in a nursing home way outside of town. It was a very hard time for her. She would leave the Millsaps library on those dark winter nights and travel out there. She'd get in her car and drive out there alone and sit with her mother until eleven or twelve o'clock at night, until they'd kick her out of the nursing home. It was a desperate, long, hard time for her. She loved us. She would tell us later, "You all meant so much to me." And of course we all worshipped her.

Lampton: You met in the Millsaps library?

Gilchrist: Yes we met at the library in a beautiful little room upstairs. There were about twelve of us. The next year Jane asked her if we could do a revue of her stories. I didn't know how to write a screenplay. I'd seen plays, but I had no idea how to write one.

Lampton: So you came down here to the coast to write it?

Gilchrist: It was near here. We stayed at Jane's aunt's house. We stayed for two weeks and wrote the thing. I did most of it.

Lampton: The production came out; it was well received?

Gilchrist: Yes, who was that wonderful critic that came from down in the Delta, at Greenville. He was a friend of Faulkner's?

Lampton: Ben Wasson?

Gilchrist: Yes, it was. He said I looked like a dream. I had on a pink dress that momma had bought me. It flowed all around. It was pink chiffon.

Lampton: Now where was this? At the premiere? [*Ellen nods*] Where was the premiere? It was in Jackson right?

Gilchrist: We ran it for about two and a half weeks, and then the Public Broadcasting Company came over and asked if it could be the first color production that they produced there in Jackson. To write it, we had to get the books from the library. That's what we brought down here to the coast with us to transcribe. It was hard to find her books. The only place we could get them was the library. And every word in the play was Eudora's, but she would call it Ellen and Jane's play. She gave us little pewter cups to commemorate it. I still have mine on my desk, full of pencils. Every word of it was hers. I just lifted the stories right up off the page. I didn't have to do anything to them, except keep Frank from cutting them.

Lampton: There is a story about you running into Eudora at Millsaps with your children.

Gilchrist: I was walking across campus with my three boys, these wonderful, beautiful, sturdy little boys, little redheaded boys. We were on the Millsaps campus, in sight of the library. She'd never seen my children. She didn't know I even had children. I wrote about it in *The Writing Life.* [*Retrieves a copy of the book from the bookshelf and reads.*]

"Oh, my," Eudora said. "Are they yours? Do they belong to you?"

"They're mine," I said. "Aren't they funny."

"Why would you ever need anything else?" she said. "Why would you need to be a writer?"

[*She sets the book down.*]

Then later, when my first grandchild was being born, it was at the same time that my first book of fiction was being published, and I told her I wasn't sure which thing I was more excited about, and she said, "Oh Ellen, they aren't in competition."

Lampton: She was a beautiful and gracious friend. She really was.

Gilchrist: She certainly was. She was exactly my mother's age.

Lampton: You sent Scott a letter and it was all taped up.

Gilchrist: I had edited that.

Lampton: . . . and I remember Eudora once told me that after she typed her manuscript she started what she called "cut and paste" with a pair of scissors.

Gilchrist: Yes . . . yes . . . I still cut and paste.

Lampton: Then she would start with blank sheets of paper, and tape, and glue, and paste, and a typical copy of her manuscript would look exactly like the letter you sent Scott. You still do that; you still do cut and paste.

Gilchrist: I just did it this morning.

Lampton: What is your mode of writing now?

Gilchrist: I type . . . on a typewriter.

Lampton: Can you even find a typewriter? Can you find one to buy?

Gilchrist: I have seven of them. My grandson Marshall found them for me, on the Internet. I have three or four in Fayetteville, plus two of another kind, not the one I like best.

Lampton: Are they electric typewriters?

Gilchrist: Well yes, yes, they're electric. They're IBM Wheelwriters. You have to have tape, a ribbon of tape. I've been hoarding tapes for so long that all of the eraser tapes have gone bad, but that's okay. I've tried writing on a computer but it annoys me so much. [*To Scott*] Can you write on a computer?

Anderson: Yes, when we were writing screenplays I was part of a writing team and one of them was my son, he was an IT in the Navy. The other was Kevin Ivey, who'd won an Emmy for technical engineering. I didn't have a choice.

Gilchrist: So they made you do it.

Anderson: I wrote *Time Donors* on a yellow pad with a pencil, and then I paid a secretary to transcribe it. We ended up going to dictation. She could understand my mumbling better than she could read my writing. My son forced me to learn to work quickly and effectively when we were collaborating.

Gilchrist: I beg my students to have children.

Lampton: Women are in a difficult period right now. . . .

Gilchrist: It's the boys, too. Young men don't want to have babies. The men in my family all want to have babies. I have the Pope to thank for half of my grandchildren. My sons married lapsed Catholics, but they never really lapse for long. Not when it comes to having babies.

Lampton: Is a woman's perspective in writing different than a man's? Do you see a difference when it comes to writing? You for one have a keen feminine instinct in your writing.

Gilchrist: I like women a lot more than I used to. I spent half of my childhood trying to kiss my elbow. I didn't want the boys to call me Shorty.

Lampton: What other writers have influenced you, I mean on a broad scale, from Chekov to Mark Twain? You mentioned Rilke earlier.

Gilchrist: Not Rilke, not when I was young. It's just that this latest translation is so beautiful, but all of the poets. God forbid, Edna St. Vincent

Millay. Of course her only influence was Shakespeare. We studied Shake-speare at Vanderbilt. Your first trimester there you read Shakespeare. That's all you do. I think I was the only person that really read it. I would have a class at night at the Kappa Sig house where I would teach them the plays we were reading. They couldn't read it; well, they wouldn't read it.

Anderson: I read about your Shakespeare group years ago. That every Sunday you and your friends get together and read plays out loud. I thought it was funny when I read that. For years, driving around the country, before we had children, Charlene and I would take turns. One of us would drive and the other would perform Shakespeare. We had *The Complete Globe Shakespeare* or something like that, this huge volume in the car with us, and that's how we would drive around the country. Coming back from San Diego when we lived there, driving down to New Orleans or up to Virginia. And it was fun. It was great fun.

Gilchrist: Good, good, good.

Lampton: There is a new edition of Audio Shakespeare and it is a book of Shakespeare but it has a CD in it. And on the CD there are famous actors giving their renditions from the various old, old plays. Sir Laurence Oliver, for example.

Gilchrist: I have to find one of those.

Lampton: But Shakespeare has influenced you critically is what all this gets down to.

Gilchrist: Yes, of course, yes, along with all the Irish poets, the great poets, Dylan Thomas. "Poem in October," which I read out loud to myself every year on my birthday [*quoting from memory*]: "It was my thirtieth year to heaven / Woke to my hearing from harbor and neighbor wood." I wish I still had my books down here. I lost them all in Katrina. Marshall has some of them, but I really need to go to the bookstore. I mostly fly down here now.

Lampton: In the mideighties, right after you won the American Book Award, you were featured on National Public Radio, and that started a new phase of your life.

Gilchrist: I was their first commentator.

Lampton: Tell me about that.

Gilchrist: It was the night of the award and I was there with my pub-lisher, my editor, and my agent. Tom Royals from Jackson had flown up and all we wanted to do was go out and celebrate. I wouldn't have gone to the awards ceremony if it weren't for Tom. Tom was on the phone with my agent all afternoon on the day of the awards ceremony. I didn't mind going to the event if I knew I had won but I wasn't going to sit there and act like

I didn't care if I lost. Either I had won the award or I hadn't. It was such a stupid process.

Tom finally talked me into going on the basis of Little, Brown having paid thousands of dollars for their table at the party afterwards. Plus, my editor told me that the "elves" around town all said I had won.

I had bought a beautiful dark red velvet suit, and I had a woman from Saks Fifth Avenue coming over "to do my makeup," so I got in a better mood. Tom put on his tuxedo and the woman from Saks put a lot of junk on my eyes that I washed off as soon as she left, and then Tom and I went to join my editor and my agent and the wonderful president of Little, Brown, who had come down from Boston because they all believed I had won. And I did, so it turned out well.

After the award, many people were interviewing me for radio and television. The nicest one was a young man named Jay Kernis, who was producing the new public radio show, *Morning Edition*. We had been doing everything we could in Fayetteville to get an NPR station. So, I was being especially nice to that reporter and talked to him for a long time. They put large segments of the interview on *Morning Edition*. Bob Edwards called me up the next day and said, "We love your voice. We want to put you on *Morning Edition*." I said, "Doing what?"

"Anything you want to do?" he said. We were laughing by then. So I told him I would make a diary or journal and answer the questions people were always writing to ask me, which mostly meant, "Who are you?" and "How do you get to write these books?"

Bob said, "Well, at least twice a week. We want your voice." So we made up the idea of the commentaries. It was a lot of fun at first and I only talked to Bob Edwards or to Jay Kernis, who really was a funny, brilliant young radio genius.

Many of the pieces I put on the air were based on the things the Mississippi writer, Jim Whitehead, said to me. We talked nearly every day. The pieces quoting Jim were the funniest ones. A man in Washington almost drove his car off the road listening to me one morning when I quoted Jim on the idea of diets: "The thing I can't believe, the thing I can't fathom is that a grown man would take off his underpants to weigh himself." [*All laugh*]

Lampton: But they will.

Gilchrist: Then my editor called me up and said, "What is all this fooling around about? Now you need to get back to work writing." I said, "Oh, Roger, come on, I'm having fun." And then a funny thing happened. My book sales skyrocketed, all my book sales, even my books of poetry. And so he backed off and thought it was a good idea.

Lampton: Was it very good money?

Gilchrist: A hundred dollars a week.

Lampton: And you did it for a couple of years, right?

Gilchrist: For a year and a half. All I did was write the pieces, go tape them at an NPR station, and Bob Edwards would put them on the air exactly as I wrote them.

Then it grew, and young women fresh out of Vassar would call me up with their politically correct ideas and say, "Are you sure you want to say that?" For a hundred dollars a week I was going to talk to these brainwashed children?

So I lost interest and started making fewer entries. Finally, we called it quits. The fun was over. But it was fun at first. I reviewed Abraham Pais's biography of his good friend Albert Einstein, and Pais called me to thank me and became my good friend. He would take me to Indian restaurants when I was in New York, and we would talk for hours about how to save the state of Israel. There were many nice things that happened because of *Morning Edition*. I just couldn't put up with being edited. Like everything in media, after it begins making money, the language police come in and ruin the fun.

Lampton: Well, it made a wonderful book, *Falling Through Space*. There is some wonderful stuff in that. That's why I say you are a woman of letters: the poetry, the fiction, and such wonderful essays.

Gilchrist: You know I answered all of the fan letters from that program. Hundreds of them, real letters, not just thank you for writing. . . . I had this long exchange with a ballet dancer when I wrote, "There should be no rules in dance." I was quoting Walter Anderson, the painter.

Anderson: I think Matisse would have agreed with that.

Lampton: Well, we've covered a lot of ground. Thank you for your gracious hospitality. I guess we'll let you get back to your day.

Gilchrist: To get ready for Christmas and the grandchildren.

Notes

1. From William Shakespeare's *The Tempest* 4.1.148–58.

2. Twenty children and six adults were killed in a mass shooting at Sandy Hook Elementary School in Newtown, Connecticut on December 14, 2012.

3. Jane Reid-Petty was a director, playwright, and founder of New Stage Theater in Jackson.

Telling True Stories:
An Interview with Ellen Gilchrist

Erin Z. Bass / 2017

From *Deep South Magazine* (September 2017), 1–5. Reprinted by permission.

Upon the publication of *Mojo Rising,* which includes a never before published story by Ellen Gilchrist, this pillar of Southern literature talks about the strange and miraculous true stories that have inspired her fiction.

On Saturday at Faulkner's home of Rowan Oak, Sartoris Literary Group released *Mojo Rising, Volumes 1 and 2.* Featuring the short stories of the South's greatest writers and stories from twelve of the region's more recent trendsetters, *Mojo Rising* is groundbreaking for its ability to gather so many of the South's top writers in one place.

Joining William Faulkner, Eudora Welty, Tennessee Williams, Richard Wright, and Willie Morris in volume one is Ellen Gilchrist—one of only two living writers (in addition to Elizabeth Spencer) in the collection. Her previously unpublished "A Christmas Story" is told in her signature style, blending humor and family life with the gritty details of childbirth.

Born in Vicksburg, Mississippi, Gilchrist has taught writing at the University of Arkansas in Fayetteville for many years. She ran away to get married at an early age but later went back to college and took a fiction writing class with Eudora Welty. She splits her time between work in Arkansas and summering on the Mississippi coast in Ocean Springs. She has written novels like *Sarah Conley,* but is best known for her short fiction and characters, like Rhoda, that reappear over and over. Her latest story collection is 2014's *Acts of God,* but she also published *Things Like the Truth: Out of My Later Years,* a collection of nonfiction essays about life, family, home, work and aging, in 2016.

We talked to her by phone in Arkansas earlier this month about watching babies being born, how she became a fiction writer rather than a poet, what she learned from Eudora Welty, and the story she's writing next. It was a delight to talk to Gilchrist about both her work and personal life, and it's obvious that she's succeeded at both being a matriarch of her family and a career woman. We're thrilled to hear that she's still writing and are convinced that she still has plenty to say.

Erin Z. Bass: Why was this the right time to publish your *Mojo Rising* story "A Christmas Story," and when was that story originally written?

Ellen Gilchrist: That surprised me when I saw that it hadn't been published before. I've written about five or six really wonderful Christmas stories. I like that time of year, and I have sixteen grandchildren and four great-grandchildren. I had a wonderful, wonderful mother and father and a wonderful, wonderful family life, and most of my childhood Christmases were during the Second World War, when there wasn't much stuff in the US and we made Christmas trees and we strung popcorn on them. I had a wonderful early life of sort of handmade Christmases.

That's a recent story, the last three or four years, because I never saw a child born. All these children, I had Cesarean sections. I would never even look at a movie of someone being in labor. I would turn the television off and run from the room. All I ever did was lie down, get a shot that made you think you were God, and watch while someone cut open my stomach and took babies out. I thought that God had been so good to me never to make me do that [labor], but if they're a strong, healthy woman and like my granddaughter . . . my oldest granddaughter owns and runs a yoga studio and it was hard work, but Ellen never looked like she was in pain. The very short, who was my size, woman doctor who was in charge of it pulled me over to stand with her behind where the baby was going to come out.

It's such a beautiful experience. Have you ever held a placenta in your hand? I thought that it was absolutely the softest and most beautiful thing I had ever touched in my life. And because of that I know why babies love satin. I did not want to let go of it. I must have held it for five minutes. I just was so knocked out by that birth, and I probably wrote that Christmas story because of watching Ellen have that baby.

EZB: I read another short story of yours, "Love of My Life," and it's a Rhoda story. In that one, she says "They had tried to kill me with the babies." Would you say your view of childbirth and having babies has changed over the years?

EG: I would imagine Rhoda meant that to be funny. I just thought having Cesarean sections was the coolest thing in the whole world. I have a family with a lot of doctors in it. All the doctors I ever had all my life were my uncles or great uncles and since then it's been my grandson. If I have an X-ray made anywhere, it has to go to Marshall. I love them and I appreciate what they go through to become physicians.

EZB: Let's go back a bit further. I read in a *Clarion-Ledger* interview that you learned to write poetry working for a newspaper in Kentucky?

EG: I'd been writing poetry ever since before I could actually write. My dream was to be a poet, to get to the point where I could call myself a poet, and then later in my twenties or thirties I would have told you that what I wanted to do was to write one poem that was so good it would be in the canon for a hundred years. I never intended to be a fiction writer, and then a man named Bill Harrison begged me. He was having dinner with me and he said, "Ellen, please write something about what it's like to live with those snotty rich people in New Orleans."

I've always thought it was so incredible that except for that poor town that got flooded a couple of days ago, Charleston—that doesn't mean that I don't love New Orleans and all the many different parts of New Orleans—but that uptown society thing is really hard to take. It's like living in the eighteenth century or something and those people take it seriously. Because of that I wrote a story for Bill. He happened to be the main fiction writer at the University of Arkansas. He'd just written a story called "Roller Ball Murder" that was made into a movie [*Rollerball*]. I wrote him this story called "Rich." It was only about six pages long and he loved it. He said, "My God, please, please finish this story and I want it to have a really killer ending." And I did it. It was just a second draft and so instead of being a would-be [poet]— I mean I've published a lot of poetry everywhere and I was doing what I wanted to do—but it was so easy to write that short story and I got so much praise for it. . . . And then agents were calling me and then I wrote a book of stories in about three or four months and I let the university press publish it and then I got famous and started getting money and stuff.

Writing fiction's so easy for me to do and writing poetry was easy, but writing great poetry is agonizing, hard, hard work. Randall Jarrell, a California poet, once said, "A poem is never finished if it's only abandoned in despair." It really is hard to finish them.

EZB: Do you still write poetry?

EG: No, I don't and for a long time I did still write poetry, but I haven't done it in a long time.

EZB: What do you remember about the class that you took with Eudora Welty?

EG: I took a fiction class with her. Her father and her brother had recently died and her mother was dying in a nursing home, and Eudora spent every afternoon from 5:00 or 6:00 until pitch black dark when they'd kick her out sitting by her mother's side in a nursing home. She'd never married and she had no children. Her friends at Millsaps, to try to cheer her up—it's not that Eudora was depressed, but that would knock out anybody—they talked her into teaching a class for one year, one day a week, and I read about it in the newspaper. I went out to the library and took out all of Eudora's books and read them in one or two nights. I thought, *my God, I want to be in that class,* so I drove out to Millsaps College and walked into the head of the English Department's office and handed him all the newspaper articles that I'd written, and I said I really want to be in this class, and the class was full but he let me in. I had never finished college at Vanderbilt because I ran away and got married and had children, so I signed up for all the poetry classes I could find at the same time and I ended up getting my degree there.

I wrote short stories for Eudora. I wrote her about one a week, and she would edit them and put these beautiful little pencil marks on them, very gentle, very light little pencil marks and I'd get it back and I'd say, "Well, that must not be any good," and I'd throw it away. I'd never heard about rewriting. There was one that she thought was publishable, and I think I published it somewhere. The myths that go around about writers are not really the true stories. I'm telling you some true stories. I had a wonderful time knowing Eudora. She was my mother's age and they had friends in common and she was just a lovely, lovely lady.

EZB: What classes are you currently teaching now [at the University of Arkansas in Fayetteville]?

EG: I had to be gone for a semester, so when I came back I didn't know any of the students, and so last semester I only taught one class, and that was just wonderful. You know, "money for nothing and the chicks were free," but to make up for it I'm teaching two, fifteen-person undergraduate classes. I'm teaching a graduate class with eight or nine of my favorite graduate students, and it's called "Craft of Fiction," but I don't think there is such a thing.

I think the way to write fiction is to write it all the time. Every Wednesday, Thursday, and Friday afternoon I'm up at the university for three hours teaching writing, which is kind of like walking down a treelined street to teach something you know. Also, at the moment, I'm finishing a novella in six stories that works like one long novel. This is just a first draft, but my typist loves it and my agent loves it and so I'm having fun doing it.

EZB: Did you spend part of the summer in Mississippi?

EG: I spent from the first of May, the last day I had a class, until the nineteenth of August down on the coast living in my condo with my oldest granddaughter [Ellen] and her two-year-old child. I watched her learn to talk, and she has all kinds of little things she says that I say all the time, but I didn't know that I said them. She tells people all the time, "There you go." I would say that to her when she did something right.

EZB: Let me ask you about *Acts of God*, because it has a theme of disaster and disaster relief, and so with our two recent hurricanes, why was that a theme that you wanted to explore?

EG: I didn't. I just started doing it, because I wrote that story about the boy that finds the baby. I don't read newspapers very often. I want to exercise an hour and a half every morning and I want to write, so that doesn't leave a lot of time for daily news. I read in the newspaper, maybe I was in New Orleans. I always pick up *The Times-Picayune* when I'm in New Orleans and I'm there a lot. It was just about a four-line story about a young man in Nebraska or one of the states near Arkansas where they have a lot of tornadoes who had found a baby while out with a group. There were no details, just a statement that he had found the child, and I have three sons and eight grandsons. I know what boys that age are like. To imagine a twelve-year-old boy or a thirteen-year-old boy finding a baby. I kept imagining him figuring out how to bend over and pick up that baby and hold it. A girl would just literally know how to do it, so I brought his girlfriend in to take it away from him, but sort of like holding a placenta for the first time in your life, it's strange and miraculous. He'll never forget that moment as long as he lives, and I could never forget it and all of a sudden I wanted to write it as a short story. I had so much fun writing that story. That may have been the first one that was very definitely a theme. And then I started writing other hurricane memories and tornado memories. The amazing thing about what we've been through the last three weeks in the United States are the people, the heroes.

I know what happened . . . a girl in my class, she was a journalism major, had come to take a writing class with me. I think it was a nonfiction class. I love to teach nonfiction, because it's all really nonfiction in the end. I really liked her. She was always on time, she'd always be there before the class started. She was an athlete, worked out every day and looked extremely strong and healthy, and when Hurricane Katrina [came], her National Guard group were called up and what they do is you go fly up in helicopters and send people down to get people off of roofs. That's why she was such an athlete and she got called down to Louisiana, and she called me late at night. She'd just gotten the call and had to leave in the morning and she said, "Ellen, I don't know when I'll be back to the class," and I said, "My God, forget about the class. While you're at it, that's material for a pretty good story and I'd better see it before this class is over." So I wanted to write that story because I'd gotten to know her well enough. I could just imagine her having the courage to go down on a chain from a plane and pick up someone from a roof, maybe even a man, someone even larger than she was, and put a harness on them and take them back up to the helicopter. I don't know if I'd have the courage to do that. I hope I would.

EZB: I also really enjoyed the title story "Acts of God" about the elderly couple that basically steals their own car.

EG: I know, they didn't mean to die. I love it. They went to the grocery store.

EZB: I was wondering about your thoughts on aging and if your kids tell you to do certain things and you ignore them or listen to them?

EG: They would never tell me to do anything that they wouldn't do themselves. And we agree on all of that. My sons would never put me in a position where I couldn't do exactly what I wanted to do. That was a story that my lawyer had told me. His grandparents, who were quite old in Texas, had had a bad wreck. They weren't supposed to be driving and they just got in the car one day and went for a ride. I love that. If you thought you could drive, wouldn't you just go get in the car and drive?

My father used to do that when he couldn't drive anymore in his eighties. He would get up at three or four in the morning and go out and get in his car and drive around the neighborhood very slowly. He had a diesel Mercedes. It had 400,000 miles on it. He was a Caterpillar tractor dealer so he could keep the thing fixed. He'd just go drive his great big diesel Mercedes very slowly around the neighborhood because he liked to drive. And he'd have a loaded gun on the passenger seat in a holster with the safety on. He didn't break laws. That little quiet neighborhood. He'd just cruise around a bit.

EZB: Is there a theme to the novella you're working on?

EG: It's a murder mystery. Not really. It's about a woman police detective in a small town in Mississippi on the coast, Ocean Springs. She's a graduate of Princeton University, but what she always wanted to be was a policewoman and she is one and she's good and she's the top detective, except for her partner who she finally marries. They start a war on drugs.

In Conversation with Ellen Gilchrist

Holly Lange / 2022

From the 2022 Mississippi Book Festival in Jackson, Mississippi. Printed by permission. Transcript by Tracy Carr.

Holly Lange: Good morning, everyone. Thank you all for being here in a very surreal experience. This is my first time to be an official panelist, and I got an email like everyone else who participates that says, "Congratulations, thank you for agreeing to participate as a panelist. Here's the schedule," and I looked at it and thought, "We're going up against Jericho Brown?" And I finally discovered how it felt to be on the other end of that email. But it is an honor to be here. I'm glad that I kind of pulled a card and they said, "What would you like to do?" And I said, "I would really like to interview Ellen Gilchrist," and they said, "Well, would you call her and ask her?" and I said yes, and she said yes. So without further ado, we will begin. Ellen was born—so I'm going to do the perfunctory thing and then we're gonna get right to it. But I kind of have to do this because we're recording it for all of eternity and we want to act right to begin with.

Ellen Gilchrist: I like hearing it. I like to be reminded. I've lived a long time and like to be reminded!

Lange: Before I reveal her age to you, I will just share that she was born in Vicksburg and by her own account, grew up with a wonderfully loving family, and her brother Bob is here, who we love, and Julie, and their daughter Whitney. And I think someone else is coming, too. So family is key to Ellen. Ellen earned her BA from Millsaps College, and I think Rob and Phoebe Pearigen are here representing Millsaps? I think so many of us are repping Millsaps today. All right, and she studied under Eudora Welty. She later did her postgraduate study at the University of Arkansas at Fayetteville. She has worked as an author and a journalist, as a contributing editor of the *Vieux Carre Courier* from 1976 to 1979, and as a commentator on National Public Radio's *Morning Edition* from 1984 to 1985. She was a professor of creative writing and contemporary fiction at the University of Arkansas and has since retired to Ocean Springs. She has three children, fourteen grandchildren, and I think it's updated: two great? How many greats?

Gilchrist: I have sixteen grandchildren and fourteen great-grandchildren. No, six great-grandchildren. I can't remember which is which.

Lange: It is my delight to welcome Ellen to the Book Festival today. I'm often asked who is my favorite author, and it's much like being asked who is my favorite child. When I was running the Festival, I dodged this question, but I have always known the answer. As a teenager, I had read Willa Cather and Flannery O'Connor and Katherine Anne Porter, and while I love their writing, their characters, and their role in literary history, it was Ellen's writing that grabbed a hold of me. I was mesmerized by her characters. And when I read *Victory over Japan*, I fell totally in love with Rhoda Manning. And then I read *In the Land of Dreamy Dreams* and I realized it's in reverse—it's not chronological, but that's how I read them. *In the Land of Dreamy Dreams*, which was published in 1981, sold more than 10,000 copies in its first ten months and won immense critical acclaim. *Victory over Japan*, a collection of short stories, won the National Book Award for Fiction in 1984. Gilchrist has won awards for her poetry, although it is her short fiction for which she is most well-known. And when I read *In the Land of Dreamy Dreams*, I went back thinking about this interview, and John Evans and I agree that this is our favorite quote from *In the Land of Dreamy Dreams*. And an apology to my mother, I'm going to say it in full: "When she had bought one of each of every single thing she could possibly imagine needing, she felt better and went on out to the Country Club to see if anyone she liked to fuck was hanging around the pool." And I read that line in Austin, Texas, in 1986—

Gilchrist: She cleaned it up.

Lange: I did clean it up just a smidge. I thought, "Ellen Gilchrist is all right." And I first met her in Austin in 1991. Do you remember this? You don't remember this, do you? *I Cannot Get You Close Enough* had just come out and we were visiting at the home of Cindy and Jack Keefer. Their daughter was one of our dearest friends, and you were dating someone named Hoyt?

Gilchrist: Purvis!

Lange: Whose daughter was rushing Tri Delt at the University of Texas, and they were having drinks together. And so we all got to hang out and my sister, who is here with us, ended up babysitting for the woman on the cover of *I Cannot Get You Close Enough* for a couple of years. We're all connected. Several decades later, and unaware of the connection, her niece Whitney Gilchrist started babysitting for me. When she told me she was Ellen's niece, my husband said that was the first time he had ever seen me truly speechless. And when we started the Book Festival, Jere Nash asked me what it would take to make the Festival successful, and I immediately replied, "We need Ellen Gilchrist and John Grisham in that order."

For me, Ellen is a feminist, a poet, and a philosopher, and now a friend. As Sabine Durrant commented in *The London Times*, her writing "swings between the familiar and the shocking, the everyday and the traumatic. . . . She writes about ordinary happenings in out of the way places, of meetings between recognizable characters from her other fiction and strangers, above all of domestic routine disrupted by violence." The world of her fiction is awry; the surprise ending, although characteristic of her works, can still shock the reader. "It is disorienting stuff," noted Durrant, "but controlled always by Gilchrist's wry tone and gentle insight." The quote I shared is a perfect example of Durrant's point. Simply, Ellen Gilchrist is a true Southern literary icon, and her work will endure for all time. Ladies and gentlemen, Ellen Gilchrist.

Gilchrist: Thank you all for coming out on this hot summer morning. I'm so glad to be back in Mississippi for good. Oh my gosh, you know, the makeup.

Lange: It is what it is. So Ellen, you had your first reading at Lemuria for *The Land Surveyor's Daughter* in 1978.

Gilchrist: I did, and Jane Petty and Patti Black. I was in Jane's living room getting dressed to go read from a little book of poems when Lemuria was new, and all of a sudden—and I've never been afraid of anything in my life—all of a sudden I laid down, lay down, however one does, behind a chair in Jane's living room, and I said, "I'm not going." And Patti somehow or other got me up. She said, "Johnny's[1] gone to all this trouble" and you know, and I said, "No, they'd already sold all the books anyway." Anyway, they had a hard time; it was a while before they could—they sold the 10,000 books that they printed and it was a while before they could get a second edition, much less the paperbacks. Finally, Patti and Jane—Jane just was contemptuous. You know, I'm with the people that started New Stage Theatre and somebody doesn't want to go read from a little book of poems to what we assumed would be ten people, but it was a lot of people. And I have loved Johnny ever since and I have loved Lemuria. He kind of has a wall of my books, oh my gosh.

Lange: He does, and in fact, you know, Ellen, what I have here?
Gilchrist: What?
Lange: It's your very first copy of *The Annunciation*. It's the first manuscript.
Gilchrist: No!

Lange: And I will tell you that John gave it to me last night and he said, "You're going to get Ellen to sign this," and I said I am, and he said, "Then I'm going to give it to you," and I burst into tears.

Gilchrist: My first novel, and I didn't know how to write a novel, but Little, Brown offered me—I mean, I signed a contract for a lot of money to write a novel and a book of short stories and they wanted the novel and I'm a poet. I had written and read nothing but poetry for most of my life. But Eudora's short stories, because they were about the place where I'd lived, maybe that's why you liked my stories. All of a sudden, here was real literature being written about the places that I love in the voice that I've been hearing on porches all my life. That's why I can read Faulkner just like some people can read the ABCs. That's the way I heard people talking all of my life. Saying those long sentences and they all have Latin and Greek in their backgrounds, were taught Latin and fourth, fifth, sixth, and seventh grade. Everybody was. I know when I have students and I want them to read Faulkner, I just have to go on and read about forty pages of it to them, and then finally, but they didn't hear that when they were children, so I can understand when they can't read it. I've forgotten what we were talking about.

Lange: Well, we're gonna talk about, let's talk about Jackson. So you're in Jackson, and what I want to know, and I think maybe most everybody wants to know, are all these characters based on people you really knew?

Gilchrist: I think that every single thing that a human being does is autobiographical.

Lange: That's true.

Gilchrist: My mother's rose garden, it looks just like her. You know, it did. She'd go out there in the morning in high-heeled shoes and pick the bugs off, distressed that a bug would eat the bud of her rose, of her Americana. But sure, everything you write is hopefully from real life. But with my family, the only complaints I've ever had is one time: my brother's wife, who had had two liver transplants, one from her father and then one from her mother. And when they went to Birmingham to the second liver transplant, they went two days early and they were the same size. So they shopped; they bought like fifty pairs of expensive shoes and I don't know what all, so whoever was left alive would have all these clothes. But I mean, what a story. But one day she told me in the summer, we were sitting out on a porch somewhere and she said, "Ellen, this is one thing I want to ask you." She said, "Why have you never written anything about me? I think I've had a real interesting life." And so I wrote a book for her called *The Blue-Eyed*

Buddhist. But I mean, it's a short story that's only been published in a couple of small books.

Lange: Do you have a favorite character?

Gilchrist: I love them all. I love Nora Jane. I love Rhoda because Rhoda is so autobiographical.

Lange: So, are you Rhoda?

Gilchrist: She's, I mean, I've given Rhoda a lot of adventures that I've never had. But the heart and soul. . . . You know, I really did get left out of a real high jump pit. I was not allowed to touch it. And that's from a story called "Revenge," I think.

Lange: [*To audience member*] That's your favorite?

Gilchrist: I don't know why, there was a certain time when I was beginning to write when a lot of reviewers would really make fun of people for using their real life as the basis for their writing. Oh, you know why? It's what you have! That's where the real heart and soul of it is, so I love biographies and autobiographies. I like it when they just go on and tell you . . .

Lange: Everything.

Gilchrist: That's why you like David Rae Morris's book about his daddy. But mostly it's Willie's letters. They are the letters that anyone would wish they were writing to their children. You know, Willie with all his incredible verbal skills would still, you know, remember that he's got to be a father and stick a line in there about, you know, morals or occupation or something, then he's back to being Willie and talking about the ball games. Or the great football player that he discovered. What was his name?

Lange: Marcus DuPree.

Gilchrist: Marcus DuPree. But what was his nickname? It was a great nickname for him, too.

Lange: I have no idea.

Gilchrist: He wrote me a lot of the letters about Marcus DuPree. And we used to write each other about the women's basketball teams and our respective universities.

Lange: Did you save all those letters?

Gilchrist: Yes. You know, I want David to go and collect all the letters that he wrote to all the rest of us. I mean, the only thing wrong with *Love, Daddy* is it's not long enough. When you finish it you think, "No, I want more."

Lange: That would be awesome to have a collection of letters that Willie Morris has written people.

Gilchrist: I'd be glad to put mine together for him.

Lange: So what is your plan for your papers? Do you have a plan for all your manuscripts and everything?

Gilchrist: I sold a lot of my papers, a lot of my things from when I began writing, when I was trying to learn how to write. When I was reading all the time. Anything about writing, especially Hemingway. Hemingway has a little book, it's very small, called *On Writing*. And anyone that wishes to be a writer should have that on his desk with the Bible. I mean, a lot of the best stuff are things that he wrote to Scott Fitzgerald. To cheer Scott Fitzgerald up and get him to continue to write, but they're really wonderful. Just about the mechanics of how you get it done. How you never write until you're dry. Always leave—when you leave the page, or the typewriter, or whatever y'all will be using, *computers*, God bless. I know they're wonderful. It's just that I can't adjust myself to the keyboard. So I gave mine away.

Lange: How did you write? Did you longhand, type?

Gilchrist: I wrote, I always wrote poetry longhand, but I'd have to type it up so I could publish it. So occasionally I would type poetry because I wanted to see it on the page. You know, but then I would just count syllables. But anyway, maybe I'll go back to writing poetry.

Lange: Well, are you writing? What are you writing these days?

Gilchrist: I haven't written a word since I cleaned out my office and left the University of Arkansas. They got mad at me and yelled at me for teaching *Go Down, Moses* by William Faulkner.

Lange: Tell them what you said when they fired you. Well, there's a story to it, with it. Do you want to tell the whole story? You argued with them, not surprisingly.

Gilchrist: Oh, I said, "How dare you." I marched down Capitol Street behind Martin Luther King with my brothers standing guard on either side because my father was afraid I'd get killed. I mean, you know, I helped start the breakfast program in schools. How dare you tell me that I'm a racist because I taught the writer who was the first person to ever write brilliantly and truthfully about African Americans as full and complete human beings. I mean, you know, the heroes of *Go Down, Moses* are people of mixed African American, Indian, magic, and English blood. They got mad at me and screamed at me. Or the head of the department did. We were just letting him be the head of the department because nobody that was any good wanted to do that. It was a little guy that had published two tiny books of poetry in his whole life. And then we had to have a meeting at the chancellor—not the chancellor but the head of the Humanities Department. What do they call it at a university here? Chair? And I called a lawyer. I called the meanest lawyer in Fayetteville, Arkansas, and I said, "You know, I'm not actually going to sue these people but I want them to be afraid and I want you to write to the chancellor," the head of the humanities or whatever, head of the Arts and Sciences. There's a word for that I've forgotten. *Dean.* Yeah, the dean of the Arts and Sciences, whom I knew and who was a friend of mine. And so the lawyer wrote him a letter and said I just wanted to inform you that I'm gonna accompany Ms. Gilchrist to the program, I mean, to the meeting that we're gonna have, so all right, all right, that'll do it. And all of a sudden everything in the English Department got very quiet. Everybody, all of those—there wasn't a single good writer left in and I had stayed on at age eighty-two working there in order to get someone who was a real writer to take my place before I left. Because I was the only person left who was teaching real literature.

And I would have classes—[*points to audience member*] an English teacher who's a good English teacher, she'll love this—I had classes of twenty and thirty undergraduates. I would teach graduate classes and [undergraduate] who had never read *The Old Man and the Sea*, and I would give it to them to read and they would just, you know, they didn't want to read it again. They don't want to read anything.

Lange: Did they find—

Gilchrist: So anyway, the head of the department wrote back to the lawyer and said, there's no need for you to do this. There's not going to be anything, that no one in my office is going to say anything rude to Ms.—*Doctor*—Gilchrist. I've got all these honorary doctorates. But I would never, never call myself a doctor. So finally the day came for the meeting. Now I was excited about it. By now all my friends know about it. Everybody in Fayetteville knew about it because I always tell everything to everybody.

And the lawyer said, "Do you want me to come and sit outside the office?" And I have forgotten now whether he actually did or not. And I walked in and I said hello to the dean, and I said, "I want you to know that I'm here for one reason only, because I was called a racist and a misogynist by the head of the creative writing program. And I'm going to defend myself about that and tell you what I did during the civil rights movement." And he said, "Ellen, you don't have to say a word." And he handed me a letter. He said there's nothing, and I said, "Oh, I want an apology. I want an apology from that man." And by then he was there. The people in the English department who loved me, a couple of them were there, too. The ones who had given me a professorship. I didn't even know it was something you should want. It was a $10,000 raise.

I could have asked for it any of the fifteen or twenty years I worked there, but it never occurred to me to want one. I mean, you know, I'm not a scholar. I don't even know what they're talking about when they talk scholarly English department stuff, but anyway, they handed me a letter offering me a year's salary. The same huge salary they were giving me and all of my extra things . . . you know, what do you call the things that they give you?

Lange: Benefits.

Gilchrist: And all the other benefits for a calendar year if I would give them back my professorship. And I pretended to think about it for a while. And I said, "Well, I guess I could go finish my novel, couldn't I?" And they said, yeah, and then we all had pleasant things to say, but I never got an apology. From this lapsed poet. But he was, you know, you have to live in the Deep South to understand what we all went through. African Americans and white people and Indians and everything that Faulkner understood and knew. And so actually, you know, in street talk, I got fired for teaching Faulkner. But I got enough money to live on, and within two or three months I had sold my house in Fayetteville and moved to my little condo down in Ocean Springs. And I was home. Oh my gosh, I should have done it years ago. I drove for about ten years when I was too old to do it. I drove back and forth between Fayetteville, Arkansas, and Ocean Springs, Mississippi, ten- and eleven-hour trips if you drive carefully . . . nine one time.

Lange: Downhill's one thing. Uphill's another.

Gilchrist: No, but I got to see it as the highways got better and better and better all the way down. You know, golly, getting from Fayetteville to the road that goes to the Mississippi border for two terrible, dangerous highways. That first hour was, you know, taking your life in your hands. And I did this at night, in the rain, but I had to be down here. Had to see the makeup.

Lange: The makeup. I think getting fired for Faulkner is an excellent end to your tenure at the University of Arkansas.

Gilchrist: It was really all a wonderful experience. I loved the part when I knew how terrified that Yankee poet was of my—he literally thought I was gonna sue him. Can you think of anything sillier?

Lange: So John tells me in *The Annunciation*—did you write that while you were in Jackson?

Gilchrist: No, I wrote that because I had signed a contract saying I would write a novel.

Lange: You had to.

Gilchrist: I had no idea. I mean, you know, I was a poet. Writing short stories was one thing. It's very close. And my poetic skills were what made me a good fiction writer right off the bat. Because, you know, the opening line of a short story and in a poem are the same things, and the paragraph is—it all just makes sense. And it taught me how to lift the ending of a story. The reason they're surprising is because that's what you gotta do, some really good writing. In fact, I need to go back to writing poetry because it made me a better writer. The further away I got from being a poet, the less I liked what I wrote. But I started there writing *The Annunciation* because I was very concerned at the time and all my friends and I were talking all the time about abortion versus adoption. And it wasn't so much about pro or con abortion; it was about whether a fifteen-year-old girl should be forced to have a baby and give her away. Because I had a friend that had that happen to her. And so that was the beginning of the story, and I set it down in Hopedale Plantation, which I named Esperanza. Well. That'll really, that'll hide it. And I started, you know, I would just write on it all the time, but I didn't know what was gonna happen in the novel all the way through it until I wrote it. And parts of it. And I would send drafts of it to my editor and he would actually—the only thing I've ever written that's actually been edited in the sense that somebody really edited. Mostly I won't let anyone touch it. But I was never satisfied with it, and I was shocked at how many people liked it.

Lange: Loved it.

Gilchrist: No, I was really shocked. Not by the reviews, which were quasi, not as good as, you know, wonderful, but not as good her short stories, not as good as her poetry, which I agreed with completely. But the readers liked that book and they still do. Because in the end, she gets her baby back. That's good. That's the way that it should end.

Lange: John Evans tells me you dated the singer-songwriter character in *The Annunciation*.

Gilchrist: That what?

Lange: That you dated the singer-songwriter in *The Annunciation*.

Gilchrist: Oh, yeah, my young man, yeah. My mother and father were so appalled about that. I brought him down to Jackson to meet them and they liked him. Very, very personable. And pretty, smart, and a great athlete. I mean, you know, they liked him, but "This won't do." And I said, yeah, but this *does*. This works.[2]

Lange: It is working!

Gilchrist: It is a great thing to do while you're going through menopause. You don't even notice you're going through menopause—think you're pregnant.

Lange: Well, you're not pregnant.

Gilchrist: No.

Lange: What did you write when you lived in Jackson?

Gilchrist: I don't know, but Whitney was telling me the other day about something I was writing, that she thought I was writing.

Lange: *The Cabal*?

Gilchrist: Two or three times I've tried to move home to Jackson because my parents were still alive—my wonderful, wonderful mother and my wonderful, wonderful father. I was a lucky—I consider myself one of the luckiest people in the world. And my brother over there who was the rotten, spoiled baby—knows it, too. I mean, we had, we had a glorious life. We had a daddy who taught us how—we rode horses and when we were in our fifties and sixties, he learned how to ski. He was seventy and taught us all how to ski. He taught me every game, but the worst—I have a brother who was—I have an older brother who's a genius, and learning card games with Dooley Gilchrist in the house was not a way to love cards. Fortunately, he did not play bridge, and so my mother taught me how to play bridge. I have forgotten how to play bridge. I wonder how many hours I spent doing that. They taught us everything. And they were strict. Daddy was a Presbyterian and Mother was an Episcopalian. And they went to their different churches, and you could go with them. You could go with either one. But mostly I'd go the Baptist Church with my best friend because that's where all the cute boys were.

Lange: Did you write anything while you were here? Or just . . .

Gilchrist: No, I moved here because my brother had just gotten custody of a beautiful, beautiful, beautiful daughter that he had and she was about twelve or thirteen and she was so talented that she—she still is—that she could play the piano by, you know, just by ear. She would just sit down at the piano, and I wanted her to take real piano lessons. You know, I would see concerts in New York, but mostly I just wanted to be near her. And Whitney was a baby, you know. This was before Whitney. Her name is Trina.

Lange: Did she make it? She was coming. She'll be here in a little while.

Gilchrist: I would have spells of wanting to be in Jackson because my family was here. I could just never make Jackson work for me. I'm better off in a real small town, Ocean Springs. I've had a house down there, a little condo down there since my oldest granddaughters were in the like, third and fourth grades and they needed to go to Donna's School of Dance in order to have a chance at being cheerleader. So, and their mother was working, so I bought a condo and moved down to Ocean Springs so I could drive them to Donna's School of Dance. I mean, you know, it's life or death in Ocean

Springs. I had more fun at Donna's School of Dance standing on a chair looking over the top of the window watching this brilliant woman teach down in Ocean Springs, Mississippi. We have a dance school that has won awards all over the United States and maybe in Europe. Oh, she's just amazing. I learned how to teach writing by watching Donna. She's like a German that used to crack your knuckles when just teaching. I mean, Donna. So, I don't know. All of those things will probably end by writing.

Lange: It ends up there. It all ends up there. What are you reading?

Gilchrist: Oh, I've just had, I have had the most wonderful time since I left Fayetteville and came home to live. I have been reading a great, big, thick book, sometimes one a day and I don't go to sleep till I finish it. Like, I read Winston Churchill's history of the Second World War,[3] and I literally would not be able to—I *lived* through the Second World War. I had an uncle flying the airplanes over Germany and later in the Pacific with the Flying Tigers. My family, you know, the paper came early in the morning and it was all, you know, I was *part* of the Second World War. I collected more scrap metal than anybody in the fourth grade. I know I did. Being out with my wagon, I really thought that the little things I did like paper drives and collecting scrap metal, I thought they were important, and they were. And anyway, Winston Churchill is such a good writer. I mean, it's like saying you've never read Faulkner if you've never read his history of the Second World War or his *History of the English Speaking Peoples.* If you start reading them, and you can probably buy these beautiful books at any secondhand bookstore for not much money. And go get the big hardbacks, because these books are too big in every sense to be read in paperback. But you won't get much sleep. I don't know why, and I keep saying to myself, "You know who won the war, you know! You know what happened on D-Day, it's 1:30! You don't have to read any further!"

Lange: You know how the story ends.

Gilchrist: Then I wake up at 4:00 in the morning and read a few more pages. I have to get to D-Day, at least. We may never, I hope, see those sorts of wars again. If we see the wars, they're gonna kill us all and everybody and everything, so we can't have any wars. So I read them. I read it all twice. *The History of the English Speaking Peoples* and the history of the Second World War in six volumes, that big, and including the last one, which my editor and my agent were the people that made sure that William Manchester's history of the Second World War. That is so strange that I'm reading for about three or four months things that I've lived through. I lived through the Second World War. I was about six years old, standing outside of the bank with my father when we heard about Pearl Harbor.

Lange: Where were you? Were you in St. Louis?

Gilchrist: No. We were in some small town where my father was, my father was building levees. He built the levees around where the Mississippi meets the Ohio. [*To her brother Bob in the audience*] Is that right, Bob?

Lange: He worked for the Corps of Engineers.

Gilchrist: He was in charge of it.

Lange: Head of the Corps.

Gilchrist: He was in charge of it. He loved those big tractors. He was building levees when they did it with mule teams. If you've ever seen pictures of these, these huge amounts of what, fifty mules pulling a wagon that was made out of slats of wood and they would close the slats and put the dirt on top of it. The mules were pulling up to the top of the levee, and the levees have always fascinated me because I watched them being built! My father would show me, he would stop the car and show me a place on the road to Issaquena County where the train had delivered the first tractor. Big, heavy, dirt-moving machines to the Delta to help with the [war]. And I lived in a house full of people at my granddaddy's plantation who had lived through the '27 flood. So that's what I've been reading. But I've also been reading, I've been rereading all the wonderful books of science and anthropology that I have bought during the last ten years. I don't have a grounding in biology and chemistry. I didn't study at the school because it was too hard. It was so easy just to take English classes. Take a Dexedrine, read the book, take the exam.

Lange: Those were the days. That doesn't happen anymore. One of the things that John Evans and I talked about prior to this for my prep talk was, what do you think is going on in the world today that we don't know about?

Gilchrist: My sons will tell you and my grandsons. They will talk your ear off. It can't be that bad. I know that much. I mean, I believe in democracy and I believe in the Constitution of the United States and Supreme Court of the United States and I have a hero named Tom Cotton who I think is the best senator in the world. They all think that the government lies to us, and a lot of my friends my own age think the government has a plan to immunize us all for Covid but it's really going to make us too dumb to know what they're doing. There are so many—*The Demon-Haunted World*[4] is a book I'm rereading right now by a great scientist about all the things that people pretend to believe. *The Demon-Haunted World*. I can't remember the name of the author. It's wonderful, but I don't believe that. I believe that there are many people governing the United States that are well meaning, that are intelligent, that are knowledgeable. Mostly Republican.

Lange: Mostly.

Gilchrist: I think the United States is what it's always been. It's a beacon of hope and brilliance left us by our ancestors. I believe in the Second Amendment. I think all guns should be locked. I don't know what's going on in the big world. I think that we should not allow Iran to have a nuclear weapon, no matter what it takes to prevent that. But I also think, because I read a lot of spy novels. I love spy novels. I've got a new writer called Daniel Silva and I really, really—once a year he publishes a book. I think that probably our government is stronger than we're allowed to know and for good reasons. I think that our spy satellites and all, I think we know what's going on. I think we're going to be able to protect ourselves. I think we're gonna be OK. I think we're not gonna have a thermonuclear war. I don't think that there are any group of people dumb [enough] to do that. Oh, and I'll read any book ever written about the invention of the atom bomb, about the people that did that. Golly, what a story! So many books have been written, even a murder mystery, there's a murder mystery that takes place out there. What do you all think? What do you all think?

Lange: You want to take a couple of questions?

Gilchrist: Yeah!

Lange: Why don't we take, does anyone have a question or want to talk about something in particular? John?

Audience member: When did it click for you, when did the light come on that you were going to be a writer?

Gilchrist: All my life I was a writer because all of the grown people around me, grandmother, great-grandmother, great-great-grandmother who lived until I was six, I was named for her. My grandfathers. My mother and father, my older brother, the genius, all of this, you know, from the time I could walk and look around me, everybody. Oh, there's my son, Garth!

Garth Walker: Hello, Mama!

Gilchrist: One of the gifts God gave me. If I looked around and somebody wasn't cooking or serving food or eating or working, anyplace I lived, down on my grandaddy's plantation, all of the grown people—which I wanted to be, I did not want to be a little short person—were sitting at desks or tables reading, or they're in a chair reading. All of the older ladies, they were all in bed reading either books or magazines. Fashion magazines. *Look, Time,* what were all the books back then? *Good Housekeeping.* I finally published a story in *Good Housekeeping* when I was oh, maybe, about twenty years ago, and I called my mother and I said, "Mother, at last, I've really done it."

Lange: "I've made it!" You've arrived.

Gilchrist: If I could just get a serial in *Reader's Digest*. They were all either writing, especially the men, because you know, they were doing their business. They were writing or they were reading, and all the men had pencils in their pockets. I usually have a lot of pencils in my pockets, #2 lead, real sharp. And they get on your clothes and ruin your white blouses. So, in a way that a person, that a baby will want to walk—have you ever seen a ten- or eleven-month-old baby that has decided to walk? My God, it'll go on. It'll take about a week, or maybe two weeks before they're on their feet, but what an amazing thing! They'll wake up and get right back to it. And it's painful. And they fall. [*To niece in audience*] There's Trina back there! Hi, love you. I would rather watch a child learning to walk. That's one of my favorite things to do in the whole world. I mean, how many days it takes or how many Sunday afternoons before they finally, they stand up. But I wanted to read and write. And every photograph of me from the time I'm about four years old, I've got a notebook and pencils with me and I'm carrying it around. Maybe I'm just gonna scribble on it. And long before I went to school, I thought I was reading. If I didn't know all the words, I just skipped the ones I didn't know and go on. And I liked to have the same—and you should do this for your children—I liked to have someone read the same book over and over to me. Has anyone in here ever read *Tommy Tomato Saves the Garden*? I've got to get Johnny—I've got to get a copy of that. *Tommy Tomato Saves the Garden*. God, how many times? I mean, they read it to me every day. I'm sitting on a cotton plantation with things growing all around me and outside, people waiting for rain or cursing the rain, whatever it was that day. I love that book.

Lange: Alright, I think we have time for one more question. Yeah, one more. OK. You, English teacher.

Audience member: Hi, yeah, as an English teacher and aspiring writer, can you talk a little about studying under Eudora Welty? I mean, was she a really hard and demanding teacher, or was she—

Gilchrist: Can you imagine Eudora being hard or demanding? Miss Welty was a lady and she was my mother's age and she was out of that generation. And one of my mother's close friends, with whom she played bridge every Tuesday, had known Eudora really well. And they all, all of her young friends, remembered the time they were at a house party. And Eudora had on a long white dress and was all dressed up. And she walked down to a pier where they were all swimming, and she was reading a letter and she walked off the pier. I love that. That is a literary story to me. That's how much she liked reading and writing, so I feel like it was probably from one of her famous poet friends who none of the people she ran around with even knew the name of. But I was sitting in bed one late afternoon reading the newspaper, and I read that Eudora Welty—right after, my family had not lived in Jackson very long—that Eudora Welty was gonna teach a class at Millsaps. And I ran to the library and took out every copy of her books that was available and there weren't many. There were about four collections of short stories. It was during the time she was writing *Losing Battles*. Her father had died, her brother had died, her mother was in a nursing home, and she spent every afternoon from the time our class, you know, from about five and until they closed, she spent every afternoon with her mother. Watching your mother in a nursing home is not fun. And the reason she was teaching at Millsaps was because her literary friends at Millsaps had decided that it would be good for her and get her in a better mood about all this death she had to put up with. If they could talk her into teaching a class. And we met two afternoons a week in the library, the old library at Millsaps in a room not quite this big, and there were about eighteen of us, handpicked. But anyway, I was not in college. I had quit college to run away and get married and have babies. [*Points to son in audience*] That's one of 'em.

Lange: There's the evidence right there.

Walker: Couldn't have done it without you.

Gilchrist: But so I was about a year and a half away from having a degree. And I don't, you know, having degrees is not very important to me. I think the honorary doctorates, I'm honored, but you're not a doctor because you get an honorary doctorate. Where was I?

Lange: We're on Eudora. And we have about a minute left.

Gilchrist: Alright, I wanna talk about Eudora. And so I grabbed, after I read all the short stories, and I was just blown away by these short stories and I thought they were so funny, and I read "Why I Live at the P.O." and I laughed until I thought I was going to choke to death. I still think it's the funniest story in the world, but the students now don't seem to get it. I don't know why they don't get it. God, it was so funny. So I grabbed up all my newspaper articles—I've been writing for newspapers since I was fourteen years old. I had a real column in a real newspaper when I was a sophomore in high school. I grabbed up everything I could find, I don't know how I knew where it was, and ran up to Millsaps and went to see the head of the English Department. What was his name. George?

Audience member: Dr. Boyd.

Gilchrist: Dr. Boyd. Was it George Boyd?

Audience member: George Boyd.

Gilchrist: Yes. And I just handed them to him and I said, "You've just got to let me in this class. This woman is—what a genius! I want to do this. I can write." And he stood there, he read for about five minutes and he said, "OK, the class is full but I'm letting you in." So while I was there I was standing in line to register and I thought, "You know, I might as well just go on and finish school." So I took all the poetry classes, and Miss Welty's class, and that's how I got to go to Millsaps, which was a wonderful story. But we would go up there and Miss Welty would come walking up the stairs and when it became winter, she would wear a little hat that kept her head warm. We just worshipped her. And we would write short stories and she would take them home and edit them. [*To audience member*] I didn't do that. I mean, the good ones. She would edit every single one and she would give it back to me and it would have these little tiny notations in pencil, very light and they were very kind things and I'd think, "Well, that's no good" and I'd write another one. I must have written about forty short stories for her 'cause if she wrote on 'em [*gestures flinging paper over her shoulder*] like that. Finally, I wrote a story about a woman who was addicted to prescription drugs, and it was just about two pages long, and she loved it. And I thought, "So that's how you do it. You just write it in a hurry and she doesn't put any little marks on it." So I don't know where the stories are that she wrote on, but mostly she was just so loving, gosh. And she told us all later, she told Jane and Patti—I had met all the New Stage people by then, gotten drawn into my life with the gypsies. She was just wonderful, that's all. She was wonderful. And the main thing was, here was a real writer with an editor and an *agent* and she was just like my mother and my mother's friends except, that, you know, that was a genius. She grew roses.

Lange: She was lovely.

Gilchrist: She was an ordinary person with ordinary relationships with us. Loving, kind, gentle, thoughtful relationships with us. She taught me what a writer was. I was not interested in writing short stories. I was only a poet. My desire was to write one poem that would still be in print in 100 years. That was what I was trying to do with my life.

Lange: I think you accomplished it. I think you're doing great. We do have to end. There's another session coming in. Ellen, thank you.

Notes

1. John Evans, owner of Lemuria Books, Jackson, Mississippi's premier independent bookstore since 1975.

2. In *Falling Through Space* (University Press of Mississippi, 2000), Gilchrist writes, "'This won't do,' my father said, when he got me on the phone. 'This business with the young man has got to stop'" (169).

3. Winston Churchill, *The Second World War*, 6 vols. (Houghton Mifflin, 1948–1953).

4. Carl Sagan, *The Demon-Haunted World: Science as a Candle in the Dark* (Random House, 1995).

Index

About the Editor

Photo by the
Mississippi Library Commission

Tracy Carr is a researcher, editor, and writer in Jackson, Mississippi. A former English instructor and librarian, she has a BA in English from the University of North Texas, an MA in English from Mississippi State University, and an MLIS from the University of Alabama. In her career as a librarian, she was responsible for several statewide literary programs, including the 2017 update of the Mississippi Literary Map. She serves on the board of the Mississippi Book Festival.